Teacher-Pupil Conflict in Secondary Schools

Published in 1987, the central question with which this book is concerned is what can, and should, teachers do about teacher-pupil conflict in schools? Few teachers in secondary education would need to have this sort of conflict described as even if that have been fortunate enough to avoid it themselves they will know of it from staffroom discussion and from the media. In can be seen in disorderly classrooms where pupils 'mess about' and 'have a laugh', and in the bleak expression on the face of their teacher. Equally it can be detected in those classrooms where the teacher is in firm control, but where pupils gaze listlessly out of the window, or only minimally comply with work demands. It is characterized by sudden blazing temper on both sides, and also by long periods of weariness, boredom and disengagement. It is not that conflict which might arise from temporary private troubles, from having a bad day or going through a bad patch, for it is there week in week out, and involves significant numbers.

Such conflict has been of interest to both psychologists and sociologists of education and important contributions have been offered by both of these disciplines. Sociologists have mapped out the differing cultural values and norms which appear to promote it. They have identified the social constraints present within the environment in which it is produced, constraints which emanate from the socio-economic organization of society and from the maintenance of an institutional framework, and which affect the micro-dynamics of teacher-pupil interaction. Psychologists have described the effects on behaviour of genetic factors, environmental conditions and cognitive states. Important though such insights are, however, they can only speak indirectly to teacher practice. This book provides an educational approach to the subject discussing topics including theoretical considerations, teacher-pupil discussion and relationships between classroom behaviour and the curriculum. It will appeal to those involved with schools and education, as well as psychologists, educational sociologists and researchers.

Teacher-Pupil Conflict in Secondary Schools

K. A. Cronk

Routledge
Taylor & Francis Group

First published in 1987
by The Falmer Press

This edition first published in 2018 by Routledge
2 Park Square, Milton Park, Abingdon, Oxon, OX14 4RN
and by Routledge
711 Third Avenue, New York, NY 10017

Routledge is an imprint of the Taylor & Francis Group, an informa business

© 1987 K. A. Cronk

Publisher's Note
The publisher has gone to great lengths to ensure the quality of this reprint but points out that some imperfections in the original copies may be apparent.

Disclaimer
The publisher has made every effort to trace copyright holders and welcomes correspondence from those they have been unable to contact.

A Library of Congress record exists under LCCN: 87045768

ISBN 13: 978-0-8153-7974-4 (hbk)
ISBN 13: 978-1-351-21502-2 (ebk)
ISBN 13: 978-0-8153-7977-5 (pbk)

Issues in Education and Training Series: 9

Teacher–Pupil Conflict in Secondary Schools
An Educational Approach

K.A. Cronk
Brighton Polytechnic

The Falmer Press

(A member of the Taylor & Francis Group)
London. New York. Philadelphia

UK   The Falmer Press, Falmer House, Barcombe, Lewes, East Sussex, BN8 5DL

USA   The Falmer Press, Taylor & Francis Inc., 242 Cherry Street, Philadelphia, PA 19106-1906

First published 1987

Library of Congress Cataloging in Publication Data

Cronk, K. A.
  Teacher-pupil conflict in secondary schools.

  Bibliography: p.
  Includes index.
  1. Teacher-student relationships. 2. Conflict
(Psychology). 3. School discipline. 4. Education,
Secondary. I. Title.
LB1033.C76 1987 371.1'02 87-45768
ISBN 1-85000 263-0
ISBN 1-85000-264-9 (pbk.)

Jacket design by Caroline Archer

Typeset in 10½/12 Caledonia by
Imago Publishing Ltd, Thame, Oxon

Contents

Acknowledgements

This volume is based upon my D Phil Thesis presented to the University of Sussex in 1985. I would, therefore, like to thank Terry Sexton, my supervisor, for the generous help he gave me, and Kathleen Moxon for her efforts in typing the manuscript and her uncomplaining good humour in making alterations. I must also, of course, particularly thank the pupils of 3Y and their teachers, without whose cooperation my field work would not have been possible.

Copyright

1 Introduction

The central question with which this book is concerned is what can, and should, teachers do about teacher-pupil conflict in schools? It is about that conflict that few teachers, in secondary education at least, would need to have described. For even if they have been fortunate enough to avoid it themselves they will know of it from staffroom discussion and from the media. It can be seen in disorderly classrooms where pupils 'mess about' and 'have a laff', and in the bleak expression on their teacher's face. Equally, it can be detected in those classrooms where the teacher is in firm control, but where pupils gaze listlessly out of the window, or only minimally comply with work demands. It is characterized by sudden blazing temper on both sides, and also by long periods of weariness, boredom and disengagement. It is not that conflict which might arise from temporary private troubles, from having a bad day or going through a bad patch, for it is there week in week out and involves significant numbers.

Such conflict has been of interest to both psychologists and sociologists of education and important contributions have been offered by both these disciplines. Sociologists have mapped out the differing cultural values and norms which appear to promote it. They have identified the social constraints present within the environment in which it is produced, constraints which emanate from the socio-economic organization of society and from the maintenance of an institutional framework, and which affect the micro-dynamics of teacher-pupil interaction. Psychologists have described the effects on behaviour of genetic factors, environmental conditions and cognitive states.

Important though such insights are, however, they can only speak indirectly to teacher practice. There are a number of reasons for this. The difficulty is not merely that between, and even within, disciplines there seem to be unresolved contradictions, though this certainly creates problems for a teacher who is seeking guidance.[1] It is, also, that the type of remedies which are suggested by sociological and psychological research are often beyond a teacher's power. They either require substantial reform of the social system or the institution, or the deployment of complex psychological techniques which are not within a typical teacher's repertoire of skills. In addition they can require the existence of financial resources which are simply not available. They do not, in short, provide the sort of solution which any teacher could put into operation immediately in any classroom.

Most importantly, however, sociology and psychology do not provide professional solutions because they can not address the central educational question which faces teachers who are in conflict with pupils. this question is not merely 'What can I do?' but, 'What ought I to do?' Clearly this latter question is a moral one, demanding a consideration of the rights of persons and the purpose of education. Equally clearly, however, any solution which did not take social and psychological realities into account would not be persuasive. What is required is a solution which, while based on a view of persons which is compatible with a moral educational stance, does not violate the insights of other disciplines.

Finding such a solution is not easy but it is too important a task to avoid. For the danger of relying solely on sociological and psychological theories is that persons, the object of education, can disappear from view as entities in their own right. They can appear either as mindless stimulus-response machines, as bundles of needs and drives, as ghostly realizations of cognitive states, or as epiphenomena of their genetic blueprint. Alternatively, as Lacey suggests, they can appear as '. . . an exegesis of some sociological force working itself out in a corner of the social world.'[2] More sophisticatedly, perhaps, they often appear as the mechanical interaction of a selection, or all, of these factors, recognizable as a machine which can be modified by manipulating one of its parts. It comes to seem as if persons, as persons, can be improved by, for example, feeding in a few more IQ points, or increasing the octane of their cultural norms.

This view of persons, as the product of factors beyond their control, is profoundly antithetical to the concept of education. That concept rests on the belief that persons can transcend physiological drives, psychological set and cultural milieux through the acquisition of knowledge, which enables them to pursue goals which are their own. Knowledge is not regarded as a stimulus which produces a mechanical response, no matter how complex the mechanism. The concept of education assumes that, however constrained teachers and pupils might be due to social, psychological and physical factors, what they do with their knowledge is in some real sense 'up to them'. It assumes, therefore, a core of the person which is distinct from, not the product of, its environment; a core which, because it is distinct, can be turned against the environment, resisting it and transforming it deliberately. Without these assumptions the concept of education is indistinguishable from the concepts of indoctrination or training. Without these assumptions teachers as well as pupils are caught in the iron laws of cause and effect and decision making is merely the production of the inevitable.

The theoretical focus of this research will be upon this essential core of human nature, which, it will be argued, transcends cultures, personalities and physiological differences. It will be described as the power which creates personalities and cultures, and whose presence makes diversity coherent. Significantly for this research, it will be suggested that it is this essential core of persons which demands rights for itself, and moves into conflict with others when those rights are transgressed. Thus, in making persons the central concept of this research the perspective is not only educational, but is focused on the specific problem of teacher-pupil conflict.

The view of human nature which will be taken is not a new one. It underlies much of the work of sociology and psychology. Neverthless the Social Sciences have tended to take it as given, rather than to spell out its characteristics and consider fully its implications for personal interaction. It is best identified in the literature with Mead's unpredictable and invisible 'I', with Piaget's 'centre of activity' and Sartre's 'no-thing of existence'.[3] For such theorists its presence was indisputable as the source of thought, structure and action. It is within the Existentialist Movement that it has perhaps been most consistently highlighted. The thought of writers such as Sartre and Nietzsche, however, does not form part of the orthodoxy of education, and it is only through the work of Rogers and Maslow that existentialism gains a foothold in teacher consciousness.[4] Rogers' view is, indeed, very similar to the one which will be taken in this book. His belief is that persons can be trusted, not only to know what is in their own best interests, but also to be concerned with the interests of others. This belief was derived initially from his work as a therapist, which led him to conclude that where a client seemed bent upon hurting himself and those around him, the problem lay in a failure to accept himself as someone of value. In Rogers' experience the solution was to provide an accepting relationship, within which the client could learn to know and trust and accept himself, which in turn led him to trust and accept others.

Rogers has applied this theory to Education. In *Freedom to Learn for The 80s* (1983) he appeals to teachers to recognize pupil-persons as trustworthy and to work with them in an egalitarian person-to-person relationship, rather than in a teacher-pupil relationship founded upon the exercise of formal power. If they did this, he argues, pupils would not use their freedom to threaten teachers, but would work with them in a relationship which would liberate the personal power of all involved. In recognizing the other as person, rather than as teacher or pupil, the fundamental moral attitudes of altruism, responsibility and forgiveness would be invoked. Socially derived conflict would disappear in the face of fundamental human unity.

My own experience of teaching intransigent pupils led me to a similar view. It appeared to me that many of the battles fought in schools were phoney — but none the less acrimonious for that. Beneath the specific cause of a specific argument, it was possible to catch sight of a fundamental agreement, and the hurt which teachers and pupils regularly inflicted upon each other appeared to derive from a colossal and complex misunderstanding. This misunderstanding seemed to consist of a failure to acknowledge the other as a person, and was fuelled by an apparently deliberate policy by those involved to hide their personhood within a role, whether within the role of teacher, or intransigent pupil. I, therefore, like Rogers, came to believe that the only way out of this impasse would be for teachers to take the initiative, and deliberately expose themselves as persons, encouraging their pupils to do the same. In this way I believed that the social differences which divided teachers and pupils would be exposed as externally derived constraints which should not be allowed to contaminate personal relationships. In the cessation of conflict which would follow. I believed that teachers and pupils could then work together powerfully to make the most of their opportunities. Like Rogers, I believed this, because I believed in the intrinsic morality and trustworthiness of pupil-persons.

The research reported in the following chapters was initiated to explore the validity and practical applicability of these beliefs. Their theoretical and professional implications are so complex, however, that is is useful to clear away three potential misunderstandings which might arise to obscure the more important issues. Firstly, in suggesting that teachers should interact with intransigent pupils on a person-to-person basis, so that their common humanity might be revealed, no suggestion will be made that the teacher should naively join the opposition and, so to speak, 'go native'. The view that is taken here is that teachers, as teachers, have something to offer to pupil-persons. They know things by virtue of their age and education which are of value. If this is not so, no amount of identification with the language, dress and values of the counter-school subculture would gain them credibility as teachers, or as persons. With nothing to offer the teacher-role would be empty. With nothing to offer in return for a substantial salary, their personal morality would be suspect. Alternatively, with something to offer, the mere trappings of a common humanity (the behaviour and the fashions of youth-culture) would be irrelevant, and a teacher who artificially adopted these would be treated with suspicion or even despised. The person-to-person relationship requires the exposure of the real person, not the presentation of an image intended to please.[5]

Secondly, it is important to emphasize that this research is not advocating a 'child-centred' approach to education. Indeed it will be suggested that the concept 'child' is a sociological, or psychological, or physiological construct which has little to do with either persons or morality. This proposition is contentious and will be argued more fully in Chapter 2. For the moment, however, it is important to demonstrate the difference between person-centredness and some of the cruder versions of child-centredness. The point can be illustrated by the practice of the teachers studied by Sharp and Green.[6] Those teachers, in rhetoric at least, claimed that because the pupil knew her own needs best, child-centred education was merely a matter of providing opportunities from which the pupil could 'choose'. In this way the child would learn to read when she was 'ready', and if she wasn't ready she could play away her psychological and social hang-ups in the Wendy House. All that the teacher demanded was that the child should be 'busy'. Beneath this rhetoric, however, Sharp and Green identified teachers who in fact believed that certain forms of 'busyness' — notably an interest in reading — were more valuable than others. They, therefore, sponsored pupils who either by chance, or inclination, showed an interest in this activity, and in so doing created a stratified classroom. Sharp and Green's analysis has, of course, been criticized, but for the present purpose that does not matter. The point of the illustration is that the teachers hid, or at least obscured, their real person from the pupil's view. The pupils had to guess at their teachers' beliefs and at the problem which large classes and a shortage of time afforded. Moreover they had to guess in a situation where their teachers' actions belied their words. By denying their pupils direct access to their beliefs, these teachers were, in effect, denying pupil personhood. They did not entrust themselves to pupils, thus remaining in a teacher-expert to child-client and not in a person-to-person relationship.

Thirdly, it is important to understand that the suggested approach to pupil-teacher conflict does not contain a naive hope that if persons are 'nice to each other' all their problems will disappear. Teachers would still be faced with a shortage of resources, and would still be constrained by the expectations and demands of powerful others. Society would still contain injustices and inequalities; and pupils would still be under pressure from a competitive system and from the problems of poverty and broken homes. They would still be seduced by the greater excitement of life outside the school. These socio-economic and social-psychological factors would not be removed. Even at an inter-personal level there would be no guarantee that pupils and teachers would come to agree with each other's point of view, merely because they recognized it as the view of another moral person. At the heart of all human relationships is a moral dilemma — the appropriate balance between the rights of one individual and those of another. Thus morality is not conceived here as a body of 'right' answers, but as a constant search for the 'best' answers in a continuously changing present. In this view it neither requires, nor expects, agreement about what 'should' be done.

Thus a person-centred approach to education and classroom conflict promises neither victory for one side over the other, nor friendship, nor even consensus. It might result in any one or more of these states, but they are not inevitable. What it does promise, if Rogers is correct, is an elevation into consciousness of the problems of classroom reality, including those problems which derive from outside the classroom, so that the persons involved can freely and openly discuss them. They may still disagree with each other about the best solution, but they would recognize that their alternative solutions were sincerely and morally held, however mistakenly. Inter-personal conflict would be replaced by tolerance and bargains. Classrooms would become places where persons stopped fighting each other and discussed ideas, where they cooperated in an attempt to find ways in which their contradictory evaluations and insights could be made to cohere. Teachers and pupils would in effect be engaged in a research programme in which they put all their disparate evidence and views in front of each other and, together, attempted to see what it meant and how they should proceed.

This process is arguably profoundly revolutionary. Rogers describes the surprise he experienced when he was first challenged about the politically radical nature of his method.[7] Since then he has developed this theme. Certainly, a person-centred approach as outlined above, has much in common with the approach advocated by some Neo-Marxists. Willis (1977) argues that teachers should help intransigent pupils to consciously explore their 'penetrations' into the contradictions of society and schooling.[8] As long as such insights remain unconscious, he argues, 'the lads' can only express them through action. Because the lads trust their intuitional penetrations, they come to oppose the dominant ideology which they equate with teachers and school. They, therefore, reject mental labour which they regard as the weapon of their teacher oppressors. As a consequence they celebrate manual labour, recognizing the oppression of this latter in capitalist forms of production, only when it is too late.

Furthermore, Willis argues, the failure of 'the lads' to explore their insights consciously, leads them to assume that oppression is natural. They presume that it is in the nature of teachers and bosses to oppress, and fail to recognize that it is the system which is to blame, a system which constrains the behaviour of both the dominant and the dominated. Thus:

> Instead of a centred world of oppression from a specific and determinate social organization of thought, production and intersets, (they see) a naturalistic world of a thousand timeless causes. Multi-determination brings misery and is the human condition. A single enemy might be fought, but never a million little ones...[9]

The failure of the lads to use rigorous mental labour to identify the cause of their problems, and the failure of teachers to help them to do this, leaves the lads, Willis argues, with only one alternative. Because they believe teachers and bosses to be fundamentally different from themselves, they see no hope in any attempt to persuade them to change their ways. So they concentrate on subversion and laughter, on personal salvation and on making the best of a bad job. Without mental labour they have no means of fighting the premises upon which the system is built, and so they become agents in perpetuating that system.

Willis's arguments outlined above have clear links with those of Rogers. A person-to-person approach would put mental labour at the heart of the pupil-teacher relationship in a way which could not be avoided. Teacher-persons would challenge pupil-persons to raise into consciousness, and attempt to express, their insights into the failure of schooling, because teachers recognizing pupils as persons, would want to listen to the way pupils felt. Equally, teachers would need to bring into consciousness and communicate to pupil-persons their understanding of the situation. In the consequent discussion, both parties might come to recognize that the cause of their difficulties was not a plethora of naturally oppressive teachers or naturally rebellious pupils, but a system which placed them in artificial opposition.[10] Schools would become sites where hegemony was challenged and where teachers would be enabled to perform the role of educators rather than that of agents of social control. This raising into consciousness and communal evaluation of unconscious insights is arguably the core, and the promise, of Education.

Significantly it is not only theorists who have recognized the revolutionary potential of person-centred education. One of the most interesting chapters in the 1983 edition of *Freedom to Learn* is that which describes the collapse of a number of experiments as a result of social opposition.[11] Thus the white suburbanites of Louisville could not tolerate the power which a person-centred education gave to the black inner-city population. The new system was, therefore, dismantled in a groundswell of traditionalism which fought to preserve the old hierarchies of power relations in schools, hierarchies which favoured the white middle class. Rogers argues that this opposition to personal freedom for all, displayed in Louisville and elsewhere, cannot be simplistically dismissed as an attempt to preserve privilege. He argues that, at a fundamental level, it is caused by a belief that order must be imposed and that freedom would lead to social chaos. Elites, therefore, from the best motives fight tenaciously to preserve their power. Rogers writes:

> This is not, I believe, a genetic characteristic, but is highly characteristic of our culture. Along with it goes a mistrust of the person which has deep roots in religious conceptions of man as essentially evil. Until and unless the human organism is perceived as trustworthy, those in power see it as their obligation to control. It is in these deep-seated philosophical areas that change must come about before we can have lasting organizations based on a person-centred approach.[12]

The failure to believe in the morality of persons is not, however, merely an entrenched idea — a matter of psychological set, or over socialization into historic ideas. All around there is evidence of behaviour which not only hurts others, but is deliberately intended to hurt. Such behaviour is endemic in schools where teachers and pupils use psychological and physical aggression in their attempts to control each other and win space for themselves. A belief in the immorality of the other is, therefore, sustained by a commonsense reading of evidence, and Rogers' person-centred approach can easily be brushed aside as idealistic nonsense. Even where a teacher is prepared to be open-minded, the difficulty of engaging disruptive pupils in discussion can be enough to overwhelm an incipient belief in their moral personhood. Rogers writes:

> Occasionally, I have known 'miracles' to follow from such discussions, but much more often it is painful, growthful struggles that ensue — in the instructor, in each student, in the interaction of the whole group.[13]

For a teacher to continue to facilitate such 'painful struggles', a belief in the intrinsic morality of disruptive pupils would be of paramount importance. Pupils who believed deeply in teacher immorality would not be won over quickly; and the constraints of large classes, limited resources, an externally controlled curriculum and socio-economic inequalities would continue to create situations which all too readily promoted conflict. A teacher who was not already convinced of the morality of their disruptive pupils would be unlikely to stay the course, for their doubts would be confirmed by the pupils behaviour. They could dismiss research findings as biased, or as inapplicable in their own situation; and the desire for self-preservation could lead to a reversion to control techniques which would abort the development of a person-to-person relationship.

This important link between belief and practice is a major theme of this book. Thus Chapter 2 presents a theoretical argument for the intrinsic morality of persons which is capable of accounting for the wide range of evidence which teachers have to accommodate, whether in the form of research results, or day to day experience. Unfortunately this involves the resurrection of long-standing debates about freedom and determinism, about the relationship between the mind and the body, and between conscious and unconscious thought. It also necessitated the use of slippery concepts — not only that of morality, but of intelligence and creativity, responsibility, forgiveness, unity, and even human nature itself. Chapter 2, therefore, undertakes the crucial task of demonstrating a way through this theoretical minefield which promotes the concept of intrinsic morality without denying important bodies of evidence. Indeed, it identifies a core of agreement between different disciplines and perspectives which is often lost beneath their more obvious differences, but which contains the necessary theoretcial insight to sustain a person-centred approach to conflict.

In considering a theoretical argument for intrinsic morality Chapter 2 also develops further a theory of how moral persons can come to find themselves in conflict. Chapter 3 explores whether these theories are adequate to explain the experiences of one particularly difficult class, 3Y, and their teachers. Using evidence drawn from discussions, interviews, written statements and an observation of lessons, it was possible to demonstrate that all the data was compatible with a view that the actors were behaving morally and also, that where conflict occurred this was a consequence of a failure to perceive the other as person.

Chapters 4 to 7 contain an account of a series of experimental lessons undertaken with a notoriously disruptive class. Chapter 4 gives an outline of the experimental design. Chapter 5 describes the problem for the teacher in holding onto a belief in pupil morality in the face of their disruptive behaviour. It illustrates how and why the suspicion that pupils need to be controlled, not trusted, can gain a foothold in a teacher's consciousness and how at such critical times a consciously held theory of intrinsic morality can prevent belief from being overwhelmed.

Chapter 6 continues by discussing the effects on the behaviour of both pupils and teacher of persevering with a person-centred approach to conflict. Specifically it discusses the effects of open-ended discussion about the problem of disruptive behaviour and demonstrates that order not chaos ensued. In this way, it also demonstrates how the evidence of experiencing a particular course of action would feed back into, and strengthen, the belief and theory which had promoted it.

Finally, Chapter 7 illustrates the complexity of classroom reality, and the way in which moral persons in interaction need to take into account not only each other's personhood, but a plethora of constraints and opportunities which form the context in which moral decisions must be made. Using the curriculum as an example, it considers how persons evaluate constraints and opportunities in order to identify appropriate courses of action. It also demonstrates how the changing nature of classroom reality constantly throws up new moral dilemmas, which demand new solutions and create an ever present challenge to the person-to-person relationship.

Notes

1 For example, teachers have been told that it is a pupil's home background, or the organization of the school, or the capitalist organization of society which creates conflict in classrooms. Alternatively they have been told that some pupils are genetically 'thick' or aggressive, or that they have been disturbed by traumatic childhood experiences, or that they have not yet reached the intellectual/social stage of development necessary for a stable moral stance towards their teachers. Faced with this variety of theoretical explanations teachers do not know whether to engage in compensatory education, institutional reform, or social revolution;

whether to impose discipline, engage in Behaviour Modification, set up a coun-
selling unit, or just sit the problem out and wait for pupils to mature. It is,
therefore, not surprising that many of them reject theory, and attempt to work on
a day to day basis with their own human intuitions.

2 LACEY, C. in BARTON, L. and MEIGHAN, R. (1979), p. 168.
3 Sartre, of course, rejected the term 'human nature' but in so doing he was
rejecting the idea that a person's character was a consequence of genetic or
environmental causes, a set of identifiable traits, rather than a matter of choice.
Thus in *Existentialism and Humanism* (Eyre Methuen, 1973, page 28), he writes

> ... man first of all exists, encounters himself, surges up in the world —
> and defines himself afterwards. If man as the existentialist sees him is
> not definable, it is because to begin with he is nothing. He will not be
> anything until later, and then he will be what he makes of himself.
> Thus, there is no human nature ... Man simply is ... he is what he
> wills ...

This line of argument still leaves the problem of the nature of the will and how it
decides what to choose. In considering human nature, therefore, this book
addresses questions about the nature of the 'will' of existentialism which is not a
'thing', but the 'no-thing of existence'. It also addresses questions relating to why
Mead's 'I' is so unpredictable, and why Piaget's 'centre of activity' busies itself
with the assimilation and accommodation of information, in order to build an
intellect.

4 I am using the term 'existentialism' very loosely here, to refer to belief in the
freedom and power of the human organism as a unitary phenomenon.
5 WILLIS (1977) makes a similar point by suggesting that a 'tactical withdrawal from
confrontation with the counter school culture' should not be accompanied by a
'simplistic expression of sympathy' (p. 190). He suggests that although teachers
should recognize the 'submerged meanings behind attitudes and behaviour', those
attitudes and behaviour might need to be 'strictly condemned' (p. 187).
6 SHARP, R. and GREEN, A. (1975). See especially Chapters 5, 6 and 7.
7 ROGERS, C. (1977), page 3.
8 Other writers make similar points. For example, CORRIGAN (1979) emphasizes the
importance of transforming consciousness, suggesting that,

> It is necessary within the institutions of the capitalist state to raise issues
> and consciousness which will, in alliance with vast struggles throughout
> the whole of society, transform not only the schooling of the Smash
> Street Kids but also all social relationships of exploitation and oppres-
> sion. (p. 154)

And APPLE, (in YOUNG and WHITTY, 1977) in an analysis of the dangers of
de-schooling suggests that teachers have an important role to play in making
pupils socially and politically aware.

9 WILLIS, P. (1977), pp. 163–4.
10 Evidence from a series of interviews undertaken at the commencement of this
research with teachers and disruptive pupils from several local schools, indicated
that the problem of consciousness was much more complex than this bald statement would imply. This was particularly true of the teachers who were interviewed. They clearly operated with a number of levels of consciousness, so that
while in their initial responses they appeared to equate 'natural rebelliousness'
with innate aggression or faulty socialization, it became clear as they talked at
greater length in the comfort of their own homes, that by 'natural', they meant
'natural in the circumstances'. Moreover, the ultimate circumstance which they
identified was the organization of society, which they blamed not only for the

inadequacies of schooling but for the intolerable burden which some families had to bear. For these teachers at least, conflict with their pupils was not a matter of false consciousness, and suggestions that teachers are unwitting agents of capitalism fail to get to the centre of the problem of classroom interaction, which seemed to be as much one of a failure to communicate the contents of consciousness, as of false consciousness itself.

11 ROGERS, C. (1983) PP. 227–52.
12 ROGERS, C. (1983) p. 250.
13 ROGERS, C. (1983) p. 29. WILLIS, P. (1977) also acknowledges the problem. While suggesting the use of 'more collective practices, group discussions and projects', he recognizes that 'the possibilities for a principled pedagogic practice with disaffected working class youth are fraught with difficulties', (p. 188) which create problems for individual teachers who have to continue with their awkward and demoralizing class contacts' (p. 189) and means, therefore, that they must somehow refrain from being 'alientated by . . . possibly personally insulting elements'. (p. 187)

2   *Theoretical Considerations*

The proposition that if teachers systematically abandon control techniques in their relationships with pupils and replace them with person-to-person discussion of classroom issues, then a creative order rather than chaos will ensue, raises some important theoretical issues. In particular it raises questions about pupil morality. Indeed, the proposition depends upon the belief that morality is neither a consequence of learning, nor maturity, but rather that it is an intrinsic and inalienable dimension of human nature which impregnates all human action. Only by subscribing to such a belief is it possible to argue that once teachers and pupils come to understand each other's behaviour then, irrespective of their age, their socio-economic position or cultural background, their genetic inheritance, IQ gender, or personal histories, all pupils (and teachers) can be trusted to work together in a partnership for the good of all involved. The purpose of this chapter is to consider the theoretical implications of this belief.

Morality on its own is a controversial concept and intrinsic morality even more so. Both commonsense and academic theories exist which suggest that some pupils are too young, or too unintelligent, or too disturbed, to consider the interests of others, or be responsible for their own behaviour; or that some people are too wicked, or wayward, to be accorded moral status. Additionally, there is a widely held view that people act morally and immorally at different times, as if acting morally were a matter of choice not nature. Further, there are those who regard it as a consequence of achieving spiritual grace. Such theories are both persuasive and pervasive and cannot be dismissed lightly. Importantly, they cannot be dismissed merely by mustering evidence, for morality is not a 'thing' whose existence can be demonstrated empirically. Rather it is inferred from an interpretation of behaviour and how one interprets behaviour depends largely on one's beliefs about human nature. Thus, if a major aim of this book — to influence classroom practice — is to be achieved, the plausibility of the argument which is presented in this chapter will be as important as the fieldwork which follows later.

That said, the identification of a satisfactory theory was not easy, and it proved necessary to move beyond the currently fashionable theories of the social sciences before an adequate solution could be found. This is no criticism of the important and growing body of sociological research into teacher-pupil conflict, but merely a reflection of the fact that that research does not take morality as its central concept. Importantly, the theory which is proposed in this chapter is regarded not only as compatible with other theories in the social sciences, but as complementary to them.

The chapter is divided into five sections. The first clarifies the concept of intrinsic morality as it will be used throughout this book. It identifies, and elaborates upon, seven statements which must necessarily be true if persons are to be regarded as intrinsically moral. Although this section contains some references to the work of others in the field, the ideas it contains are a sort of theoretical omelette made from a number of eggs whose precise source it is now difficult to identify. Where there is a direct link with the work of another writer this will of course be stated. At the outset, however, my debt to Spinoza needs to be acknowledged, for it was only after reading his *Ethics* that my ideas began to crystallize. By and large, though, Section One should be read and criticized as an exercise in logic, rather than in the history of ideas. It is an important section because it provides the criteria against which the literature of the educational disciplines can be judged, in order to discover which theorists subscribe to the concept of intrinsic human morality and which oppose it.

Sections Two and Three consider each of these groups in turn. Specifically, Section Three considers the problem of determinism in the social sciences. This can appear to threaten the concept of morality by suggesting that a person's behaviour is determined by factors outside his control and that people cannot, therefore, be held responsible for what they do to each other. It will be argued that in spite of the 'scientific' aura which surrounds deterministic arguments, they are as metaphysical as a belief in intrinsic morality. Section Four extends this argument by suggesting that the metaphysic of intrinsic morality is, moreover, more consistent with important bodies of research than that of determinism. It confronts the fact that persons as physical beings must in some way conform to the laws of the physical universe and addresses the problems which this raises for a belief in their freedom to choose their behaviour and act altruistically. Finally, Section Five considers the implications of these arguments for an investigation into teacher-pupil conflict.

1 The Concept of Intrinsic Morality

As has already been indicated there are many views about what morality is and is not and the subject has produced a massive literature. There are few, however, who would dispute that, in order to be considered moral, a person must *(a) be capable of choosing his behaviour and, thus, of being held responsible for that choice* (otherwise he would be regarded as amoral); and *(b) act altruistically,* that is take into account the rights and interests of others (otherwise he would be regarded as immoral). The concept of morality as it is used throughout this book is based upon these two statements. *Thus, an intrinsically moral person is defined as one about whom these statements are always necessarily true,* because to be altruistic and responsible for his behaviour would be inalienable dimensions of his nature.

Although this is a fairly simple definition, which with luck will offend no-one, its simplicity is deceptive, for it has a number of more complex logical sequences. These can be summarized in seven statements which, if the definition of an intrinsically moral person outlined above is true, are also necessarily true. Each will be considered in turn. They are:

(i) Morality is a problem-solving activity involving the need to make choices about how to balance the rights and interests of the self against those of others.

(ii) When intrinsically moral persons engage in long-term conflict with each other this is a consequence of misunderstanding.

(iii) If persons are intrinsically moral and, thus, by definition responsible for what they do they must be free.

(iv) If persons are intrinsically moral, they must also be intrinsically intelligent, creative and purposive.

(v) If adults are intrinsically moral, so are children.

(vi) If persons are intrinsically moral, their behaviour will be unpredictable except at a statistical level.

(vii) If persons are intrinsically moral, the criteria they use to evaluate situations will derive from their own nature and not from an external moral code, whether internalized through socialization, or through divine revelation.

(i) Morality is a problem-solving activity

For many people morality is a matter of obeying moral law. If they perceive any problems with the concept, these are to do with deciding what that law is and then persuading themselves to follow it, even when they would prefer to do otherwise. This is not the sort of problem-solving activity which is referred to here, however. Indeed the definition of morality given above does not imply that some behaviour is always moral — that it can be regarded as 'good-in-itself'. It simply requires a person to take an altrusitic stance towards others. This requirement, however, stands in need of some further explanation. For example, while some might expect a saint to act solely in the interests of others, the concept of a moral person does not generally have this force. Thus, it is not on the whole considered to be immoral to stand up for one's rights, so that some would argue that even a violent response might be regarded as moral, if such rights were unjustifiably and consistently violated by others. Certainly the concept of justice is closely related to the concept of morality and justice implies some form of equality of treatment, with the rights of the perpetrator of an act being weighed against those of others who are affected by it. Indeed, it can even be argued that unless a person is concerned for herself, she would have difficulty in showing concern for others. Thus, some psychologists suggest that anti-social behaviour is often associated with a poor self-concept; and the Christian exhortation 'Love thy neighbour as thyself' requires that we love ourselves in order to know how to love our neighbour.

A moral person, therefore, is not someone who need always and automatically give way to the interests of others, irrespective of the damage which this might do to herself. Indeed, to claim that this was an intrinsic tendency of human nature would fly not only in the face of moral justice, but in the face of the facts. People do care about themselves. A better statement of this aspect of morality might therefore be: *a moral person is one who is as concerned for the well-being of others as for her own*. It therefore follows that at the centre of morality is the ongoing existential problem of balancing the rights and interests of others against those of the self. The problem derives from the fact that, in the world as we know it, the interests and needs of one person can often only be fulfilled at the expense of the interests and needs of another. In some situations the choice might be one of utmost gravity, as in the case where only one life can be saved. More often the moral dilemmas which confront people are less serious. Tired parents long to sit and rest. Their child wants their active attention. Whose interests should prevail? Such examples are potentially infinite. Moreover, it is inconceivable that they will ever go away, for even in a social Utopia they would regenerate themselves as long as moral persons were in interaction.

Thus, the view that persons are intrinsically moral, that is that it is in their nature to be concerned both for the well-being of others and for their own, necessarily means that it is in their nature to confront problems which an intrinsically immoral, or amoral, person would not even perceive. The problems of these latter would be of a different order — how to maximize their own interests in the face of social and physical constraints. For such persons to qualify for a sort of moral status, they would need to be seen to obey some accepted moral code, to behave in ways which others had decreed to be 'good'. But the cause of their behaviour would be either fear, or hope of gain, or indoctrination. However, for intrinsically moral persons no externally imposed moral code would ever entirely suffice. No such code could ever be sufficiently detailed, or subtle, to cover the wide range of moral dilemmas produced by an ever changing present. Their morality would of necessity, therefore, be a matter of problem solving, not obedience.

Importantly, because human life is complex, the problem of balancing conflicting rights would be equally so, and only on rare occasions would an ideal solution be available. More often a number of less than ideal solutions would appear and there would inevitably be times when moral persons disagreed about which one was best. Indeed, there is nothing in the definition of a moral person which is being invoked, which necessitates a view that he will be able to find solutions which are satisfactory in some objective sense, and sometimes a solution might prove disastrous. Nevertheless, if it is in the nature of persons to be concerned about the well-being of others, one would expect neither disagreements nor disasters to lead to long-term conflict, even if the initial discussions were heated. Rather, and as a result of their mutual concern, one would expect moral persons to make compromises and bargains, to accept some personal inconvenience, to monitor the effects of their decisions, to apologize and where possible make up for any hurtful consequences and to forgive mistakes. Thus if it is true that persons are intrinsically moral, it is also necessarily true that long-term conflict is a consequence of some sort of misunderstanding.

(ii) When intrinsically moral persons engage in long-term conflict this is a consequence of misunderstanding

This second logical consequence of the concept of intrinsic morality is awkward, for everywhere there is evidence that individuals and groups consistently, and often deliberately, ignore the well-being of others and act in ways which are destined to hurt them. To represent all this behaviour, and the conflict which can ensue, as a consequence of misunderstanding might seem to put an unnecessary strain on belief. Nevertheless, if, as this research requires, altruism is to be regarded as an intrinsic quality of human nature, then this explanation of conflict must stand, for intrinsically moral persons could never engage in conflict out of selfishness or greed. That 'misunderstanding' is, in the light of the evidence, a sensible explanation of conflict, will be argued later. For the moment it is worthwhile illustrating how misunderstanding might lead intrinsically moral persons to engage in long-term conflict with each other. In general terms such conflict might result from a misunderstanding about the nature of persons, or from a misunderstanding about the nature of situations. In both cases the misunderstanding would justify a continuation of hurtful behaviour.

Misunderstanding about the nature of persons would consist of a belief that either an individual, or a group, or indeed the whole human species was intrinsically immoral, or amoral, and that moral behaviour, therefore, had to be learned or imposed. The doctrine of original sin is an example of such a belief, as is the view that children have to be taught to be moral, or that certain groups and individuals fail to learn. In many cases, as Rogers[1] argues, these beliefs are deeply held; but if, as will be argued later, persons are in fact intrinsically moral, such beliefs are erroneous. Nevertheless, on the basis of these beliefs moral persons would feel justified in treating severely anyone who offended them, opposing their supposed immorality with whatever force was deemed necessary. Indeed, they might even consider that, as a consequence of their offences, such persons had forfeited any rights they might once have been accorded. Thus there would no longer be any need to consider their well-being and certainly any hint of compromise, or collaboration, with such persons would be regarded as moral weakness.

Alternatively, the misunderstanding might be about a situation, or event.[2] For example, it might be that someone whose morality you had never doubted suddenly acted in a way which seemed so outrageous and hurtful, that your faith in his morality was shattered. You would thus redefine him as immoral and act towards him in the way described above. If, however, he were in fact intrinsically moral, this redefinition would be a mistake. The explanation for his behaviour would lie in his evaluation of the circumstances in which he found himself, and not in a lack of concern about you. Clearly, you could not know of these circumstances, otherwise, as a moral person yourself, you would understand his dilemma and forgive him the hurt he had unavoidably, or mistakenly, caused. Meanwhile, he, ignorant of your ignorance, would be offended by your changed behaviour and retaliate in kind for the same reasons. Unless both you and he come to fully understand the situation, this could go on for a very long time.

One would, of course, expect an intrinsically moral person to be at pains to discover circumstances under which another person was acting, so that long-term conflict could be avoided. This often happens in close relationships. However, there are difficulties in the way of this obvious solution. The initial shock and hurt might be so great, and the angry response so violent, that discussion would become difficult, and as retaliation followed retaliation, communication might break down completely in a surfeit of hurt feelings and moral indignation. Alternatively the circumstances might be too sensitive, or too complex to discuss easily; or forgiveness might be given without question and without revealing the depth of hurt. Such forgiveness without understanding could only increase the problem if the act was then repeated — perhaps unwittingly.

Clearly, therefore, the concept of intrinsic morality does not preclude the development of long-term conflict, for it is indeed possible to explain its existence (even at national or international levels) as a function of misunderstanding. Whether or not this would be correct or an adequate explanation is another matter. The point here is that if it is true that persons are intrinsically moral, then this explanation of conflict must, of logical necessity, also be true. For while the concept of intrinsic morality is compatible with the view that people can make mistakes, it is incompatible with the view that they will engage in conflict purely for their own ends, irrespective of the damage that this will do to others.

(iii) If persons are moral they must be free

The concept of morality as it is being used in this research includes not only the idea of altruism, but also the notion that people are responsible for what they do. This implies that they have free will, the ability not only to choose a course of action, but also to translate that choice into appropriate behaviour. Indeed, it must necessarily be true that, if a person is to be held responsible for her behaviour, then irrespective of her genetic code, her psychological set, her social and cultural background, or her personal biography, she must (in the phrase which Ayers claims is 'dear to the heart of the free-will contraversialist') have been able to 'act otherwise'.[3] Without this ability, both choice and responsibility would be empty concepts and persons would be amoral machines, either programmed to act in ways which were beyond their control, or acting in such ways by chance.

The whole controversy about whether or not free will is a reality is fraught with difficulties. Some of these stem from confusion about the meaning of the terms in which the debate is expressed. Others stem from the logical consequences of a belief in free will. The following paragraphs will therefore contain a discussion of the terms which will be used in this research relating to the concept of free will, in the hope that this will avoid confusion. In addition some of the problems which arise out of the logic of freedom will be identified.

To begin with, the statement that, if persons are moral they must be free, is not meant to convey the idea that for persons to be moral they must always be able to do what they want, nor that things never 'happen to them'.[4] Such a claim would clearly defeat the notion that morality is an inborn, inalienable dimension of all human nature, for things are always happening to people and only rarely do circumstances allow us to do exactly as we please. Throughout this research the term 'free' will rather be used as the antithesis of 'determined'. Determinism is that theory which argues that every effect has a cause, and that that cause, too, has a cause and so on back to a first cause (whether God or the Big Bang). Determinism has its problems, of course. 'What caused the Big Bang?' or 'What caused God' and so on, into an insanity of infinite regression. Nevertheless, determinism is a powerful theory. By applying the laws of cause and effect, we have been able to build technologies which allow us to control our environment with some success. As a theory, therefore, it has a good record.

The problem which the theory of determinism poses for this research, however, is that if everything can be explained by chains of cause and effect, human action cannot be represented as the consequence of human choice. For the concept of intrinsic morality to stand, it is necessary to hold that the human species is free from such causal chains, and it is in this sense that the term freedom will be used. This will be contrasted with the notion of personal liberty which will be defined here as a function of the constraints upon persons. This distinction between freedom and liberty is crucial to the argument presented in this research, and rests upon a differing conception of causes and constraints. Thus, causes, as defined here, would leave no spaces for personal choice because they would enter into, and reside within, a person's being. He would become their effect and, as such, he would be programmed to create further effects through his actions. Indeed, only our blindness to the operation of these determining causes would prevent us from seeing that he and his environment were indistinguishable. As a link in a causal chain he could never confront his environment in order to change it. Rebellion would be as determined as conformity, each the result of differing causal factors.

Constraints, on the other hand, are defined as existing outside the person. They could box him in and severely limit the opportunities which were open to him, but because their existence was separate from his, there would be nothing illogical in claiming that he could work to remove, or circumvent them. Such attempts might be over-optimistic, or be enterprises which awaited a future technology; or they might always remain beyond fulfilment by the human species. The point is that the attempt could be made, whereas no determining cause however small could be confronted in this way by a person who was its effect. Moreover, no matter how severely a person was constrained, as long as that person still lived, there would be some choices which could be made. Thus, even a prisoner could choose to collaborate with his keepers, to go on hunger strike, or to adopt a stance of sublime resignation to his fate.[5]

Importantly, the distinction being made here between causes and constraints has a further logical consequence. Thus, whereas liberty would be open to growth and decline with an increase or decrease in environmental opportunities and constraints, freedom would be incapable of either. It would be an absolute state. It could not grow because it is nonsense to describe something as more free than free; and it could not decline because, just as it is meaningless to suggest that something is part-caused (either it is caused or it is not), so it is meaningless to suggest that it is part-free. The existence of the smallest determining cause on human nature would not, therefore, lead to a small reduction in personal freedom. It would destroy that freedom and destroy it absolutely. Such a cause would either act upon the whole person, thus destroying that person's freedom directly, or it would act on part of the person — say on his liver. This latter eventuality would mean that a person would need to be conceived as a bundle of discrete components, each with its own nature and, therefore, each either susceptible or not to the effects of differing causes. As a consequence the person could no longer be regarded as a unitary phenomenon. He would be a machine of interacting parts and his nature would be determined by the way in which those parts interacted. Importantly, like any machine he could not be held responsible for his behaviour, any more than an engine can be blamed if it fails to start because the points are damp.[6]

Thus, if a person is to be regarded as responsible for his behaviour the following three statements must also necessarily be true:

(a) He is the first cause of that behaviour — that is, it is not caused by factors outside his control, however insignificant these factors might be.

(b) This ability to choose his behaviour is not divisible and therefore not open to growth or decline. A person is either able to choose his behaviour, or he is not.

(c) A person is a holistic, unitary phenomenon and not a collection of objects — brain, heart, liver, genes and so on, in mechanical interaction.

The concept of responsibility, grounded as it is in the logic of freedom, therefore presents grave problems for anyone who would believe in it. It appears to set the human species aside from the rest of the universe which, according to the theory of determinism, dances to a very different tune. This is the problem which many of the great religions claim to have solved, but for the atheist, or agnostic, religious solutions have little appeal. It is not surprising, therefore, that much common sense and academic thinking is based on a deterministic view of human nature. Section Four of this chapter will consider these competing claims and will argue that a belief in human freedom does not necessarily require a belief in a God, who allows just one part of his creation — the human species — to flout the laws of cause and effect.

(iv) If persons are intrinsically moral, they must also be intrinsically intelligent, creative and purposive

It was argued in Section (iii) above that the concept of intrinsic morality is incompatible with the theory of determinism. Here it will be argued that it is, also, incompatible with the theory of indeterminism. This latter theory, as its name implies, rejects the view that the universe, and all the events which take place within it, can be explained through the iron laws of cause and effect. It substitutes instead, the capricious law of chance. It is an extraordinary theory for, by suggesting that things happen for no reason at all, it confounds our deepest instincts. Thus, although it has a foothold in some academic analyses (for example Neo-Darwinism[7]) it is not generally popular. This lack of popularity, however, is not a sufficient reason for rejecting it. Rather it must be rejected in this research because, although it (like this research) denies determinism, it also threatens the concept of choice. This concept requires that whatever a person did in any given situation, she not only had the ability to 'act otherwise', but also that she had reasons for acting as she did. Unlike determined, or chance-like behaviour, reasoned behaviour is based on an evaluation of situations and such evaluations enable people to prefer one possible course of action to another. It is this ability which gives the concept of choice its full force.

Thus, if persons are intrinsically moral and, therefore, capable of choice, it must also be true that they are:

(a) intelligent — that is able to receive, understand and act upon information about their environment;

(b) creative — that is able to manipulate this information into different patterns, in order to discover both what it might mean and, also, what possible courses of action such meanings would allow; and

(c) purposive — so that the search for the best course of action is both intentional in itself and deliberately translated into appropriate behaviour.

Without these qualities the behaviour of free persons would be indeterminate, a matter of chance. Persons could not, therefore, be held responsible for their behaviour. They would not be moral.

Importantly, any suggestion that there are times when a person does not act intelligently, creatively and purposively, leads logically to the conclusion that, at those times, that person is not acting morally either. Thus, if a person is to be described as intrinsically moral, these qualities would need to be regarded as intrinsic too. They would be inalienable dimensions of that person's nature and, as such, they would have to obey its logic — the logic of freedom. They, too, would be beyond the reach of determining causes and would be indivisible into more primitive parts. They would be absolute qualities, incapable of growth or decline. (See Section (iii) above.) Clearly, research which claims to measure intelligence or creativity by separating them out and dividing them up into discrete components, or which claims to identify the differential effects of nature and nurture upon them, is working with a definition of these concepts which is not acceptable here.[8] Indeed, those who attempt to measure intelligence and creativity must, in spite of their protests,[9] regard them not as qualities of human nature but as components of it — as some sort of object. Objects can be divided and measured; qualities can not.[10]

The view that people have reasons for what they do rather than that their behaviour is predetermined, or a matter of chance, thus leaves some awkward theoretical problems for this research. The challenge to the concept of intrinsic morality which is posed, not only by the large body of research into IQ and measures of creativity, but also by developmental theories which suggest that intelligence, or creativity, or indeed morality itself, can grow, cannot be left unanswered. This challenge will be taken up later in this chapter. Section (v) below will first explore in more detail the way in which theories of development can threaten the belief that human nature is intrinsically moral.

(v) *If adults are intrinsically moral, so are children*

This statement is a further consequence of the logic of human freedom discussed in Section (iii) above. It is especially important for this research, because any suggestion that children are less morally mature than adults would mean that an indiscriminate abandoning of control techniques by teachers would be foolhardy. Any one, or more, of their pupils might not yet have reached the stage where they could be trusted to react sympathetically and the result could be disastrous. Once again, however, the view that children are as moral as adults flies in the face of much commonsense thinking and academic analysis. In particular, developmental theories which suggest that children grow through stages into fully-fledged moral persons have to be rejected.

In order to substantiate this claim it is useful to start from the statement that for a person to be moral they must be responsible for what they do. In Section (iii) above, it was argued that the concept of personal responsibility necessitated the concept of personal freedom and that freedom, being an absolute state, is incapable of division and, therefore, of growth or decline. Clearly, then, it is not a state which one can achieve gradually, or in stages, and if adults are responsible for their behaviour (that is free) then children must be too. The only alternative to this line of reasoning is to adhere to a 'Sudden Miracle' theory. Such a theory would argue that at some specific moment in time (perhaps when an adolescent was in the middle of construing a particularly irregular French verb) genetic and environmental factors simultaneously and instantaneously lost their causal power over him and he was free. While such a theory would enable one to argue logically that whereas adults were responsible for their behaviour children were not, it would create as many theoretical problems as it solved. It would, for example, raise questions about how and why such a metamorphosis could occur. Certainly this freedom could not be 'caused' by anything, for freedom is beyond the power of determining factors. Moreover it would divide humanity into two species whose fundamental nature would be diametrically opposed — one determined and one free. Moral adults would belong to the latter; while not only children, but presumably any adult who had not been the recipient of the sudden miracle (perhaps the mentally ill), would be members of the former.

Significantly the 'Sudden Miracle' theory is not one which is generally argued and there certainly seems to be little evidence to support it.[11] It therefore does not seem improper to suggest that the most convincing logical consequence of a belief that adults are responsible for their behaviour is that children are too. This in itself, however, does not demonstrate that children are as moral as adults, for a second ingredient of the concept of morality (as defined in this research) is that of altruism. It might be the case that although children, like adults, are responsible for what they do, they are less concerned for the well-being of others. Fortunately, for present purposes, this too would be an illogical conclusion. Thus, if free persons are altruistic, then their altruism cannot be regarded as a component of their nature which can grow in power (like yeast in a bread mixture) or be replaced if faulty (like a broken fan-belt). As was argued in Section (iii) above, to be free a person must be a holistic, unitary phenomenon and not a machine of interacting parts. His altruism must, therefore, be a dimension, not a component, of his nature. As such, like intelligence, creativity and purposiveness, it would have to obey the logic of freedom and, therefore, miracles apart, if adults are intrinsically altruistic, then children must be too.

This is an interesting conclusion for it illustrates the fact that whatever else 'childhood' is, it is not a moral concept — if by 'moral' one means someone who is responsible for their behaviour and altruistic. This does not, of course, mean that it is not a useful concept in other spheres — physiology, sociology, or even psychology. Such disciplines are dealing with phenomena which can grow (bodies, cultures, states of mind) and whose growth is caused (by food, by people in interaction, or by an increase in knowledge). Significantly, however, such disciplines do not take 'a person' as their central concept. Intrinsic morality, on the other hand, must by its logic have a belief in a unitary person at its heart. To be a moral person is to be a whole person who exists (barring sudden miracles) unchanging through time. This accords well with the universal human experience that, in spite of even dramatic changes in our circumstances, our emotional state and in what we know or choose to do as the years progress, we are, in fact, the same person who has lived through it all, learning perhaps through bitter experience, but fundamentally the same. Throughout this book therefore the term 'person' will be used to refer to this fundamental being, who is nothing but her continuing self, expressing in a multitude of different ways her inalienable nature — intelligent, creative, purposive and moral.

(vi) *If persons are intrinsically moral their behaviour will be unpredictable except at a statistical level*

This statement is so obvious that it hardly needs discussing. It is mentioned here merely because it is one of the criteria which will be used in order to discover whether other work in the social sciences is compatible with the concept of moral personhood. Thus, any research — and there is a considerable amount of it — which claims to be able to predict a person's behaviour by identifying its environmental or genetic causes would need to be treated with care, for it would imply that a person's behaviour was determined not chosen. This is not to deny that, as a matter of fact, we are often able to predict how an intrinsically moral person will behave — especially if we know them well. Nevertheless, if persons can choose creatively they will always be capable of surprising us. Importantly, any positive statistical correlation between a person's past, present and future behaviour would need to be explained, not through the presence of determining causes, but through the fact that the reasons which had prompted the original behaviour still held good in the eyes of the person concerned. Thus, a person who had been ill-treated when young might become so convinced of the immorality of others that he consistently ignored their rights in his later inter-personal relationships. His behaviour would be 'predictable' in the everyday sense of the word. But he might make exceptions with people whom he got to know well and who, he came to believe, cared about him. He might even come to learn and understand the reasons why he was originally ill-treated and, thus, decide that his views about people in general had been mistaken. Or, alternatively, finding little satisfaction in a life in which he cut himself off from others, he might decide to try an experiment and see what would happen if he began to smile at them.

Thus, while it is true that people are unlikely to act unpredictably all — or even most — of the time (for it would be unintelligent to abandon behaviour which is known through experience to 'work') the statistical correlations which will then be discovered could not be taken as evidence that our behaviour is anything but chosen. To suggest otherwise would be to deny the concept of moral personhood and to treat the future as if it were closed.

> (vii) *If persons are intrinsically moral, the criteria they use to evaluate situations will derive from their own nature and not from an external moral code, whether internalized through socialization, or through divine revelation*

This final statement is true by definition. For, were moral law the creation of society, or of God, so that it had to be imposed, or learned, or revealed, then, by definition, persons would not be intrinsically moral. Because this is necessarily the case, it is possible to say something more about the contents of intrinsic moral law — what rights and responsibilities it demands; for, whatever these demands are, they will be grounded in human nature. Importantly, these rights and responsibilities will be grounded in the inalienable dimensions of, and not in some privileged part of, a person's nature (perhaps in his soul). For, as was argued in Section (iii) above, the logic of freedom and responsibility demands that persons are unitary phenomena and not a collection of bits and pieces — no matter how moral one of those pieces might be. It follows, therefore, that intrinsic moral law will be concerned not only with altruism, but with intelligence, creativity and purposiveness too.

Nevertheless, in considering in more detail what this moral law might be, it is useful to begin with altruism. In Section (i) above, it was argued that an altruistic person would be one who was as concerned for the well-being of others as for her own. The concept of well-being suggests not only physical, but mental and, perhaps, spiritual health, or 'wholeness', too. A person will, therefore, be well when her whole being is able to express itself. She will be 'well' when she is able to 'be'. A minimum requirement of moral law would therefore be the safeguarding of life (it being difficult to 'be well' if one is dead[12]): More generally, however, intrinsic moral law would be concerned with ensuring an equitable distribution of opportunities for persons to express their intelligence, creativity and purposiveness. It would be a basic moral right for persons to so express themselves; and a basic moral duty to ensure that by so doing they neither hurt others, nor took more than their fair share of the available opportunities, thus unwarrantably restricting the liberty of others to do the same.

The argument that if persons are intrinsically moral, then moral law is natural law to be discovered by a consideration of human nature, leads to a view of morality which is quite familiar. As importantly, because it can only be expressed as a general principle (and not as a definitive 'code of behaviour' which specifies certain actions as good, or bad, whatever the situation) it allows one to understand how morality is experienced as a series of dilemmas (see Section (i) above). Moreover, even on such grave issues as the taking of a life, or fighting a war, it is possible to see how intrinsically moral persons might disagree, with some arguing that taking life could never be the best solution and others that, in some cases, it is the optimum solution for the resolution of a widespread or greater evil. More significantly for this research, which is concerned with teacher-pupil conflict and not with matters of life and death, it is also possible to see how persons would apply this law in more mundane situations. Thus, intrinsically moral persons would resent being compelled to perform mindless tasks which did not allow them to express their intelligence and creativity, and they would resent this especially if those who benefitted from such tasks appeared already to be over-privileged. Indeed, they would only perform such tasks if there was no way out, or if they believed that they themselves would benefit in the long run, or that their performance was a service to the underprivileged who deserved their help. Significantly, in this latter instance, monotonous or uncongenial work would bring pleasure by allowing the performers to express their intrinsic concern for others.

Generally speaking, however, intrinsically moral persons would regard boredom as an evil which was naturally, and therefore morally, intolerable. They would feel morally justified in doing everything in their power to avoid this state of being. Moreover, if the blame for their boredom was laid at the door of others — whether properly or not — those others would be required to account for their actions. If they could not, or would not (perhaps because they felt that the moral basis of their behaviour was obvious) they would be in danger of being defined as immoral and the seeds of long-term conflict would be sown (see Section (ii) above). Thus, while natural moral law provides criteria against which *all* situations and social systems can be judged, having implications for the equitable distribution of resources such as wealth and power, it very particularly here allows one to understand one aspect of the moral indignation which sets pupils against their teachers. Thus, Woods, describing his time in Lowfield School, writes:

> One of my one or two outstanding memories from the enormous mass of experiences of the school is that of pupils talking to me about boredom. They managed to convey, in a very few words largely, years of crushing ennui that had been ingrained into their bones. A great wealth of expression was got into 'boring', 'boredom', 'it's so bo-or-oring here'. The word, I realise now, is onomatopoeic. I could never view lessons with this group again without experiencing that boredom myself. They would occasionally glance my way in the back corner of the room with the pained expression on their faces, and I knew exactly what they meant. (Woods, 1979, p. 267)

Woods' experience (which many teachers will recognize) is clearly consistent with the view that these pupils were condemning a situation which denied them the right to express their creative and purposive nature. That pupils often submit to such boredom can be explained as a consequence of their belief that a teacher is too powerful to oppose, or has done his best in a difficult situation and should, therefore, be tolerated. Where pupils hold neither of these beliefs they might be expected, if they are intrinsically moral, to act disruptively, for the situation would both allow, and demand, active moral opposition. Either way, it is possible to represent pupil responses to boredom, and indeed the boredom itself, as a consequence of pupil evaluations of the situation and the teacher, in which they invoke criteria which stem from a knowledge of their own nature and their natural rights. Importantly here, if pupils are to be represented as intrinsically moral, then this would be the logically necessary explanation of pupil boredom in school and would, therefore, provide the proper way of analyzing a prime source of teacher-pupil conflict.

In the preceding paragraphs seven of the logical consequences of the concept of intrinsic morality have been identified and discussed. One purpose of this exercise was to clarify the way in which important terms will be used throughout the rest of the book. It is, therefore, worth re-emphasizing three of the more important points which have been made. First, a distinction has been drawn between freedom and liberty which depends upon a different definition of 'causes' and 'constraints'. This distinction is vital to an understanding of the argument which will be presented in this research. Thus, while no attempt will be made to deny that constraints upon persons can sometimes horrendously limit the choices which are open to them, the optimistic message is that constraints, unlike causes, do not in themselves make conflict between teachers and pupils inevitable and, moreover, that they can, in many cases, be removed. Secondly, a distinction has been drawn (especially in Section (ii) above) betwen long and short-term conflict. Here again, no attempt has been made to deny that even if long-term conflict can be avoided by person-to-person discussion, in the short term, in the heat of a moment of hurt and before discussion can begin, tempers might blaze and angry scenes ensue. The promise of person-to-person discussion is not that such scenes can ever be totally avoided, but that they would become less frequent and never escalate into long-term antagonism. Finally, and perhaps of paramount importance, the concept of 'a person' has been discussed. Whereas some other analyses define personhood as a state which must be achieved, perhaps through socialization, the term is used here to denote the state of being human. The term 'a person' is thus used to signify that which is fundamental and unchanging in a human being, the ultimate self who is the same at birth and death. This self is depicted as intrinsically moral, so that when the term 'person' is used the adjective 'moral' is generally implied. Thus, the phrase 'person-to-person discussion' indicates a discussion between two intrinsically moral persons.[13]

A second purpose of Section One of this chapter was to identify the criteria against which other work in the social sciences could be judged, in order to discover which theorists support the concept of intrinsic morality and which oppose it. If the arguments presented above are valid, then the seven statements themselves provide these criteria. Unfortunately the result of this appears to be that important bodies of research must be rejected. While it will be argued later that there is a way round this problem, such a wholesale rejection might already seem to be so preposterous that the reader is no longer prepared to suspend her disbelief in intrinsic morality. It is, therefore, worth remembering some of the equally undesirable logical consequences of such incredulity. Thus, a definition of human nature, or morality, which did not include the notion that people are responsible for their behaviour and are, therefore, free, would mean that no-one could be blamed or praised for anything they did. Both their altruistic and hurtful behaviour would be determined by factors outside their control. Indeed, the concepts of responsibility, altruism and morality itself, would be left with little meaning. They would become descriptive, not explanatory, concepts. Statements about who was responsible for an action would merely be statements about who did it and not about what had caused it, for the person himself would not be its cause. The phrase 'altruistic behaviour' would merely signify behaviour which hurt no-one and not behaviour which was chosen because it would not hurt; and the term 'morality' would indicate simply that set of behaviours which a given society happened to value. It would be a relative concept leaving no grounds for criticism, for there would be no universal moral standard against which the morality of a society could be judged. Any rejection of the concept of intrinsic human morality would, therefore, solve some theoretical problems by creating new and equally formidable ones; for it would leave us in a stark world where human feeling would not arise out of human nature, but would, like everything else, be merely another link in a causal chain. Clearly much more needs to be said before we write off kindness, love and sacrifice in such a drastic manner.

2 Support in the Literature for the Concept of Morality

It is a relatively simple matter to demonstrate the logical consequences of a particular definition of morality. However, this still leaves the problem of whether the initial premise — that persons are intrinsically moral, is in fact true. As was suggested earlier the problem is a difficult one, for no matter how much data is provided which illustrates altruistic behaviour, the cynic could always argue that such behaviour was merely a consequence of successful socialization. Moreover, because the concept of intrinsic morality seems to be logically incompatible with received educational orthodoxy about the nature of intelligence, creativity and childhood, he would have powerful friends to call upon to substantiate his case. Before moving on to consider the validity of that case, therefore, it is worth bringing forward here some of the witnesses for the defence. The evidence which will be produced is necessarily circumstantial for the reason given above. Nevertheless, it is substantial in the sense that the names associated with it are as prestigious as those which the opposition can claim. As importantly, widespread support for the concept of intrinsic morality can be found in commonsense thinking. Thus, people do regard themselves as unitary entities who act intelligently and purposively. They believe they make decisions which result in actions; and, while constantly experiencing moral dilemmas for which they can find no ready-made answers, they go to great lengths to justify to themselves and others the morality of what they do.

Support in the literature of the social sciences for the concept of intrinsic morality, is equally widespread and it is only possible to record a fraction of it here. Some key aspects of this support will, therefore, be demonstrated. Thus, the work which is quoted will illustrate:

(i)   Support for the theory that persons exist as purposive entities, who are distinct from their environment and who are, therefore, free and responsible for what they do;

(ii) Support for the concept of intrinsic altruism;

(iii) Support, in research, for the view that conflict between such pupils and teachers can be explained through the concept of misunderstanding.

(i) Support for the view that persons are purposive entities who are distinct from their environment and responsible for their actions can be found in many places. For example, symbolic interactionists and pheno-menologists focus upon creative intelligence, emphasizing the effect on behaviour of the meanings which people attribute to events. Equally, many structuralists in both psychology and sociology recognize that, be neath statistically significant patterns of behaviour, lie human actors. Piaget, for example, argued that a distinct 'subject', or person, existed who was engaged in constructing his intellect through a process of 'assimilation' and 'accommodation'. He argued that this was so because '... the being of structures consists in their coming to be, that is, their being under construction'.[14]

Similarly, Durkheim, writing from a position sometimes regarded as deterministic, argued of collective social values: 'Each understands them certain elements and adds others'.[15] Of society he wrote:

> A day will come when our societies will know again those house of creative effervescence in the course of which new ideas arise and new formulae are found which serve for a while to guide humanity.[16]

Existentialists and marxists, while being more sceptical about the freedom of the intellect, recognize the power of persons to act freely even when their consciousness is heavily socialized. Indeed, this potential for creative action is at the heart of the marxist message giving it its revolutionary dimension, so that most of the disputes between marxists are disputes about the severity of the constraints under which persons labour, and therefore about the degree of their liberty.

Others emphasize the relationship between freedom and purpose. Thus, for example, Hampshire argues:

> In (the) act of referring to myself as the source of my action, and of referring to myself intentionally, I have that peculiar guarantee of my own distinct existence that Descartes put into the

Cogito. The guarantee lies in the intention behind the act of reference, an intention that I could not mistake for anything but my own.[17]

(ii) The literature also provides support for the view that persons are intrinsically moral. For example, Maslow writes of intrinsic conscience and Strawson, in an attempt to by-pass metaphyscial questions about freedom and determinism suggests that the question of human morality can be settled empirically. He argues that if the superficial differences in moral codes and behaviour revealed by anthropological and psychological studies are set aside, one is still left with evidence that concern for others is as universal a characteristic as concern for self, and that it is, therefore, in the nature of human persons to be moral. Thus, he claims that in all cultures a person who cared only about his own well-being '. . . would appear as an abnormal case of moral egocentricity, as a kind of moral solipsist . . . (which) is barely more than a conceptual possibility, if it is that'.[18]

Wherever one looks, Strawson argues, persons feel resentment towards, and condemn, those who offend them. Importantly, if the offended party then comes to recognize that there were mitigating circumstances, for example that the offence was unavoidable, or committed in ignorance, or good faith, then the offence is forgiven. He suggests that in this ability to forgive, persons demonstrate not only that they are intelligent enough to take new information into account, but that they are moral enough to empathize with the other's point of view. However, in taking offence, Strawson argues, we clearly believe that the other is a moral agent, who is responsible for his action and towards whom, therefore, a moral stance is appropriate. If we did not believe that he was capable of acting morally we would not condemn him, but act towards him as if he was an object, who merely posed 'problems . . . of intellectual understanding, management, treatment and control'.[19] We would regard him as something to be '. . . handled, cured or trained, (or) perhaps simply avoided'.[20]

Thus although we might be afraid of, or repelled by, or even feel a certain kind of love for such 'person-objects', we could never quarrel, nor reason, nor feel angry with them. Nor could we feel gratitude towards them. Being amoral and therefore not responsible for the effect of their actions on others, they could be accorded neither praise nor blame.

If Strawson's advice — to look at the evidence — is followed, it does indeed reveal that there is support for his views. For example, a consideration of the findings of sociological research into teacher-pupil conflict reveals not only that pupils and their teachers act morally, in Strawson's terms, but that they act intelligently and creatively and, in the light of the evidence and opportunities available to them, pursue their human purpose. Pupils resent and resist their teacher's attempts to engage them in 'boring' activities and they become angry when teachers use inhuman control techniques such as sarcasm and violence, to maintain order. As a result Willis's lads 'wag' and 'blag' and 'doss' their way through their lessons, and messing about and having a 'laff' become a way of life.[21] The pupils' attitudes are not blindly indiscriminate, however. Some teachers are valued because they display moral concern for the pupils, for example when they are helpful and explain work, or provide variety in the curriculum to alleviate boredom, or allow pupils some liberty.[22] Moreover teachers are liked when they display an interpersonal stance of friendliness, and when they express their own creative joy in life through a sense of humour. As a result, in different situations and with different teachers, pupils adapt their behaviour, sometimes conforming, sometimes retreating, sometimes rebelling.

Equally, research evidence illustrates the moral stance which teachers take to their pupils. They engage not only in an assessment of a pupil's academic abilities, but of their personal qualities. Moreover, it appears to be this latter form of assessment which is uppermost in their minds. Nash found that although he used professionally-orientated questions to elicit the criteria used by teachers to judge their pupils, 'All the (criteria) related to aspects of the child's personality ... (and) ... none dealt specifically with the child's abilities'.[23]

Willis, using a different theoretical perspective, found that even when it was accepted by teachers that their teaching role had broken down in relation to 'the lads', they still expected to be treated with politeness — arguably because, in their view, their rights as persons still remained after their rights as teachers had disappeared.[24] And Hargreaves illustrates in detail the complex way in which teachers evaluate evidence before imputing a label of deviance; and that even when a teacher is satisfied that the label is accurate, it is still possible that he will change his mind in the light of new evidence.[25]

Additionally, many research studies provide evidence that teachers, however misguidedly, go to great lengths to find mitigating circumstances for disruptive pupil behaviour. Often they draw upon the explanations given in educational literature blaming a poor home background, or a low IQ, or a weak or disturbed personality, or maladjustment.[26] In some cases such explanations take them very close to a perception of pupils as amoral objects who are not responsible for their actions. Nevertheless, the stance taken by such teachers is arguably a moral and intelligent one, in that they search for information which will allow them to forgive. Moreover, in the light of such information teachers appear to adapt creatively to the situation. In *The Divided School* Woods describes no fewer than eight categories of teacher responses, and although, as he suggests, these were undoubtedly strategies for survival, their variety expressed both creativity and differing evaluations of the situation and of the morality of pupil behaviour.[27] Back in the staffroom, with less to constrain them, teacher creativity was celebrated in a humour which paralleled pupil laughter.[28]

(iii) There is evidence, then, from a number of studies, which suggests that schools are populated with moral, intelligent and creative persons. Importantly, there is also evidence to suggest that when such persons engage in long-term conflict this is a consequence of misunderstanding, based on ignorance. The distribution, form, and manner in which this ignorance appears to be perpetuated does not lend itself to simple description but a few examples can be given. As already noted some research suggests that among teachers there is a tendency to view pupils as child-objects and to explain disorderly behaviour by reference to social and psychological causal factors. In this tendency teachers come to regard pupils as amoral objects to be 'treated and controlled', rather than as persons with whom they should communicate and reason. If, however, their pupils were instrinsically moral, this would be an example of a misunderstanding of human nature, which, it was argued in Section One (ii) above, promoted conflict.

Others, such as Sharp and Green and Willis, suggest that the teachers they observed were unaware of the societal and institutional constraints which limited both their own and their pupils' options.[29] Woods even argued that some teachers 'resisted' knowledge of those constraints which were beyond their control, because to acknowledge them would be to 'undermine commitment'.[30] As a consequence teachers would fail to take into account in their assessments of situations, factors which were visible to pupils. With teachers and pupils working from a different understanding of situations they would inevitably arrive at different conclusions about a proper moral response,[31] and unless they communicated the reasons behind their behaviour they would, as was argued in Section One (ii) of this chapter, be tempted to regard each other either as immoral persons who were pursuing their own interests and who should therefore be opposed, or as amoral persons who could not be trusted to understand.

In both the examples given above, research suggests that it is a form of ignorance about the nature of pupil persons, or of situations, which perpetuates conflict. Clearly, however, if intelligent persons interact on a daily basis, one might expect them to discover the truth about both and, if this did not happen, one would expect to find some mechanism at work to keep their ignorance intact. Lacey, in *Hightown Grammar*, posited the existence of a 'semi-permeable social membrance', which prevented teachers and pupils from seeing each other clearly, and which was 'particularly opaque from the pupils' point of view'.[32] This social membrane seemed to be sustained, in Hightown Grammar at least, by organizational rules — for example the one which, by preventing pupils from entering the staffroom, also prevented them from seeing their teachers in moments of human relaxation, from seeing them as persons. Moreover, Lacey noted systematic attempts by some teachers to hide their persons under their role during classroom interaction. For example, one teacher described how he would '. . . don the old mask and walk in like the Lord of Creation'.[33] That teachers often succeed in hiding their thoughts from pupils is further evidenced by Bird's study, in which she discovered a girl who '. . . was clearly surprised that a teacher had considered her to be a nuisance during the previous year'.[34]

If, however, teachers are to be represented as intelligent it must be shown that they have good reasons for hiding themselves. Once again there is evidence that these reasons exist. They are vividly described by Woods, who represents teachers as being caught in a

> . . . powerful pincer movement with the 'professional demands' on one side, and 'recalcitrant material' in the form of reluctant or resentful pupils on the other, with shrinking aid or ability to resist either. In the crush, the kernel of their real job, teaching, is lost, and only the cracked shell of their personal defences remains.[35]

Thus, externally derived constraints are, in Woods' view, compounded by pupil behaviour, forcing teachers into less and less productive ways of operating. In a situation where teachers are already heavily constrained by the expectations of powerful others and a shortage of resources and where, therefore, their moral dilemma (how best to teach) is already intense, disruptive behaviour appeared to be the ultimate constraint which prevented them both from finding a solution which was acceptable to their pupils and from communicating with pupils about their difficulties. For example, Woods found that attempts by a teacher to make lessons more interesting were aborted in the face of such behaviour[36] and it is possible to argue that the well-documented change of heart by young teachers from the idealism of their college courses which exhort students to 'motivate' pupils, to the chalk-face wisdom of experienced teachers which exhorts them to 'control' pupils, is as much a response to pupil intransigence, as it is to pressure from colleagues. Probationary teachers, faced with pupils who seem determined not to give them a chance, must sometimes wonder whether typical accounts of the effects of labelling have got the direction of causality exactly wrong, with the teacher rather than the pupil being the victim.

On the face of it, therefore, the concept of moral personhood which this book wishes to employ, dovetails with a number of different theoretical perspectives and with evidence from a number of substantive studies. Moreover, in all these studies the gap between teacher and pupil perception is emphasized, a gap which, it has been argued, promotes and sustains conflict. Whether this difference is represented as culture clash, or false-consciousness, the result is the same. Lacey's semi-permeable membrane prevents teachers and pupils from understanding each other.

Moreover, as research studies have suggested, teachers tend to explain disruptive pupil behaviour by reference to social and psychological pathology. Such explanations inhibit the open discussion of classroom issues, which would be necessary to dispel inter-personal ignorance, by suggesting to teachers that such discussions would not address the cause of the problem. Ironically, these explanations also emanate from the social sciences, creating confusion and inertia. If a person-centred approach to classroom conflict is to be persuasive this confusion must be dispelled.

3 The Problem of Determinism in the Social Sciences

The major challenge to the concept of moral personhood comes from deterministic theories which represent persons and their behaviour as the product of more primitive causes. By denying the distinct, unitary existence of persons, such theories deny the possibility of human choice, and therefore the possibility of human morality. Disruptive behaviour is seen as the consequence of, for example, a low IQ, inadequate socialization, or genetic bloody-mindedness.

Such challenges are not confined to work in the social sciences. There is a large body of commonsense thought which takes the same view. Thus, it is often argued that no matter what philosophers, or sociologists, might say, 'everyone knows' that some people are corrupt, or immoral, or not responsible for what they do. Such declarations are often illustrated with examples — Margaret Thatcher, Arthur Scargill, or Fred Bloggs in 4D. The commonsense attack, also, takes the form of arguing that, although adults may be moral, children are not; or that although some people may be intelligent and creative, this is hardly an appropriate description of little Susan Brown, who spends her time gazing morosely out of the window and resisting all attempts to engage her interest. Alternatively, persons are viewed as having two natures, so that they are only moral when their 'better nature' is in control. This better nature, which presumably resides somewhere in the recesses of the mind, is like a high court of justice to which the outside world can 'appeal' if the person's 'worse' nature is getting out of hand. All these views are deterministic, either because they divide persons into more primitive parts, or because they leave a person's morality and intelligence open to the vagaries of age, inheritance, or environment. They are sometimes accompanied by a sense of fatalism — that 'people are what they are' and that 'what will be will be', and that there is nothing that anyone can do about either.

All these commonsense views are represented somewhere in educational literature, and the names associated with them are often prestigious. Unfortunately they cannot be challenged by a single line of argument, because determinism in the social sciences presents itself in at least three different forms. Firstly, there are those theorists who appear (I tread warily here) to believe in determinism. Secondly, there are those who clearly do not believe in it but whose work can be misread in a deterministic way. Finally, there are those who do not believe in it but whose arguments ignore the logical necessity of the indivisibility of freedom, and are, therefore, as deterministic as the arguments which they attempt to confound. Each of these positions will be discussed in turn, in order to consider the nature of the threat they pose to the concept of intrinsic morality, and the ways in which that threat can be averted.

The case for a deterministic view of persons is generally based on the belief that, as physical organisms, they are controlled by the laws of cause and effect. Thus human behaviour is regarded as the outcome of environmental factors in interaction with bodily mechanisms and genetic inheritance. The logic of this view is that conscious thought must be dismissed as a by-product of a physical state of the brain; and it is this physical state of the brain (not its by-product) which must be accorded causal status. Thus Honderich writes:

> (1) Actions are movements caused by states of the brain. (2) These latter, the physical correlates of consciousness, are themselves the effects of other physical states.... The propositions expressed in these two sentences have as their subject matter the whole of human experience.[37]

Later, discussing the behaviour of a mythical Tom Green, he writes:

> The central point is that *anyone* in an R-like state would come to be in an S-like state, and furthermore would perform an action like Tom Green...What I have in mind is only this, that what Tom Green did is *explained* if one accepts the causal propositions (quoted above) by something that is not individual to, or peculiar to, Tom Green. More precisely, it is explained by properties of his, which no matter who else had them, would issue in an action like his.[38]

Clearly, in this view, Tom Green has no freedom to break the chains of cause and effect which control him, and although he might produce an unexpected response, it would be difficult to characterize this as a creative choice. It would, in effect, be the consequence of a hidden variable.

On the basis of the assumption that persons are purely physical organisms, such theorists then proceed to explain away the commonsense experience that we actually do have purposes which are our own and that we do make creative choices. They argue that the causes which act upon us operate at such a deep physiological level that we are unaware of them. We, therefore, cannot incorporate them into our descriptions of ourselves. Perceiving only that we cause an effect, and not that we are caused, we mistakenly imagine ourselves to be a first cause. Some even suggest that this state of affairs is not important. Gibbs writes:

> A person is free if he can do as he chooses. An act is an exercise
> of optative freedom if it is an exercise of its author's intentions. If
> his intentions have been determined by other things outside his
> control, it does not matter.[39]

Unfortunately, from the point of view of this research, it does. For if
Gibbs is right, persons in schools might be programmed to perpetuate
inhuman, though humanly constructed, social systems; or, from another
perspective, they might merely be sophisticated weapons constructed for
deployment in the wars of 'the selfish gene'.[40] Either way, any attempts to
resolve conflict by appealing to their morality, could only succeed by
chance.

Alongside attacks on the freedom of human purpose there are attacks
on intrinsic human morality. For example, Eysenck argues that conscience
is a 'conditioned reflex'[41] and Freud was in no doubt that moral behaviour
had to be imposed from without. He wrote:

> To put it briefly, there are two widespread human characteristics
> which are responsible for the fact that the regularities of civiliza-
> tion can only be maintained by a degree of co-ercion — namely
> that men are not spontaneously fond of work, and that arguments
> are of no avail against their passions.[42]

For Freud, described by Sulloway as 'Biologist of the Mind',[43] the turbulent, passionate, physical, 'Id' was clearly the nasty side of human nature,
and often in need of external control.

In spite of the gloomy message of these viewpoints, it is easy to see
why they have a widespread appeal. For those caught in heavily constrained situations they legitimate fatalism and lethargy.[44] For those in
positions of power they justify the use of that power;[45] and for the
theorists who base their research upon them, they promise equivalence of
status with highly successful and prestigious physical scientists. Thus, if
the statistical significance of psychological correlations do not yet match
those produced in, say, physics, this is perceived as a challenge. To meet
such a challenge would mark psychology's coming of age. As a consequence deterministic psychology is full of statistics and mathematical formu-
lae. Teachers are informed by Cattell and Child that motivation can be
split into 25 per cent of this and 25 per cent of that;[46] and Kline suggests
that a person's behaviour can be predicted 'with some degree of success'
by applying the formula:

$$ai_J = b \, J \, I \, A \, L \, i + \ldots b \, J \, k \, A \, k \, i + b \, J \, I \, T \, L \, i + \ldots b \, J \, k \, A \, k \, i +$$
$$b \, J \, I \, D \, L \, i + \ldots b \, J \, k \, D \, k \, i + b \, J \, I \, S \, L \, i \ldots + b \, J \, k \, s \, k \, i^{47}$$

One is left maliciously pondering whether Kline could have predicted the
production of his formula by applying it.

A malicious response, however, is no answer to sincerely held beliefs and careful research. Nevertheless, it does give a lead to where the weakness in such beliefs lies. What both commonsense and theoretical determinists have in common is a tendency to regard other people as determined, but not themselves. Both, for example, are complacent about excluding children from full free human status; and both adopt a highly moral tone in identifying the immorality of others. In this tendency the person-on-the-street is perhaps more consistent than some of her academic counterparts. She, at least, divides humanity clearly between those who are free and moral, and those who are not. She shakes her head sadly over these latter, and righteously advocates, in true Freudian style, the imposition of moral order. Academics, perhaps with more sensitivity to the issues involved, brand themselves with their own labels. They then, in a masterly example of double-think, attempt to persuade others to a deterministic point of view by the power of their arguments. It is as if they believe that persons can both be determined by factors beyond their control, and free to make intelligent distinctions between truth and falsity. This belief is clearly untenable. As Popper points out,

> ... according to determinism, any theories — such as, say, determinism — are held because of a certain physical structure of the holder (perhaps his brain). Accordingly, we are deceiving ourselves (and are physically determined to deceive ourselves) whenever we believe that there are such things as arguments or reasons which make us accept determinism.[48]

Popper's argument, of course, does not defeat determinism. It merely demonstrates that, like a belief in freedom, it is a metaphysical theory which cannot be proved. However, this is an important demonstration, for it sweeps away the pseudo-scientific aura which typically surrounds deterministic research, and makes it respectable, rather than naive, to consider alternatives. This respectability is enhanced once it is recognized that much of the determinism which emanates from the social sciences is so plastic that, as Popper comments '... a physical determinist who understands this matter at all, can hardly take (it) seriously'.[49] Indeed, it is often not intended to be taken seriously in the sense that the theorists involved do not intend to deny human freedom, and its apparent denial is a consequence of a number of confusions.

One of the confusions which can occur derives from an improper reading of sociological and psychological models which can lead to a category mistake. It is a truism, but one which is not always adequately emphasized, that sociological and psychological descriptions are not descriptions of persons, but of groups of people, or groups of their attributes and behaviour. Social and psychological facts are, therefore, facts about social and psychological categories. Thus, although these categories refer to persons, they are true of persons only at a statistical level, and this is the case even when the method used to process evidence is not statistical.

All such accounts recognize that, once the focus moves from the category to the individual person, categorical deviancy will be observed. Moreover, that deviancy will not stand in need of explanation. It will be there because categorical descriptions do not claim to describe in detail the behaviour of their members. It will be there by definition.

Thus structural-functionalists recognize that some working class pupils achieve well in a middle-class educational system. Labelling theorists recognize that a deviant label sometimes results, not in further deviance, but in conformity. Ethnographers point out that pupils rarely fall neatly into such categories as 'conformists' or 'rebels' and that the concept of a 'counter-school subculture' says nothing very precisely about any of its members; and even marxists allow that few teachers suffer from total false-consciousness. Given these truisms it is clear that to construe such accounts as deterministic at the level of persons would be a mistake.

That this mistake is often made, however, is certain[50] and it stems at least in part from linguistic problems. The confusion in the language of the social sciences is too large a topic to be addressed here. One aspect of it is, however, especially pertinent. This is the lack of clarity and precision in the use of the language of freedom and determinism.[51] Thus persons are sometimes represented as being 'shaped' or 'acted upon' by their environment, when what is meant is that they are constrained by it. Persons are described as 'divided', when what is meant is that they do, and believe, quite different things at different times, or that they are unsure what to believe and do. And even theorists who are explicitly wedded to the concept of human freedom, talk sometimes as if the future is closed. For example, Bigge wrote of cognitive-field psychology that its purpose was '. . . to formulate tested relationships that are predictive of the behaviour of individual persons . . .'[52] To predict, of course, is not to close the future, nor even to believe that it cannot surprise us; but the use of the word, like engaging in the enterprise of prediction, subtlely insinuates that choice is an empty concept.

The drift into deterministic language is particularly dangerous when it is used to describe sociological and psychological patterns and categories which are relatively stable. The combination of such language and evidence can make it seem as if these social and psychological factors have the power to reproduce themselves by acting causally on persons. The alternative possibility, that patterns of behaviour represent repeated, intelligent responses to stable patterns of constraints, is therefore obscured. Thus, rather than promoting action such accounts can reinforce fatalism, and constraints which could be removed are left intact.

At the heart of the determinism which emanates from the social sciences, however, is a failure to demonstrate the unity of the person. A major stumbling block has always been that, however much we might wish to separate ourselves from the rest of the physical universe, it is clear that we have at least an associate membership. Indeed, as our knowledge increases, it becomes impossible to set ourselves apart in any convincing way. For example, the discovery that our genetic make-up differs from that of a chimpanzee by only 0.7 per cent is, as Desmond comments '... sobering for an earth creature renowned for its cosmic gall'.[53] As a consequence, social scientists have always had to take the theories of the physical sciences into account. Some, as has already been noted, abandon all idea of human freedom in favour of a mechanistic view of persons. On the principle that 'if you can't beat them, join them', they have become collaborators in the perpetration of determinism. Others with more courage, but perhaps less logic, have sought to resist material determinism and keep alive a belief in human freedom, by suggesting that persons are comprised of (at least) two things — a body, which is determined, and a mind, or soul, which is not.[54] They therefore create a problem as intractable as the one they attempt to solve, for they need to demonstrate that these two separate entities are in fact only one. As Strawson points out, any failure to do this raises delightful, but awkward, questions about whether a particular mind can move between different bodies, or indeed, whether a body can be inhabited by more than one mind at a time. It also creates conceptual problems about who the 'real' person is, and certainly does violence to common usage. For as Strawson again points out '... when *a man says* 'I', then there speaks *one* identifiable man: he can be *distinguished* as *one* by ordinary criteria as, perhaps, Professor K, the Cartesian'.[55] (Strawson's emphasis)

The solutions offered to this problem have always been ingenious but rarely satisfactory — certainly from the point of view of teachers. For they require either a belief in God, who, by divine miracle (on a once and for all basis, or intermittently) can give the soul power over the body via the pineal gland, or the supplementary motor area of the brain, or in the spaces left by quantum indeterminacy.[56] Or they require an attitude of sublime indifference to the body, as if having one didn't matter. Thus Findlay commenting on the writing of Husserl, (who argued that human action originates in the mind) suggested that although the '... notion of "acts" is scrupulously explained ... their description reads like an account of ghostly performances'.[57] And Woods, describing an interactionist perspective, argued:

> Man inhabits two different worlds: the 'natural' world wherein he is an organism of drives and instincts and where the external world exists independently of him; and the social world, where the existence of symbols such as language, enables him to give meaning to objects. This attribution of meanings, this interpreting, is what makes him distinctly human, and social. *Interactionists, therefore, focus on the world of subjective meanings and the symbols by which they are produced and represented.*[58] (my emphasis)

This is, clearly, a useful and neat device for ignoring the problems raised by evidence from the physical sciences. Such evidence is ignored because it refers to our 'animal', and not our 'human' nature, and the body is successfully edited out of the picture. Teachers faced with a very physical 5Y on a wet Friday afternoon, however, are not accorded the luxury of editing the situation in this way; and the evidence in front of their eyes suggests that God is busy performing his miracles elsewhere and is not due back until after the bell.

Thus, both 'dualists' (who divide persons into body and soul) and 'idealists' (who emphasize the power of the mind,) fail to inform action in real classrooms. An unfortunate consequence of this has been that the concept of human freedom which they strive to defend is brought into disrepute and teachers are seduced by determinism. The clearest way forward, therefore, is to declare unequivocally that persons are unitary, *physical* organisms and to explore the physical sciences for evidence which would allow them to be regarded as intelligent, creative and moral organisms too.

4 Persons as Physical Systems

Russell argued in 1921 that:

> It is a wrong philosophy of matter which has caused many of the difficulties in the philosophy of mind — difficulties which a right philosophy of matter would cause to disappear.[59]

Sixty-five years after this was written, and in spite of the fact that 'the mind' is a central concept of education, an appeal to the physical sciences in a book on education feels like a gross social impropriety. This is, perhaps, understandable. As Habermas argued, the differing research methods and training processes in the different disciplines has 'promote(d) an ethnocentricity of scientific subcultures ...'[60] with each viewing the other as 'unintelligible'. Nevertheless, it is a pity, for it leaves teachers, and, Kenny argues, many social scientists too, working from '... an extrapolation from the history of science ...'[61] rather than with the insights of contemporary thought.

This is clearly not the moment for a detailed examination of the revolution which has taken place in Physics over the last century. Nevertheless, some illustration of the debate which has led to the undermining of classical determinism is helpful in order to demonstrate the feasibility of a belief in persons who are both physical and free from the iron control of the laws of cause and effect. Material determinism was most dramatically stated by Laplace, who argued that if one could know the exact state of the universe at any given moment in time, one could, in principle, predict and retrodict every other event. He regarded the universe as a magnificent machine in which dead matter was pushed, pulled, attracted, repelled, stuck together and torn apart again by whatever was in its immediate environment. Moreover, that environment was suffering a similar fate at the hands of its environment, and so on to the end of space and time. Events, such as human action, would be momentary episodes in causal complexes, and not even the sophisticated insights of catastrophe theory[62] could prevent persons from '... danc(ing) to the tune called by mathematical rules of local origin'.[63]

Fortunately, contemporary Physics has made it unnecessary for anyone to believe in such a universe. Briefly, Einstein, in 1905, challenged the old view of matter with the publication of his equation $E = M c^2$, which Calder claims '... sums up all action and creation in the universe'.[64] This equation proposed that matter, far from being inert stuff which moved mechanically in response to environmental pressures, was energetic in its own right. Morever, as Quantum Theory then demonstrated, at sub-atomic levels at least, its behaviour was unpredictable at any other than a statistical level. It therefore became difficult to understand how any machine, let alone a whole universe, could be persuaded to behave in a law-like manner, which it nevertheless patently did.[65] Thus, although the mechanical laws of cause and effect no longer seemed an adequate way of explaining movement in the physical world, they needed to be replaced by laws which could account for order. Heisenberg's Principle of Indeterminacy published in 1927 was, in effect, a holding position. It usefully identified the degree of deviancy which was statistically predictable in a given population of sub-atomic particles, but it did not solve the problem of why some particles deviated while others conformed.

As might be predicted physicists have responded in different ways to this problem, which is interestingly analogous to that facing social scientists.[66] There are those who argue that the unpredictable behaviour of sub-atomic particles is a function, not of their nature, but of the inability of researchers to identify and control all the variables present in an experimental situation. The apparent indeterminacy of matter, they maintain, is merely a measure of scientific ignorance.[67] Others, however, argue that the behaviour of matter is actually indeterminate, that sub-atomic particles do act in a chance-like manner, but that their constraining effect on each other produces a sort of order. Neo-Darwinism is based on this view. Thus the evolution of species is seen as the consequence of random genetic change together with the effect of the environment which determines which of these changes will survive to reproduce themselves.[68]

A third group of physical scientists, however, challenge the validity of the metaphysics of both determinism and indeterminism. They argue that different explanatory concepts now need to be employed to accommodate new and substantial bodies of evidence and theory. Of interest here is the fact that a number of the concepts they suggest are drawn from the social sciences. Thus one finds 'purpose' and 'intelligence' and 'creativity' being used as explanations of biological processes, and they are used not metaphorically but as the most obvious and direct way of understanding what is observed. For example Webster and Goodwin, arguing against the Neo-Darwinist position, suggest that rather than talking of a 'genetic programme', it is more precise to talk about 'genetic information'.[69] Such information is available to the organism to use for its own purpose. Their view is based on the known ability of organisms to use some of the genetic information available to them and to ignore the rest. Moreover, they do this in a way which ensures the preservation of a successful genotype. Thus, for example, they note that '... in a comparison of frog species there is a greater genetic difference *within* one order of Anura than there is *between* sixteen orders of mammals.'[70] Yet the frogs are able to choose the appropriate information from among the great diversity available to them and reproduce perfect Anura bodies; and the mammals are able to pick out just those significant differences from a mass of common information to ensure that the distinctiveness of their order is preserved. Moreover, this seems to be more than a predetermined response. The organism seems to be capable, in a time of crisis, of searching its genetic library for different information which will allow it to compensate for any accident which has befallen it and so to preserve its identity. Thus, even when a random genetic or environmental change is introduced in experimental situations, this does not '... result in a "random" change of structure, but an orderly change to another possibility ... (so that) ... typical form will be conserved'.[71] Perhaps even more dramatically, Schaefer calls on the example of fruit-flies which have been born without eyes — a defect which can be identified with specific genes. He writes:

> ... put them together, and breed them, and their offspring have no eyes. But after a few generations of breeding some have eyes again. When you check the genes they haven't changed at all. They still have 'eyeless genes'.... This is really astonishing. Nobody can explain it, even though de Beer has been asking the question for thirty years. To my intuition the lesson is clear. The genes and the functions and the bio-chemistry of the body are not controlling us in any sense whatsoever.... They are only servants to create pathways. They are plastic; one gene or a group of genes can apparently get together to make sure that something else gets done.[72]

The ability of very primitive life not only to use genetic information but to search for such information which it can use to its advantage, is, for these theorists at least, an indication that the biosphere is purposive, creative and intelligent. Their views clearly contradict the orthodoxy of Neo-Darwinism, but that orthodoxy is under attack at every level. Thus Capra[73] and Williamson[74] argue that although it is capable of explaining evolutionary change, it cannot account for the long periods of stasis in, for example, blue-green algae and molluscs. Moreover, many have argued that it cannot account for the initial emergence of life. Schaefer claims zero probability for the random emergence of organic matter, and estimates the probability of the emergence of a living cell by chance, as '... ten to the power minus 400 or 600 — meaningless'.[75] At another level, evidence is accumulating which clearly demonstrates the flexibility, creativity and intelligence of more complex organisms with a much larger proportion of animal behaviour being learned than had been supposed.

The ultimate attack on Neo-Darwinism, however, comes from physics. Neo-Darwinism is essentially a reductionist theory which edits the biological organism as an entity out of existence,[76] replacing it with biochemical causal interactions. The revolution in Physics, therefore, poses a severe threat. As Rose, a bio-chemist, comments:

> ... in-so-far as physical rationality must, in the long run, by definition underlie biological rationality, the biologist, although confident of the extensions to the edifice being created, all the time has to build in doubt as to whether the physical foundations may not be a quagmire.[77]

It is interesting, therefore, to find in Physics those who interpret the behaviour of inanimate objects[78] in equally radical ways, and who also claim that their new way of seeing is more capable than the old of accommodating all the evidence. David Bohm is prominent among such radical thinkers. Drawing upon the insights of both Quantum and Relativity Theory he suggests that the physical universe can best be understood as an expression of two laws, the law of flux and that of unity.[79] Ultimate reality for Bohm is, therefore, 'Undivided Wholeness in Flowing Movement'[80] — the 'holomovement'. The universe, he argues, is not made up of separate parts, or things, in mechanical interaction. It is a creative multi-dimensional effervescence in which relatively stable forms are discernible which we label as distinct objects, but which in reality are part of an unbroken, energetic whole.[81]

In his attack on an atomistic view of the universe Bohm challenges both classical determinism and indeterminism, while at the same time providing a way of explaining order and change. He uses two analogies which are helpful in clarifying his view. He compares the nature of the universe to that of a stream.[82] The flowing water represents the holomovement, the ultimate reality. However, on the surface of the stream, ripples are discernible. These ripples are like objects. They cannot be divided from the stream for they cease to exist without it. Moreover, their nature is its nature — that of liquid in motion, and their behaviour can only be understood in these terms. Thus, although at one level of focus the behaviour of a ripple appears to be 'caused' by its 'interaction' with another ripple, this type of explanation is superficial. The ripples merely constrain each other, and the behaviour of both of them needs to be understood in terms of their common fluid nature, and their oneness with the whole. In a second analogy, Bohm compares the universe to a holographic plate[83] In contrast to the negatives of two-dimensional photography, holographic plates when shattered retain the whole image in each fragment. In the smallest fragement the detail of the encoded image may be difficult to detect but it is still there. In the same way, Bohm argues, the fundamental nature of the whole universe is encoded in every naturally occurring physical system, however small. Thus, Bohn argues that because Quantum Theory leads to the view that the universe is an indivisble unity, all naturally occurring physical systems within it must share its nature. For example, they, too, will be indivisible unities and, like the universe, they, too, will be in a state of flux. Equally, if the behaviour of the universe is orderly, or patterned, which it patently is, then the behaviour of smaller systems — like persons — will also be orderly. However, this combination of flux and order cannot, in Bohm's view, be accounted for by suggesting that random, or indeterminate, change is 'patterned' by the determining effect of the environment which only permits certain changes to occur or survive. Indeed modern physics has demonstrated that particles can respond to each other in a way which defies the laws of cause and effect, for, however far apart they might be, their response can be instantaneous, occurring before any possible chain of determining events has time to operate. Some other explanation is, therefore, needed for this pattern of behaviour. Bohm's explanation is that the universe is a unity of 'potentially infinite dimensions'[84] and that among these are intelligence and purposiveness.[85] The distanced articles respond to each other, therefore, not because they 'cause' or 'constrain' each other's behaviour, but because, as members of a unitary phenomenon, they have immediate knowledge (or intelligence) of each other and respond in the light of this knowledge. Order is, therefore, according to Bohm not 'explicate' — imposed from without — but 'implicate' — a consequence of intimate understanding. Moreover, in a universe impregnated with intelligence, change cannot be regarded as random or indeterminate. It would need to be seen as a creative and orderly expression of whatever was possible.

This view of an intelligent and purposive universe, which both creates, and resides within, every naturally occurring physical system, is perhaps the physicist's equivalent of an all-powerful, universal God. It certainly resolves the problem noted by Spinoza that, if God is infinite and eternal, there is neither time nor space left over within which anything, which was not part of him, could exist (*Ethics* Part One, Proposition XV). Importantly, Bohm's view that the universe is the first cause of all physical systems does not destroy their freedom. Because the nature of the universe is encoded within all natural physical systems, they too would have the power to be the first cause of their behaviour albeit with a sphere of influence proportionate to their size. Importantly, Bohm is not suggesting that physical systems do not constrain each other and that, therefore, an explanation of some events can never be found by mapping out the factors present in the environment. Hurricanes do cause things to fall over. Rather he is arguing that such explanations would merely provide a measure of the liberty of any system (see Section One (ii) of this chapter). They would contain a description of 'explicate' order. However, the ultimate explanation of the behaviour of a system within a given set of opportunities and constraints would, he suggests, need to be based upon an understanding of 'implicate' order of the creative, intelligent and purposive nature of the system itself. He writes:

> Generally speaking, the laws of physics have thus far referred mainly to explicate order. Indeed it may be said that the principle function of Cartesian coordinates is just to give a clear and precise description of explicate order. Now we are suggesting that in the formulation of the laws of physics, primary relevance is to be given to the implicate order, while explicate order is to have a secondary kind of significance.[86]

Bohm's views are, of course, not universally accepted among physicists, for the debate in physics is a real one reflecting a crisis in knowledge. Moreover Bohm's arguments are infinitely more complex than this brief description implies. However, the quotation above, even on its own, makes the important point in relation to this research that, in understanding persons as physical systems, the laws of cause and effect need to be given second place. Thus, Bohm argues that if our descriptions are not to be over simplistic and if we are not to be misled into believing that the constraints upon people have the power to determine their behaviour, we must understand persons as organisms which are expressing the universal order which is within them. Or, as Hoyle, writing from the viewpoint of his work in astro-physics, suggests in every observed situation we need to see 'the response of the universe'.[87] Importantly, as Goodwin and Webster argue, behaviour would not be a consequence of '. . . a "central directing agency" conceived as a material entity — the so-called "genetic programme" . . .'[88] Rather, the behaviour of all living organisms would need to be seen as the result of a creative urge '. . . to explore the set of structures, perhaps infinitely large, which are possible for them'.[89] Evolution and symbiosis would be expressions of this creative urge and so would human action.

These are, clearly, very powerful ideas. Their appeal is not only that, although they are based upon complex theory and evidence, their message is simple, but, also, that they express what most people believe about themselves — that they are whole beings and that this wholeness includes both mind and body. Moreover, the ideas are persuasive because, unlike the evidence which underpins them, they are not new. They closely reflect many religious conceptions of the universe, especially those found in the east and in cultures where people live close to nature; and they draw upon and make coherent concepts which idealists and dualists sought to defend in the face of classical determinism. Equally they are persuasive because they come from an unexpected source, and because their expression has not been easy. They are not, in effect, the type of 'bright idea' which wins their authors acclaim and friends in academic places for they fundamentally undermine, rather than extend, established orthoxody and are more likely to block than promote a career.

But the power of these ideas also resides in their potential. Because they speak of the multidimensionality of all existence and of all events, they speak to every academic discipline. Indeed, Goodwin's belief that intelligence is behind the evolutionary process leads him to suggest that that concept might be the integrating idea which would bring the disciplines together.[90] Such possibilities cannot be explored here. The last section of this chapter, therefore, merely identifies the implications of this view of reality for the concept of moral personhood, and teacher-pupil conflict.

5 The Implications of These Ideas for Research into Teacher-Pupil Conflict

The view that the universe and all naturally occurring physical systems are governed by the laws of unity and flux rather than those of cause and effect has two important consequences for this research. The first relates to the validity of the concept of intrinsic morality and, thus, to the theory of teacher-pupil conflict which is being proposed. The second concerns the methodology which should be used in order to study teacher-pupil conflict at first hand. Each of these will be discussed in turn.

Theoretical Implications

The major theoretical problem for this research, identified in Section One of this chapter, was that the concept of intrinsic morality necessitated a belief in seven statements about human nature, which appeared to flout much common sense and theoretical thought. Thus it was maintained that, if persons were intrinsically moral, they must also be free. That is: that their actions were 'their own' and not determined by factors outside their control; that they were holistic organisms and not a collection of interacting components; and that their nature remained unchanging over time being an absolute nature and, therefore, incapable of growth or decline. In addition, the concept necessitated that persons were intelligent, creative, purposive and concerned for the well-being of others, and that these qualities, too, were unchanging and absolute, being dimensions of, and not components of, the nature of free persons.

The excitement of the ideas emanating from the 'hard' sciences is that it is possible to substantiate these views, so that an acceptance that persons are physical systems is consistent with the view that they are intrinsically moral. Thus, while there may be some who prefer to believe that humanity is set free from the physical world by divine intervention, such a belief is not necessary. Indeed, the existence of any universe — let alone Bohm's — is surely miracle enough. In Bohm's universe people would be the first cause of their actions because, as microcosms of that universe, they, like it, would be unitary forcefields and not a machine of interacting parts, no matter how sophisticated or magnificent. Their nature, like its nature, would remain constant through time, though how they expressed their nature would depend upon the opportunities and constraints within their immediate environment. However, that environment could never 'cause' them to behave in a specific way. It could only restrict their liberty just as one ripple on a stream restricts the movement of another, but can neither cause nor prevent it acting like a ripple. Moreover, in a universe where even the old distinction between animate and inanimate phenomena begins to break down and where persons, therefore, cannot properly disassociate themselves from other naturally occurring systems, it is still possible to see them as intelligent, creative and purposive. Thus, if Goodwin and Webster are correct in their view that evolution is 'a cognitive unfolding', 'an orderly change from one possibility to another' and a creative urge to 'explore a set of structures perhaps infinitely large', then human action would be like this too. Indeed, Bohm's law of flux would be the law of creativity, a law which persons by their nature would express. How they would express it might be statistically predictable, just as at sub-atomic levels the behaviour of particles can be statistically predicted. But, like at sub-atomic levels, where some particles behave in unpredictable ways, persons, too, could surprise us.

Clearly, then, it is possible to maintain that persons, as wholly physical systems, are 'free' in the full sense which is required by the concept of intrinsic morality. However, Bohm's twin universal laws of flux and wholeness would also allow persons to be regarded as intrinsically altruistic. Thus, as microcosms of the whole, persons would experience, in their innermost being, their unity with the whole and with other microcosms of the whole. Neither religion nor human friendship would stand in need of further explanation. Empathy with others, concern for other natural phenomena, and an urge to express communion with the universe would be fundamental to human nature.

Importantly for the theory of teacher-pupil conflict which is being proposed by this book, an acceptance of Bohm's physical laws of creative flux and wholeness justifies the view that intrinsic morality is a matter of problem solving. Thus the law of flux would require persons to take up opportunities afforded by their environment and express themselves in all possible ways. The law of wholeness would require that they did this in a manner which neither hurt others, nor denied them the opportunity to do the same. These twin imperatives would, therefore, create ongoing problems about the proper limits of individual creativity. Moreover, these problems could clearly lead to disagreements and conflict. As in all descriptions of Heaven where the inhabitants are, by definition, dead, the potential for conflict would only disappear in the universe if Bohn's holomovement was stilled.

However, it would be an error in logic to view individual creativity and concern for others as competing motivations leading inevitably to conflict. This would divide a person into two, with one part of his nature at war with the other. It would destroy his unity and his freedom. With his nature divided equally between 'good' and 'evil' there would be no natural or logical reason for him to prefer either. Choice would be the equivalent of tossing a coin or submitting to the prevailing dominant force. Thus the twin motives of creativity and unity would need to be seen as inalienable dimensions of each other. Importantly, to suggest otherwise would be to ignore the logic of the universe which, itself being indivisible and in a state of flux, represents the infinitely creative potential of the ultimate whole. Indeed, the smaller the system, the fewer opportunities there would be for creative expression and, thus, any escalation of conflict into a permanent division between individuals or groups, would constitute a failure to achieve the creative potential of cooperation. In the rest of nature this potential is realized through symbiosis and delicately self-regulating ecologies. The human species, in common with some others, forms cultures and societies for the same end. Endemic conflict would, therefore, restrict creativity as well as altruism and being, thus, contrary to human nature could only occur as a result of the sort of misunderstanding described in Section One (ii) above.

These theoretical conclusions have important implications for teacher-pupil conflict and for its resolution. Firstly, it would need to be clearly understood that such conflict benefitted neither teacher nor pupils, for important opportunities for expressing creative unity would be lost and the well-being of all parties would, thus, be diminished. With this understanding there would come the moral imperative to try to resolve the conflict and to find ways in which its negative consequences could be overcome. Secondly, because conflict would be the result of some form of misunderstanding its resolution would lie not merely in an attempt to manipulate the constraints on the situation. Indeed, these might be intractable. Rather the solution would lie in the removal of the misunderstanding. Thus, teachers, whose stock-in-trade is the dissemination and analysis of knowledge, would be especially fitted to play the leading role in this process. They would need to share with their pupils, and invite their pupils to share with them, the reasons for their actions so that these reasons and the information on which they were based could be evaluated. In this way new ways of behaving could emerge based on cooperation, bargains, or an agreement to co-exist. While this latter would not open up the full potential of creative unity it would at least allow space for future discussion. Finally, the theories currently emanating from the physical sciences insist that anyone who wishes to study or resolve the problem of teacher-pupil conflict, should clearly understand the nature of both persons and inter-personal behaviour. They should know that human action is impregnated with morality and that spiralling through classroom events, shaping them and giving them meaning are the twin laws of creativity and unity, articulated through intelligence. Without this knowledge they will neither intervene effectively, nor even understand what they see.

Implications for Research Methodology

Traditionally, research into human behaviour has fallen into two broad camps. There are the 'idealists', that is those who believe in the power of ideas to promote action and who, therefore, argue that only by discovering a person's reasons can his behaviour be explained. They thus take as their data their subject's own account of situations and, in so doing, rely almost exclusively on the contents of his conscious mind. In the other camp are the 'positivists' — those researchers who maintain that people do not know why they do what they do and, therefore, that to ask them to explain their behaviour would be a waste of time. Better, by far, to identify factors within a person's make-up or environment whose presence seems to correlate highly with certain forms of behaviour and then to suggest that these factors cause such behaviour. Examples of such research have been described in Section Three above.

This is, clearly, a crude categorization for there are cases of research in which a combination of 'reasons' and 'causes' of behaviour are combined. Generally speaking, however, when this is done no attempt is made to demonstrate logically how a person's behaviour can be regarded as both 'reasoned' and 'caused' — perhaps because (as has already been argued) such a demonstration defies logic. Nevertheless, such research is clearly based on some sort of hunch that both the idealist's belief (that the conscious mind has all the answers) is over-optimistic and that the positivists' belief (that human behaviour is determined) is over-pessimistic. The implications of the theory of persons and of human behaviour which has been argued above supports this hunch and provides it with a logic. Thus the rest of this chapter will illustrate how an over-reliance on the contents of a person's consciousness in any investigation into their behaviour could lead to false conclusions. However, instead of resorting to the traditional alternative, to a search for causal factors and the development of statistical models to represent their differential effects (which clearly, destroys the concept of personal freedom) it will be suggested that a methodology needs to be devised which is appropriate to the nature of the subject under study — that is, to human nature.

At the heart of the idealist's case lies a belief in the rationality of human action. The theory of persons and of human behaviour which has been presented above, supports this belief. However it demands an extension of idealist thinking, for idealists often distinguish between 'actions' which are consciously performed and perhaps even thought out, and 'behaviour' which is not. This latter is regarded as something (like breathing) which 'the body' gets up to and over which the rational mind has little control. Here, however, all human behaviour, whether conscious or unconscious, instinctive, emotional or deliberately planned would need to be regarded as intelligent and purposive, for there is no logical room in the concept of a unitary intelligent being for unreasonable or 'mindless' behaviour.

This conclusion has some interesting and important consequences. For example, although much of the discussion in this chapter has focused on theories which deny human freedom by dividing persons into mental and physical components, there is an equally destructive tendency in the social sciences to divide the mind. At least since the time of Freud the effect of the unconscious on behaviour has been recognized, as has the fact that the unconscious often appears to disagree with what people consciously think they want. As a result even theorists who were happy to discount the body in their explanations, were left with a divided person and the problem of knowing which mind was really in control. The views emanating from the physical sciences provide a solution to this problem as well as to that of classical dualism which divides the body from the mind, or soul. They place the multi-dimensional process of human nature, involving intelligence, creativity, purposiveness and morality, unequivocally at the level of the unconscious in the hidden ground of the holomovement. The importance of unconscious intelligence is, of course, already widely recognized so that, for example, hearing or seeing, which were once regarded as mechanical processes, are now known to be highly selective, but unconscious, performances. Certainly Goodwin, in claiming evolution to be a creative cognitive unfolding of physical possibilities, is not claiming consciousness for slime moulds.[91]

With the identification of the unconscious as the seat of creative intelligence, consciousness can be regarded as one of its most interesting behavioural products so far. It can, as Armstrong suggests, be explained as '. . . simply the scanning of one part of our central nervous system by another'.[92] Its function would be, in Watson's words, that of:

> . . . a feedback system. It lets you know how you are doing.
> Feedback simply means taking some information from a system
> and returning it as part of the input. Any thermostat does this

while regulating temperatures. Bio-feedback is the return of biological information to the person whose biology it is.[93]

Additionally, as Dennett suggested, it could be used as a way of communicating with others. He draws an interesting analogy in which he likens consciousness to the press office of an organization. As in all organizations, however, the backroom boys of the unconscious might, for all sorts of good reasons, give the press officer only '... a very limited and often fallacious idea of what is going on in the system', so that he remains 'massively ignorant' and massively misinformed'.[94]

There are a number of important consequences for research methodology of these representations of consciousness.[95] Clearly, if we wish to understand the behaviour of other people, it would be best to get in touch with their unconscious which knows most fully what is going on. Indeed, our unconscious reading of, and response to, the unconscious body language of others suggests that we attempt this difficult task on a regular basis. Secondly, although the view of consciousness outlined above demotes it from pride of place in an understanding of persons, it can still be regarded as a powerful tool. It allows organisms who have it to reconsider a plan of action by feeding it back into the system before putting it into operation. Organisms which had not developed consciousness would not have this facility and if their plans were not right first time it could lead to a fatal result. In addition, the ability to externalize thought into a verbal language allows organisms with consciousness to share with others information which would otherwise be trapped within their own system, and this sharing of information leads to the creation of more powerful systems of knowledge within which new opportunities for action can be perceived; opportunities which would be lost if persons could only work from their own experience.

Nevertheless, like all inventions, if the limitations of consciousness are not recognized, the results can be unfortunate. For example, there is a clear warning in the arguments expressed above about an over-reliance on how people explain their own behaviour. The 'backroom boys of the unconscious' might be releasing an adequate story but equally they might regard it as in the interests of the organism to deceive. Alternatively, they might have more pressing business to attend to and, for the sake of economy of effort, provide the most minimal account they can get away with. Or they may simply not have an adequate verbal language within which to express the complex truth. Often we can compensate for such deficiencies by reading other messages — by observing emotional responses and what people do. Thus, research using first-person accounts would only be convincing if it was accompanied by this type of evidence too. Indeed, any descriptions of persons or human interaction which failed to demonstrate the coherence of a whole range of behaviour would need to be treated with care. For, if the theory proposed in this chapter is correct, it is to the language of the whole human organism that we should listen if we wish to understand people.

Finally, the proposed view of persons as unitary physical systems warns against the dangers of using psychological and sociological models which can appear to turn human nature into a machine of interacting parts. Human nature it has been argued is not a 'thing', a bundle of in-born or environmentally caused behaviours and traits, or of independent capacities which can be neatly mapped out, weighed, measured, predicted and controlled. However, this does not lead to the conclusion that it does not really exist, that it is merely a concept, a term which we use to make sense of the world. Human nature is not, for example, comparable to the concept of deviancy which, some argue, exists only in the eye of the beholder. Rather it can be compared to the concepts of electricity and gravity which equally do not refer to 'things', but which have a reality which is independent of human perception — as anyone who has accidentally touched a live wire or walked over the edge of a cliff will know.

This book, therefore, explores the power of the creative, intelligent, unitary nature of persons which, it suggests, can both create and resolve conflict. In order to keep this power sharply in focus the use of models has been rejected in the belief, shared by Bohm, that when they are applied to persons they are 'meaningless' and 'confusing'. Without models, Bohm argues:

> Men may ... be able to understand one another deeply, and so act from a sense of the oneness of humanity. What is needed here is not action from a 'model of oneness', but rather an action from direct and immediate perception that the deep cause of all human action is a universal formative movement. Human nature in its totality — and all the essential abstractions from it such as beauty, truth, rationality — are not 'things', but aspects of a whole move-ment. 'Things' can properly be conceived in terms of models. But the whole movement of human nature cannot be contained in any models. Rather it is capable of continually revealing itself anew in fresh and unexpected ways that are in essence inexhaustible.... The real question — which has to be explored deeply rather than given a ready answer — is then: can we live without depending on models of human nature?[96]

This is a question which is clearly important for teachers who are in conflict with their pupils and who might look to models devised by social scientists to provide ways in which such pupils can be manipulated and controlled. It is one of the questions to which this research is addressed and, clearly, has important implications for the methodology employed.

Notes

1 See Chapter 1 and ROGERS C. (1983) p. 250.
2 This part of the argument owes much to STRAWSON, (1974). His ideas are discussed more fully in Section Two of this chapter.
3 See AYERS, M.R. (1968) p. 104.
4 For example a person is not able by the power of her will to resist being knocked over by a tidal wave, or to defy the force of gravity as she jumps from a tower block window. Nor is she 'free' to speak Russian if she hasn't learned the language. I make these very obvious points because they are sometimes presented as serious objections to a belief in human freedom. The examples used are usually more subtle, but of the same order, e.g.: 'Working class pupils are not free to benefit from a middle class education because they do not have an adequate language'; or 'The worker in capitalist forms of production is not free to improve his position because of the power of the society which oppresses him'. While understanding the thrust of these objections, I shall argue that there is a form of freedom to which they do not apply. Importantly, throughout this argument, the use of the personal pronoun — as in the phrase 'his behaviour' — will be used to discriminate between something which a person 'chooses' to do and something which he is compelled to do. Thus, if someone bumps into me causing me to fall this will not be described as 'my' behaviour, even though it was I who fell. As I might in real life, I will 'disown' the behaviour because I was not responsible for it. It was something which 'happened to me'.
5 The problem of the freedom of the sleeping, or otherwise unconscious, person raises itself here. The grounds for claiming freedom for such persons will become more apparent in the discussions in Sections Four and Five of this chapter. However, in order to prevent scepticism interfering too grossly with the reader's willingness to address the logic of the argument, it is worth recalling that current medical practice, in treating deeply unconscious patients, suggests a belief that such patients can make choices. Persons in coma are played recordings of their favourite music, or messages from those they love, presumably in the hope of convincing them that it is worthwhile making the necessary effort to live.
6 I am aware here that I am touching on a debate which is gathering in momentum on the potential morality of computers. The view I take in that debate is that although a computer might be programmed to take, or develop, a moral view, it could never be regarded as intrinsically moral, precisely because it would have to be programmed by an external agency. Its moral stance might appear to be natural, that is 'in its nature' once it had been programmed, but it would never arise naturally. It would always have antecedent causes. The most appropriate analogy would be between it and a person who needed to be socialized into being moral.
7 Neo-Darwinism will be discussed in Section Four of this chapter. Briefly, it suggests that evolution is the consequence of random changes in genetic structure, which produce new species; and that, whether or not these species survive, is 'determined' by whether, or not, the environment permits them to survive. It, thus, combines both indeterminism and determinism.
8 The claim that intelligence and creativity can be regarded as (a) free from determining causes; (b) indivisible and, therefore, unmeasurable; and (c) inalienable dimensions of each other, transgresses current psychological orthodoxy to such an extent, and raises issues of such importance and interest, that a full discussion of this view has been added in an appendix.
9 I have in mind statements such as that by EYSENCK, (1981, p. 13) who suggests that there is 'general agreement that whatever "intelligence" may be, it is not a

"thing" like a table or a chair, or a pig, but a *concept* ...' which he compares to the concepts of 'heat' or 'electricity'. This appeal to the 'hard' sciences dangerously obscures the problem of how one can possibly measure a 'concept' — a problem as acute for physicists as psychologists.

10 Can, for example, something be bluer than blue, or for that matter less blue than blue, and still be blue? It could, of course, be turquoise blue, in which case it would be blue/green; but whatever the mixture, it could not be more of the colour it was, than it was. It could only become something else. Which is not to say that a colour cannot attach to twice as large an area of space. For example, if I mix two pots of blue paint I have more blue paint, but it isn't more blue. I can cover more wall but, if I do the job properly, each part of the wall is as blue as the rest. Paint and walls are objects which can be divided and measured, their quality of blueness cannot. (NB. This argument is not affected by the debates about whether colour exists independently of the effect of light waves from a surface on the retina, or of whether what you call red is in some objective sense the same as what I call red. (See e.g. ARMSTRONG, D.M. (1981, pp. 104–18). Colour, too, may be only a 'concept', but whether it has been developed as a response to the surface of an object, the nature of light or the state of the retina, it is an attempt to describe a quality of something.)

11 It is, of course, sometimes argued that miracles can happen which transform a person. Some regard baptism as a means of cleansing the person of original sin; and Paul's vision on the road to Damascus might be an example.

12 The argument still holds if one believes in life after death. In this case the life to be 'safeguarded' would be the life of the soul whose 'well-being' might — at least according to the Inquisition — require a person to be burned at the stake in order to ensure eternal life. Such burnings would have to be regarded as the work of moral persons acting, in the light of their beliefs, for the good of others.

13 An additional and important semantic consequence of a belief in intrinsic morality is that the terms immoral and amoral cannot properly be applied to persons. This leaves the problem of whether these terms would have any meaning, or whether they should, so to speak, be struck out of the language. The three terms (moral, immoral, and amoral) are an interesting trio, none of them being the exact opposite of either of the other. Thus 'moral' implies responsibility for one's behaviour and concern for others; immoral implies responsibility for behaviour, but no concern for others; and amoral implies that one is not responsible for one's behaviour, with concern for others being an open issue — depending upon how one has been 'programmed'. These semantic waters are further polluted by terms such as 'irresponsible' (which is clearly neither the exact opposite of 'responsible', nor of 'not responsible') 'good' and 'evil'. Thus, if persons are intrinsically moral to talk of a 'good' person would be to repeat oneself; and to talk of an 'irresponsible' or 'evil' person would be a contradiction in terms. It might, perhaps, be proper to talk about 'good' or 'evil' actions, or social systems, as long as by this one meant that they were good, or evil, in their consequences and not in their conception; and it, of course, would be entirely proper to designate objects as amoral. Whatever the solutions might be to these semantic problems, it is clear that anyone who wishes to defend the concept of intrinsic morality would need to use the language with care and precision, lest by inadvertently suggesting that *persons* can be immoral or amoral they perpetuate the misunderstanding which, it has been argued, sustains long-term conflict.

14 PIAGET, J. (1971) p. 140.
15 BIERSTEDT, R. (1969) p. 216.
16 BIERSTEDT, R. (1969) p. 222.
17 HAMPSHIRE, S. (1982) P. 73. The 'cogito' (Latin for 'I think') refers to Descartes'

famous conclusion: 'I think, therefore, I am', which, he claimed, proved personal existence.

18 STRAWSON, P.F. (1974) p. 15. A solipsist is someone who is convinced only of his own existence. A 'moral solipsist' would, presumably, be convinced that he was the only person who mattered.

19 STRAWSON, P.F. (1974) p. 17.

20 STRAWSON, P.F. (1974) p. 9.

21 WILLIS, P. (1977).

22 See, for example WOODS, P. (1979). p. 91.

23 NASH, R. (1973) p. 21.

24 Willis interprets the evidence in a rather different way, suggesting that the teacher's demand for good behaviour is a '... nagging vestigial but insulting attempt to reassert the old authority ...' (WILLIS, P. 1977, p. 81). He claims in the same passage that 'many teachers operate with a schizophrenic notion of the pupil', and that 'It is as if pupils were composed of two people one of whom is supposed to save the other'. Nevertheless, one of the examples he gives of typical teacher exhortations to the lads — 'Would you give me just some common decency, you haven't even got manners to listen to me, so why should you be treated like men?' suggests that my interpretation does not distort Willis's evidence. It seems quite possible to argue that teachers are declaring here the paramouncy of the moral, personal stance over all other allegiances; that they are demanding to be treated first and foremost as persons with human rights, even if 'the lads' refuse to recognize their teacher role.

25 HARGREAVES, D. (1975) p. 186.

26 HARGREAVES, D. (1975) sums up this phenomenon when he comments that '... social scientific literature has been taken over by teachers to "explain" deviant conduct ...', so that '... social scientific vocabulary has become part of the explanatory vocabulary of teachers, whether it's sociological ("He comes from a bad home, you know") or clinical-psychological ("He's maladjusted, you know")' (pp. 263–4).

27 WOODS, P. (1979), pp. 140–69. Certainly it is difficult to equate such a variety of contradictory norms of teacher behaviour with the notion of an integrated teacher culture, or teacher solidarity. Whatever teachers might have in common would appear to derive less from their membership of a social group than from their human need to survive. This lack of cultural solidarity within the teacher group is further illustrated by BALL (1981) who points out that teacher attitudes to differing classroom practices reflects their membership of 'subject sub-cultures'. These subcultures reflect not only knowledge specialisms, but also perceived 'problems and difficulties involved in teaching these subjects' (p. 182). As a consequence Ball finds that 'the difference in overall perspective and opinion about the innovation (mixed ability teaching) between the subject departments is most correctly represented as a continuum, extending from strong support (English Department) to strong opposition (Modern Languages Department)....' (p. 183). And while, as Ball again suggests, 'These subject sub-cultures are obviously related to wider subject-perspectives ...' he goes on to emphasize that 'it is important to qualify what is a generalization of attitudes by pointing out differences within the perspectives and within subject departments ...' (p. 185). No doubt the differences within subject subcultures could be linked with membership of others — political or class. But there comes a time when an explanation of a teacher's behaviour through the concept of culture is so cumbersome (because it requires an interpretation of the interaction of so many subcultures) that it is no longer a useful way of explaining the phenomenon, and it becomes easier to say that teachers behave as they do because they made this or that moral decision in the light of

28 See for example Woods, P. (1979) pp. 210–37.
29 For example, Sharp and Green (1975) argued that 'Unless or until educators are able to comprehend their own structural location and develop theories of the limits of feasible political action to transform that location, they will continue to be unwilling victims of a structure that undermines the moral concerns they profess ...' (p. 227). And Willis (1977) discussing the inability of curriculum reform to deal with what, in his view, is the real problem, a stratified society, suggests that although 'modifications of the teaching paradigm ... are in no sense machiavellian' (p. 69), they derive either from '... a genuinely and strongly-held conservative ethic concerning the organic, harmonious society' (p. 69), an ethic which Willis clearly feels to be mistaken; or from 'what might be called a pragmatic, not over-hopeful and poorly integrated solidarity with the working class — an uneasy but fatalistic sense of their basic oppression' (p. 70), which Willis, clearly, believes to be an over-pessimistic assessment of the situation. Willis, therefore, like Sharp and Green, is accusing teachers of misunderstanding the situation, not of immorality.
30 Woods, P. (1979) p. 167.
31 An example would be the different understandings which, Willis (1977) argues, teachers and some pupils have about the nature of manual labour. To 'the lads' there is little 'intrinsic' difference between one form of labour and another, so that 'there is near indifference to the particular kind of work finally chosen so long as it falls within certain limits defined, not technically, but socially and culturally ... (which) ... is in marked contrast to the sense of range and variety of jobs projected by careers advisory services and teaching' (p. 133). This difference in view leads 'the lads' and their teachers to approach Careers lessons very differently.
32 Lacey, C. (1970), p. 175.
33 Lacey, C. (1970), p. 174.
34 In Woods, P. (1980(a)), p. 101.
35 Woods, P. (1979), p. 141.
36 Woods, P. (1979), suggests that 'Many a teacher who has tried an experiment, and felt it has not been working and disorder threatening, has reverted midstream to more formal techniques. The best example is the dictating of notes'. (p. 163)
37 Honderich, T. (1973) p. 201.
38 Honderich, T. (1973) p. 210.
39 Gibbs, B. (1976) p. 39.
40 See Dawkins, R. (1978) who appears to reduce the biosphere to an arena in which genes compete for survival, and where the successful genes would be those which built the most efficient 'survival machines' (p. 21) in the form of successful species. In his words: 'They are in you and in me; they created us, body and mind; and their preservation is the ultimate rationale for our existence. They have come a long way, those replicators. Now they go by the name of genes, and we are their survival machines'. Dawkins' view is disputed by Goodwin whose ideas are discussed more fully in Section Four of this chapter.
41 In Lickona, T. (1976) p. 109.
42 Strachey, J. (1978) p. 4.
43 Sulloway, F.J. (1979) 'Freud — Biologist of the Mind' was the title Sulloway gave to his book.
44 Sartre, J.P. (1948) argues this point. In his defence of existential fiction he wrote:

What people reproach us with is not after all our pessimism but the sternness of our optimism. If people condemn our works of fiction in which we describe characters that are base, weak, cowardly and sometimes even frankly evil, it is not because those characters are base, weak, cowardly or evil. For suppose like Zola we showed that the behaviour of those characters was caused by their heredity, or by the action of the environment on them, or by determining forces, psychic or organic. People would be reassured. They would say, 'You see, that is what we are like. No-one can do anything about it'. (p. 42)

45　How else, such persons would argue, is order to be maintained, except by exerting a force which can counteract subversive genetic or social factors?

46　CATTELL, R.B. and CHILD, D. (1975) p. 202.

47　In CHAPMAN, A.J. and JONES, D.M. (1980) p. 327.

48　POPPER, K. (1979) pp. 223–4.

49　POPPER, K. (1979) pp. 220.

50　JAHODA, M. in CHAPMAN, A.J. and JONES, D.M. (1980) warns against an over use of models in psychology, pointing out that … ideas, including conceptual models of man, have consequences in the real world.… Indeed there is ample evidence that (they) have influenced the way people, not just psychologists, think and act'. P. 279.

51　Other problems stem from the use of the same term to describe different things, and the use of different terms to describe the same thing. The Appendix illustrates some of these problems further, in a discussion of the concept of intelligence.

52　BIGGE, M.L. (1982) p. 171.

53　DESMOND, A. (1979) p. 13.

54　There is of course the other great division found in the literature of the social sciences between the conscious and unconscious mind. This will be discussed in Section Five of this chapter.

55　STRAWSON, P.F. (1974) p. 176, in an essay addressed to these issues.

56　Malebranche (1638–1705) is associated with the idea of intermittent acts of God, and Leibniz (1646–1716) with a single act of God at the time of creation, which would allow the body and soul to act in harmony (see, for example, the Open University's Third Level Arts course, A 303, Units 1 and 2, pages 32 and 33); while Descartes (1596–1650) has his name inescapably linked with the pineal gland, the organ which he considered was the meeting point between body and soul. In our own century the search by Dualists for a satisfactory solution continues. POPPER (1979) describes, for example, how 'Some quantum theorists (have) suggested … that our minds work upon our bodies by influencing or selecting some quantum jumps. These are then amplified by our central nervous system which acts like an electronic amplifier: the amplified quantum jumps operate a cascade of relays or master-switches and ultimately effect muscular contractions' (pp. 232–3). Alternatively, John Eccles (a Nobel prize winner for his work on the brain) puts forward the theory that the Supplementary Motor Area of the brain is the seat of the will. Until recently the SMA was considered to be an obsolete relic of the evolutionary process, having no known function. Eccles has recently discovered, however, that it becomes electrically active a fraction of a second prior to the activation of other parts of the brain which control movement — hence his hypothesis that it is the source of decision making, the seat of the will. The scientific aura which surrounds explanations based on quantum theory, or intricate research into the functioning of the brain, should not, however, be allowed to obscure the logical difficulty that, if the mind or soul is made of stuff which is fundamentally different from that of which the body is made, so that it does not have to obey physical laws, its effect on the body must be the consequence of a divine miracle. The only difference between these twentieth century explanations and their seventeenth century counterparts is that they credit God with knowing more science.

57 In URMSON, J.O. (1975) p. 133.

58 WOODS, P. (1979) pp. 15–16

59 RUSSELL, B. (1921) p. 307.

60 In ADEY, G. and FRISBY, D. (1976) p. 225.

61 In HONDERICH, T. (1973) p. 103. My own discussions with groups of teachers in which I challenged them to describe the implications of, for example, Relativity and Quantum Theory, leads me to confirm Kenny's view, rather than the optimism expressed by Gilbert Ryle that 'the influence of the bogy of mechanism has for a century been dwindling because ... the Newtonian system is no longer the sole paradigm of natural science' (RYLE, G. (1949) pp. 309–10). My experience has been rather that of C.P. Snow, described by DAUB in CHANT, C. and FAVEL, J. (1980) p. 222: 'In his presentation of the "two cultures" issue, C.P. Snow relates that he occasionally became so provoked at literary colleagues who scorned the restricted reading habits of scientists that he would challenge them to explain the second law of thermodynamics. The response was invariably a cold negative silence. The test was too hard'.

62 See WOODCOCK, A. and DAVIS, M. (1978). The problem which Catastrophe Theory leaves is that of space for human freedom and creativity; for although it does not describe linear chains of cause and effect, but rather clusters of factors in relationship with each other, it nevertheless implies an inevitability of result which is beyond the power of persons to change.

63 HOYLE, F. (1977) p. 119.

64 CALDER, M. (1979) p. 31. The equation $E = Mc^2$ proposes that matter becomes pure energy at the speed of light, and that matter is, therefore, an expression of energy, that it is energy at rest. The significance of this proposition is not only that it provides material for authors of science fiction whose characters, by travelling at massive speeds, can return to earth with bodies which are younger than those of the friends they left behind. More importantly it has implications for persons living ordinary terrestrial lives, and for the environment in which those lives are led. For as CAPRA, F. (1982) points out 'Whenever a subatomic particle is confined to a small region of space, it reacts to this confinement by moving around. The smaller the region of confinement, the faster the particle will "jiggle" around in it' (p. 78), so that '... the velocities of protons and neutrons are often so high that they come close to the speed of light. This fact is crucial for the description of their interactions, because any description of natural phenomena involving such high velocities has to take the theory of relativity into account' (p. 79). Persons, as natural phenomena comprised of myriads of atoms, can, therefore, be described more exactly as energy in motion, than as inert stuff which is acted upon by external forces; and so can their environment.

65 It is of interest here to refer to the second law of thermodynamics, which C.P. Snow claimed his literary colleagues did not understand. (see note 61 above). This is the law which predicts the dissipation (not the concentration) of energy, so that if you bounce a rubber ball, it will eventually come to rest. In the words of WARN, J.R.W. (1969) 'It will be a little hotter than before; the molecules will be jiggling in different directions with various energies. That all these molecules should spontaneously organize themselves into a co-ordinated upward movement, so that the ball "jumps" up once again, is not impossible in terms of energy conservation. *It is however extremely unlikely*, because there is only one type of net upward movement compared with the myriads of *equally likely* schemes of

random movement' (Warn's emphasis, P. 56). This well attested phenomenon of entropy, that is the dissipation of energy through uncoordinated effort, is typical of machines and contrasts dramatically with the ability of some physical systems to 'get their act together' so to speak, so that their molecules are organized into a coordinated movement. Consider, for example, the necessary coordination of molecules to get a person out of bed in a morning. Such orderly molecular behaviour clearly stands in need of further explanation.

66 It is also of interest that it is not just the theoretical problem which is analogous to that facing social scientists, but the problem of research methodology too. The intrusive effect of the social scientist on the human situation he is observing, is well known, and it is, therefore, comforting to note that when physicists investigate the sub-atomic world, their instruments interfere in that world in a way which is equally difficult to control. (See BOHM, D. 1980, p. 73 and 74, for a discussion of this phenomenon.)

67 Einstein, for example, was never prepared to accept the indeterminacy of matter. His position, summed up in his famous dictum 'God does not play with dice', was countered by Bohm's equally famous quip 'Stop telling God what to do'. But that did not solve Einstein's problem of how to account for order.

68 Thus in 1971, the geneticist and Nobel Prize Winner, Jacques Monod, wrote: 'Chance alone is at the source of every innovation, of all creation in the biosphere. Pure chance, absolutely free but blind, at the very root of the stupendous edifice of evolution: this central concept of modern biology is no longer one among other conceivable hypotheses. It is today the *sole* conceivable hypothesis.' (Quoted in CAPRA, F, 1982, p. 109.)

69 WEBSTER, G. and GOODWIN, B.C. (1982) p. 43.
70 WEBSTER, G. and GOODWIN, B.C. (1982) p. 34.
71 WEBSTER, G. and GOODWIN, B.C. (1982) p. 43.
72 SCHAEFER, G. (1982) p. 25.
73 CAPRA, F. (1982) p. 310.
74 In SMITH, J.M. (1982) pp. 171 to 173.
75 SCHAEFER, G. (1982) p. 23. Schaefer's argument is, of course, statistical, but the weakness of the hypothesis that life emerged 'by chance' can also be demonstrated empirically. Thus, with knowledge of hindsight, it is possible to select the known chemical ingredients of living cells and submit them to primeval conditions, thus reproducing in a controlled way the situation which Neo-Darwinists claim occurred by accident. The only problem is that living material is not produced in these experiments. MARGULIS, L. (1981) p. 80, discussing this problem alongside our ability to produce viruses from a recipe which includes part of a living cell, argues 'If a plausible natural phenomenon could be found that could accumulate the organic materials and replace both the investigator and the enzymes he isolates from living cells, the problem of origin of simple virus-sized replicative systems could be solved, at least in principle.' She, herself, is sceptical about the possibility.

76 WEBSTER, G. and GOODWIN, B.C. (1982) make this point strongly, arguing that 'The organism as a real entity, existing in its own right, has virtually no place in contemporary biological theory'. p. 16.

77 ROSE, S. (1976) p. 365.

78 Many physical scientists are beginning to have difficulty in distinguishing between inanimate and animate objects, though the distinction between a machine and a naturally occurring physical system remains clear. The lack of a clear distinction between what is alive and what is not can be illustrated by the virus. In their simplest forms they are just nucleic acid (DNA or RNA). Outside cells, they appear to be inert chemicals. They can be analyzed into their constituent parts, and then put back together again. Yet even after such a drastic operation which

would finish the career of a lesser mortal, if they are implanted into a cell they come alive, and within an hour can produce thousands of new viruses (see CAPRA, F. 1982, p. 298). Moreover, as Capra (1982) again points out, 'Macroscopically, the material objects around us may seem passive and inert, but when we magnify such a "dead" piece of stone or metal, we see that it is full of activity. The closer we look at it, the more alive it appears' (p. 78). Capra also notes (1982 p. 307) that 'Detailed studies of the ways in which the biosphere seems to regulate the chemical composition of the air, the temperature on the surface of the earth, and many other aspects of the planetary environment have led the chemist James Lovelock and the microbiologist Lynn Margulis to suggest that these phenomena can be understood only if the planet as a whole is regarded as a single living organism'. Such evidence clearly challenges traditional ideas about what is alive and what is not.

79 One of the problems with which physicists have had to contend over the past half century or more, has been the apparent contradictions between General Relativity Theory on the one hand, and Quantum Theory on the other. I am in no way qualified to comment upon these differences which are discussed in BOHM, D. (1981) pp. 134 to 139. However, his statement that, 'Though quantum theory is very different from relativity, yet in some deep sense they have in common this implication of undivided wholeness' (p. 134), is supported by an argument which is accessible to a non-scientist; and his conclusion that the important differences between the two theories will only be finally resolved by 'a qualitatively new theory, from which both relativity and quantum theory are to be derived as abstractions, approximations and limiting cases' (p. 176) appears sensible in the light of knowledge of the way theories evolve. Both General Relativity and Quantum Theory are 'good' at this point in time, in that they both help us to operate more successfully within the physical environment. Bohm's search for an over-arching theory which will make sense of both in relation to each other is, therefore, an important enterprise.

80 BOHM, D. (1980) p. 11.

81 As far as I am aware Bohm does not make any reference to Nietzsche, but the latter's 'Dionysion world of external self-creation, of eternal self-destruction' (1913 p. 432) is irresistably recalled '... do ye know what "the universe" is to my mind?' Nietzsche demands (p. 431). 'Shall I show it to you in my mirror? This universe is a monster of energy, without beginning or end; a fixed and brazen quantity of energy which grows neither bigger nor smaller, which does not consume itself, but only alters its face.... It is ... energy everywhere, the play of forces and force waves, at the same time one and many, agglomerating here and diminishing there, a sea of forces storming and raging in itself, for ever changing, for ever rolling back over incalculable ages to recurrence, with an ebb and flow of its forms, ... saying yea unto itself ... for ever blessing itself....' Bohm's account is infinitely more sober than that of Nietzsche, but it does seem to add up to the same thing.

82 BOHM, D. (1980) p. 10.

83 BOHM, D. (1980) p. 177.

84 BOHM, D. (1980) p. 189.

85 BOHM, D. (1980) p. 195 Also, BOHM in BENTHALL, J. (1973) P. 108.

86 BOHM, D. (1980) p. 150.

87 HOYLE, F. (1977) p. 122.

88 WEBSTER, G. and GOODWIN, B.C. (1982) p. 16.

89 WEBSTER, G. and GOODWIN, B.C. (1982) p. 46.

90 See GOODWIN, B.C. (1976) pp. 188–9.

91 I use slime moulds as an example because Goodwin himself is particularly hard on them (see GOODWIN, B.C. 1976, P. 225).

92 In Borst, C.V. (1970) p. 79.
93 Watson, L. (1980) p. 164.
94 These particular quotations are taken from Miller, J. (1983) p. 79. A fuller discussion of Dennett's views on consciousness can be found in Dennett, D. (1981) pp. 149 to 173.

95 One, which although not directly relevant here is worth noting because of its importance to educational theory, is the consequence for Behaviourism. Behaviourism has always posed a problem for humanistic social scientists because it seems to be based on a mechanistic view of persons, and yet Behaviour Modification techniques appear to work. As a consequence it is often regarded as dangerous, or as David Hargreaves (1975 p. 258) claims 'morally repugnant', and Skinner-bashing has become a fashionable academic pastime. Once it is accepted that intelligence operates at an unconscious level, however, Skinner's repudiation of the conscious mind no longer seems so threatening; and there is no need to feel affronted at being compared with a pigeon once it is accepted that pigeons are intelligent, too. It becomes safe to trust the body which is perhaps less easily fooled than our conscious mind; and if persons respond unconsciously to their environment or to behaviour modification, one can assume that they do so intelligently. To be fair to Skinner who claims, with this book, that 'the picture which emerges from a scientific analysis is not a body with a person inside, but a body which *is* a person ...' (1973, p. 195), he does also claim that 'Man is not made into a machine by analyzing his behaviour in mechanical terms' (p. 197). The problem with Skinner's theoretical work is that it is often confused, as Dennett, D. (1981, pp. 53 to 70) illustrates. In the confusion, however, it is important not to throw away the proverbial baby. There is an important message in what Skinner says, even if the way he says it is unfortunate.

96 In Benthall, J. (1973) p. 108.

3   3Y and Their Teachers: A Case Study
of Classroom Conflict

In Chapter Two it was suggested that evidence from a selection of sociological studies into schools supported the view that both teachers and pupils were intelligent and moral, but that they sometimes acted upon the mistaken belief that the other was not. It was suggested that it was this mistake which turned disagreements into long-term conflict. Pupils, in failing to perceive the circumstances which limited teacher behaviour, interpreted that behaviour as immoral and as something to be opposed. Teachers, in sometimes failing to see the intelligence of pupil behaviour, came to see it as determined by social and psychological causes and, therefore, as something to be manipulated or controlled. The evidence, it was argued, suggested that the continued failure of teachers and pupils to recognize their mistake was in part a consequence of the availability of commonsense and theoretical models which validated their belief in the inhumanity of the other, and in part a consequence of material and social constraints. Important among these latter would be the expectation of powerful others, that teachers should use their time to 'teach'. With high pupil-teacher ratios and a fragmented secondary curriculum, interpersonal communication would arguably be an early casualty even when a teacher believed in the intelligence and morality of disruptive behaviour and felt that time taken to engage in person-to-person discussion with their pupils would help solve classroom problems. As a result, teachers would be driven into survival strategies which made communication even more difficult, promoting further disruptiveness and further survival strategies. As Desnos pointed out about all such chicken and egg situations, 'This sort of thing can go on a very long time if you don't make an omelette'.[1] This chapter contains a detailed description of the chickens and eggs which were produced in one specific instance, and investigates how it was that some teachers failed to mix an omelette which was educationally nutritious.

The investigation was necessary for two reasons and this chapter, therefore, has two major aims. In the first place the studies of classroom conflict cited in Chapter Two were broadly sociological in their focus. The evidence they contained was, therefore, collected to demonstrate the predominant characteristics of social groups. As a consequence, it cannot be relied upon to provide either adequate descriptions or explanations of the behaviour of individual members of those groups. A theoretical extrapolation from sociological studies to the behaviour of persons, clearly needs to be checked against evidence collected with persons sharply in focus. The first major aim of this chapter, therefore, is to demonstrate the degree to which person-centred evidence supports the proposed theory of classroom conflict and in so doing to clarify further the links between a sociological and personal perspective. Specifically it will emphasize that statements of the order: 'The most basic, obvious and explicit dimension of counter-school culture is entrenched general and personalised opposition to "authority"',[2] and 'Much deviant behaviour is ... the defensive counter thrust of a complete fully integrated and self-sufficient culture under attack from an alien culture'[3] are descriptions of social groups and, therefore, need to be treated with care by teachers in their dealings with individual pupils.

The second reason for exploring a specific example of teacher-pupil conflict, using a person-centred perspective, was the need to identify a class which could become the subject of a limited series of experimental lessons. The purpose of those lessons was to examine what happened when a deliberate attempt was made to resolve conflict by making the teacher's problems explicit to pupils. The second major aim of this chapter, therefore, is to demonstrate that the pupils in 3Y were just as typically disruptive as pupils in the counter-school subcultures described in other research. In so doing, the opportunity is taken to give a full introduction to the pupils who became the subjects of the experimental lessons.

In broad terms this chapter can be regarded as forming a bridge between the general theory of Chapter Two and the experimental lessons described in Chapters Four to Seven. The data upon which it rests was collected intermittently over a period of one year prior to setting up the experiment. It is drawn from discussions and interviews with the pupils in 3Y, conversations with and written statements from their teachers, and observations of lessons. After a short introduction in which the background of the school and the class is described, the data is used to demonstrate:

(i) the teachers' views about the behaviour of 3Y, and about their professional response to this behaviour;

(ii) the pupils' views of their teachers, and of their own behaviour; and

(iii) my perceptions of the behaviour of 3Y and their teachers in interaction.

Using this format it is possible to identify areas of agreement and disagreement between the actors' views, and to investigate whether any disagreements could be accounted for by ignorance of the other, fuelled by a failure to communicate at a person to person level.

General Background

The school which 3Y attended was a large comprehensive situated on the edge of a council estate which had been designated as a Social Priority Area. The problems faced by families on this estate were, therefore, publicly identified and the school was recognized as one which contained very difficult pupils. In fact the intake of the school was unusual, for as well as drawing from the neighbouring estate it also contained a fair proportion of children of professional parents Indeed, the headmaster in an initial interview described it as containing both ends of the socio-economic scale 'with nothing in the middle'.

Many of the teachers appeared to sympathize with the problems faced by the estate children, some having chosen to work in such an area from a sense of vocation. A senior teacher told me:

> I think we've got a lot of kids coming to school with many (and I think it has increased too) more problems than they used to come to school with. And they look to teachers, or to some teachers at any rate, to help them with a lot of things that are not happening at school at all. We're dealing with the pressures at home, we're dealing with the fact that the family unit isn't secure.

As a consequence of these problems a Pastoral Care System had been set up, and one member of the senior management team spent most of his time on this aspect of school life, helped by Heads of Year.

Perhaps not surprisingly many teachers felt they had discipline problems with some of their classes. The school had a system whereby offenders were put 'On Report'. This meant that they had to carry a Report Form round with them to each lesson. Teachers had to indicate on this form how a pupil had performed in their class under the headings of 'Punctuality', 'Behaviour' and 'Work'. A cross meant poor and a tick satisfactory. In addition teachers sometimes added comments such as 'Excellent' or 'Very Silly'. The more 'crosses' a pupil received the longer they stayed 'On Report', and this could lead to a parent being called in, or exclusion from school. On the other side of the coin, it was possible for pupils to earn House Points for good behaviour or good work.

In spite of these measures and a system of school rules, pupil behaviour was often seen as a problem. Apart from unruliness in class there was a constant flow of misdemeanours reported in other parts of the school premises and truancy was a major headache. The school was housed in two buildings on the same site. 3Y had most of their lessons in the Lower

School, which was characterized by long corridors, narrow winding stair-cases, and a structure which seemed to amplify every noise. Occasionally they moved across to the Upper School for lessons in specialist rooms. A number of teachers commented on the scope which the lay-out of the building and the change-over arrangements gave for absconding from lessons.

There were rules relating to movement and the seu of the buildings. For example staircases were labelled 'Up' stairs and 'Down' stairs to facilitate the flow of pupils. Nevertheless, this rule was constantly broken, leading to noisy traffic jams. At lunch times the building was locked. One door was manned by senior pupils who let in staff and other authorized persons, while repelling the illegal attempts of pupils to enter. This meant that most of the pupils spent their breaks on the extensive playing areas, but because there was easy access from there, not only to the local estate but to nearby woods and a park, this added to the high rate of truancy. A teacher with responsibility for dealing with truants described the mea-sures which had been taken to attempt to control the problem, and admitted their lack of success:

> We've tried various gimmicks, like we have registration at the end of the afternoon now, and that's supposed to keep them in for the afternoon. What it does is allow them to leave at nine o'clock and come back at half past three.

Academically the school was organized into three bands. The fourth and fifth year, however, followed Options. These were chosen during the third year prior to setting up 'O' level, CSE and Non-examination groups. Pupils were given forms outlining the option scheme, and when they had made their choices they had to get the appropriate member of staff to sign saying that the pupil would be considered for that subject. In addition to Banding and Options there was setting within bands for Mathematics. For pupils who had difficulty with basic literacy and numeracy there were 'Special' classes in a remedial unit, to which they went on a number of occasions during the week for extra help. For the non-examination senior pupils the school had developed special courses, but there was scepticism among the staff as to their value. One teacher who had spent long hours instigating such a course, and who had therefore, in Becker's terms, laid down substantial 'side-bets'[4] on it, admitted 'We thought we'd improved things by having super, interesting, practical lessons and so on. And the very thing that you think, you know, is marvellous, they don't turn up!' Perhaps unlike Woods'[5] stereotype of a 'committed' teacher, however, she did not blame the pupils but the system, arguing 'Their outside life is so much more mature, that school is ... absolutely irrelevant'.

The school day was organized into seven lessons, with five forty minute lessons in the morning which ended at one o'clock and two lessons in the afternoon which ended at three thirty. Apart from this ongoing routine, however, the school offered a rich variety of clubs, sports events, school trips, drama productions, and parent-teacher functions. The description of the school given above, therefore, must be read as a caricature of the richness of life which it contained. It provides the minimum information necessary to understand 3Y's life within it.

3Y themselves were in the bottom band of the third year.[6] They were a small class of twelve boys and six girls aged between thirteen and fourteen years. They had been marked out by their teachers not only as low achievers but as excessively troublesome, a view which was confirmed by my own comparisons with other classes I observed. They all lived on the council estate and they included pupils who were known to the police, who came from broken homes, and from homes affected by poverty. They included non-readers, truants, and habitual offenders against school rules.

Identified as a difficult class in a difficult school they, therefore, appeared to be ideal subjects for study and for the experimental lessons. Importantly, their official reputation was acknowledged and accepted by the pupils themselves. On my first meeting with them in the corridor outside a lesson I was to observe one girl, Barbara, said 'Are you going to be our teacher?' Before I could answer she added gleefully 'You won't be able to control us'. Unable to resist the challenge, I countered 'Want to bet?' But my bravado was brushed aside with the claim 'We're the naughtiest class in the school'.

3Y's Teachers

The teachers in the school knew I was there to investigate the causes of disruptive behaviour; however, they did not know the theoretical perspective from which I was working. Nor did they know initially that I intended to engage in experimental lessons. I merely said I was interested in why certain pupils were badly behaved and how they, as teachers, dealt with the problem.

I was interested in discovering not only their views of the pupils and why they behaved as they did, but also their views on how they, as teachers, attempted to carry out their role. It was of interest, therefore, that these teachers talked most readily about problems which derived from outside school and which made their job increasingly difficult. These included shortage of money and time which had been exacerbated by ROSLA and comprehensivization. They also talked of the problems of communication in a large school not only with children, but between staff. They talked of the stress which all this created, one blaming a 'lack of backing' from outside agencies, and another 'this bloody illogical society'.

When they did talk about 3Y, it was in much the same terms as teachers in other research; that is they argued that 3Y's inability to do school work was a major cause of problem behaviour. They linked this with an inability to concentrate, a lack of self control and, sometimes, with problems at home. As in other accounts different teachers varied in the emphasis they put on these factors, but they were in no doubt that they affected classroom interaction on a day-to-day basis. In addition to socio-economic and pathological explanations, however, 3Y's teachers described them as persons who demanded human rights. Their understanding, therefore, appeared to consist of different levels of explanation which they regarded as linked, but in a way which was too complex to explain briefly. They, therefore, chose what they regarded as an appropriate level of response for a specific question, taking the other levels, for that moment, as given.[7]

The teacher who spent most time with this class was their form teacher Mr Charles. He took them eight times a week for English and History. He seemed well-informed about their background. He told me that at least five pupils were without one parent (three had no father, and a brother and sister had no mother). Two members of the class had siblings who were in serious trouble with the police, one for GBH. Several members of the class had been in court themselves. Of all the teachers who taught this class he was the only one who referred directly to this background in order to explain their behaviour. He commented on '... deprivation ... unfortunate sibling example, and even parental encouragement'. However, he also put their poor behaviour down to 'frustration and lack of self respect'. Four out of the eighteen pupils he described as 'lacking confidence. Need continual contact with the teacher'. These were counterbalanced by another five who were '... always confident. They don't need the teacher'. Four were described as having an acute inability to concentrate, and three as persistent truants. One girl was described as being 'large', as having 'friends older than herself', as having plenty of money to spend, but as being 'probably unhappy at home'. He said 'When she's sensible she's a mature young lady, but most of the time she's difficult, offensive and obscene'.

Although no other teacher referred directly to home background, there were comments which suggested that this type of explanation may have been in their minds. Thus the technical drawing teacher said 'It's obvious to me that certain misbehaviour is a cry for help'. However, he quickly went on:

> Other types of behaviour I put down to devilment and quite natural. For example one boy stuck a compass in another and the other gave him a mouthful within earshot of me.

He also seemed to think that lack of ability was part of the problem. He commented 'There are one or two members of the group who require a great deal of attention, and providing I can give this their behaviour is excellent'.

The woodwork teacher also blamed their poor behaviour on '... frustration from their lack of ability and lack of success'. He claimed:

They are inattentive, have a very short concentration time — five minutes. If they have any problems that have to be thought about they give up rather than think them out.

The art teacher also commented on their lack of ability:

Usually their lack of confidence in their work and a sense of frustration with their results will cause unacceptable behaviour. They also need a lot of help and individual attention, and sometimes become impatient while your attention appears to be with somebody else. Concentration is also important here. They find it difficult to work for long spells at a time, giving their full concentration to whatever it is they are doing.

They had two French teachers. One of them, who was in her probationary year, admitted to having problems with the class at first but felt she was overcoming them. She was unable to account for this change beyond noting that, because her teaching practice experience had been in difficult schools, she was not shocked by the pupils' behaviour such as swearing and wandering about in class. Their second French teacher was the deputy head. She described the behaviour of the class as '... rowdy, inattentive, unpredictable, with sudden outbursts — usually an ongoing quarrel'.

Two pupils, Steve and Mike, were described as '... the nucleus of a cheerful, noisy section who sometimes start out with the intention of working, but rarely control themselves for more than ten minutes'. Three others, Jim, Robert and Frank, she described as '... weighed down by their own imcompetence. Quite often depressed and quiet'. Another, Tony, as '... irreverently cheerful, obsessed with sex. His hand will get stuck in one gesture position eventually!'

When asked to account for all this rowdy, unpredictable and cheerful behaviour her first thought was to blame the system — an unsuitable curriculum, lack of resources, and inappropriate timetabling:

The lesson content is largely unsuitable. They can't cope with French as a language and have exhausted the stock of simple background books. Their French studies teaching is shared, too, so there's a lack of continuity.

However she continued:

Also the class is interested in tribal squabble, and when there has been a disturbance during the lunch hour this is carried over into disruptive classroom behaviour — always unpredictable. Individuals may have private griefs and grievances that disturb their behaviour. If they are key members of the group the whole class is difficult.

This view was supported by another teacher who said:

Often I feel that a lot of the trouble is nothing to do with the teacher at all. Whatever you're doing the row that ensues in none of your making. It will be between a group of kids because one of them has turned round and pinched their biro top. And you can't say 'Alright, alright. Forget it. We'll sort it out at the end of the lesson'. They can't accept that. And so, you know, a lot of things arise, as I say, that are nothing to do with your lesson.

3Y's teachers were, therefore, not dissimilar to teachers described in other research in that they appeared to believe that disruptive behaviour was caused by a mixture of poor home background, low intelligence and personality disorders. However, as they continued to talk it was clear that they saw pupil persons beneath these social and psychological problems; persons who demanded, and responded to, a personal approach. The art teacher said:

These children sense very quickly whether you like them or not, and respond accordingly.... If they become particularly noisy for any reason you need to be particularly firm with them. They realize then that they have gone too far and quite often apologize.

The technical drawing teacher said 'They need to be treated friendly — encouraged and complimented. If they are looked after they respond beautifully . . . . This is the key'. The deputy head said 'They will not tolerate any "distance" or "side", so military attitudes to discipline are useless. The teacher needs to win their support'. She also said 'Their behaviour is accepting, not hostile. Sometimes it's consoling— "Never mind, Miss. Nobody will ever know that we didn't do any work!"'

Teachers also described the ways in which they taught the class in the light of their beliefs. The deputy head described her acceptance '. . . of certain types of behaviour which would be outrageous from another group'. The home economics teacher said she '. . . gave a great deal of praise for any small thing that goes right'. The art teacher explained how she would '. . . never expect too much from them (and) explain everything quite clearly and simply, step by step, never giving out too many instructions at once . . .' And the technical drawing teacher described '. . . keeping blackboard demonstrations to a minimum . . . (and) using work sheets (and) dealing with them individually'. Mr Charles, their form teacher, said he allowed them free time, so that '. . . the periods before lunch on Tuesday and Wednesday and the last period on Thursday are more social than didactic'.

Thus the picture which emerged was of teachers who, while recognizing the social and psychological difficulties of pupils, claimed to treat them as persons. They appeared to regard pupil behaviour as a natural rather than a pathological response to an inappropriate and, therefore, 'boring' curriculum, to difficulties with learning and to a school day which was too long. Moreover, because they ultimately blamed the system rather than the pupils, it was the system which they attempted to manipulate by keeping teaching down to a minimum and accepting behaviour which challenged the system. In short, there appeared to be a considerable amount of empathy among them for the pupils' position, which indicated a moral stance and a forgiveness based on a knowledge of mitigating circumstances.

Of course, the views expressed by 3Y's teachers might have been an inaccurate reflection of their beliefs and behaviour. They might have been concerned with presenting a good image or, as has been suggested,[8] they might not have had conscious access to their own motivation. In addition, they might have been mistaken about the motivation of their pupils. In order to explore these possibilities further their pupils' views will first be considered, followed by an assessment of the degree to which the behaviour I observed when they were in interaction with 3Y matched up to their claims. Significantly, at face value at least, the views of these teachers warn against an over simple notion of culture clash. Indeed, their scepticism about the value of their role closely parallels the scepticism of typical disruptive pupils about the value of education. Thus, far from appearing as the puppets of a culture which was 'alien' to that of such pupils, these teachers appeared to be in the business of intelligently evaluating situations and addressing moral dilemmas.

The Pupils' Views

In the event, the evidence drawn from interviews with pupils supported their teachers' views of them. They, too, described their behaviour as a natural response to an inappropriate and boring curriculum. They did not deny that they had learning difficulties, but said that in spite of this they would like to learn. The difference between the two sets of accounts was that, whereas teachers claimed to understand and to be willing to help pupils, the pupils saw many teachers as deficient in these two respects. They, therefore, gave teacher inefficiency and injustice as an additional cause of disruptive behaviour.

Once again care has to be taken in the interpretation of data drawn from personal accounts. As Woods warned, there can be a

... tendency in a conflict situation to regard an external interviewer as a kind of relief agency ... (so that) on occasions, the
actual incidence of the discussions made grievances ... (with)
people talking themselves into a temper.[9]

Like their teachers, therefore, 3Y may well have been merely responding
to an audience rather than identifying the reasons for their past behaviour,
reasons which may have been forgotten or never consciously known.

Although all the pupils in 3Y were interviewed the views of only
thirteen are given in detail. These were chosen because they were identified by the school as the most disruptive, a view which was confirmed by
the observation of lessons. They are those, therefore, who can be most
clearly identified with anti-school pupils in other research. These pupils'
views are presented here in more detail than is typical in the sociological
accounts previously quoted. As a result it has been possible first, to
identify more precisely the issues on which 3Y and their teachers agreed
or disagreed; secondly, to demonstrate that although there were links
between 3Y's views and sociological categories of pupils, these categories
could not accommodate all the evidence and, therefore, that sociological
analyses would be an inadequate basis from which to develop policies
aimed at improving personal relationships; and thirdly, to allow pupils
who were to play key roles in the experimental lessons to introduce
themselves.

I presented myself to the pupils as someone who was engaged in
teacher training and who was, therefore, interested in the pupils' views
about what distinguished a good teacher from a bad one. I also said I was
interested in their general views about school. I emphasized that whatever
they said would not be passed on to their teachers. This statement was
apparently taken seriously. The probationary French teacher told me that
when she had asked what we talked about the pupils had said they could
not tell her because 'It was confidential'.

Evidence will be presented from the interviews with Steve and Mike;
Brian, Dave and Frank; Howard, Tony and Chris; Janet and Barbara; and
Maureen, Liz and Val. These were the self-chosen groups in which they
came to talk to me.

Steve and Mike

These two boys were cheerful and outgoing. Not many minutes of the
interview had passed before they had challenged me to a snooker match at
the local youth club. Their views about school seemed to reflect this
approach to life. They seemed to have a well worked out philosophy. Life
and therefore school should be a proper mixture of enjoyment, work and

justice. In an ideal world these would be inextricably intermixed. However, they seemed to accept that in the real world compromises had to be made. What was important in the production or avoidance of conflict was the quality of the compromise. Their view was that if work was allowed to drive out all pleasure from life, this would create an unnatural and intolerable situation. If such a state of affairs was imposed by teachers it would be unjust. Good teachers were those who recognized the need to balance work with pleasure, either by making work interesting or by providing space for alternative activities. Bad teachers were ones who failed to make such provision, and who used inhuman methods to impose their will. For example:

Steve: One good thing about school is the education about it. The worst thing is that some of the teachers just get on our nerves.

Mike: Shout at you, and get hold of you and hit you.

Steve: Like Mr. Jones. If you do it wrong he gets hold of your neck and he really does hurt you. And he slaps you around the head.

They complained of another teacher who would not let them sit next to each other, which they regarded as an unnecessary restriction of a simple pleasure.

Mike: He goes 'It's a special treat to sit next to each other'. It's stupid I think.

KC: You think it's better to sit next to each other?

Steve: Yea. Like if you've finished your work you can talk to your mate.

Using the same criteria other teachers were described as good.

Steve: I can name you three people who I've liked in the past since I've been in this school. The one best teacher that I've liked, he was a geography teacher. He was a terrific teacher, cos you could have a laugh with him as well as doing your work, right? Like five minutes before the end he'd say 'Pack up,' you know, and he'd let you come out and do demonstrations of teachers, and take them off, and all that. It was really good.

Steve also said he liked Mr. Charles, the form teacher, though he recognized that other pupils did not agree with him, 'Everyone calls him; but he's good. He's alright'. They described an incident where they had 'pocketed his hanky' and 'had a laugh'. At other times:

Steve: We come in the room, and he says 'Right — History books out'. And we say 'Oh Sir!' And he gives us the books and we chuck them on the floor. And he has a laugh with us you know.

KC: But — I mean — some people might say that you shouldn't be throwing books about.

Steve: Oh no. I know that's right sometimes, cos you can blind a person. It's alright if you don't hit them. You might hit them on the head, right? Like this boy was sitting there one day and I picked up this book and I wopped it at his head, right? And he throws it back. Or I throw some paper at Mr. Charles, and he throws it back. and you can have a laugh.

The third teacher of whom both boys approved was the young French teacher. Whereas Mr. Charles and the geography teacher cited by Steve allowed alternative activities to allay boredom, she was praised for making the work itself interesting.

Steve: She's strict in a way, but she lets us do a quiz and things like that, so we like it.

Mike: She let's us play French bingo.

Where teachers did not provide pleasurable activities, the boys took it upon themselves to fill the gap. They described the games they devised for themselves some, with cars and biros, which had quite sophisticated rules. These games were not seen as an alternative to work, however, but rather as something to be set alongside work. Thus Steve described how, in lessons:

Steve: ... we go around pinching things and hitting each other.

KC: And do you think that's misbehaving?

Steve: Yea. It's only in fun though isn't it? It's only in fun.

KC: Do you think you spend more time having a laugh than you ought to?

Steve: No. Well I know it's my education, and this year I don't mind sitting down and studying, cos I know it's important this year. But the last two years I've liked to — you know — enjoy myself messing about.

Mike: And now we're coming up to the fourth year, you know you'll be good, and sit down and study it all. It's coming time to sit down and study it all now.

They went on to talk about the Options they would choose, especially English and History. Steve said 'Every lesson in History (with Mr Charles) I try to do my best. I haven't got one mark under eight out of ten'. He also said he needed woodwork because his Dad wanted him to be a joiner: 'I'm putting down woodwork, and if he says "No", I'll take it at night school'.

Mucking about and having a laugh were, clearly, not a demonstration of opposition to work in any simple way. Rather they appeared to be viewed as the expression of an existential imperative, to be balanced against an equally important need to do what work was necessary. One cause of conflict was when teachers appeared to confuse these two issues. An example of this which clearly rankled with Steve related to the way in which pupils were allocated to their Maths sets. He had been placed in the bottom set, D. In putting him in this set, Steve claimed that teachers were confusing a wish to have fun with an unwillingness to work and a lack of ability. This he felt was unjust.

> *Steve:* ... Take Brian. I'm just as brainy as him in Maths. And I'm brainier than a couple of others. But he puts me in D in the lowest group. But the point is I can do the work, but they won't give me a try.
>
> *Mike:* They put us straight down in the lowest one. Straight in D.
>
> *Steve:* Just cos we had a muck around in the second year, he goes, 'Down to the bottom'. But Brian and the others messed about as much as us and they go up.... It's stupid.
>
> *KC:* Does it matter? Can you do the same work even if you're in the D's?
>
> *Steve:* How can we do the same work as them? They say, when people ask me, they go, 'Oh what Maths group are you in? I suppose you're in the D's'. And I go, 'I know I am, but I mess about, and they think I'm not brainy but I am'.
>
> *KC:* Well wouldn't it have been worth not messing about?
>
> *Steve:* Well we didn't ought to mess about too much; but like — well when you were at school did you mess about?
>
> *KC:* [Laughs]
>
> *Steve:* See! Everyone messes about when they're at school!

Asked why other boys who messed about got put into the top set they accused the teachers of favouritism.

> *Steve:* Yea — like Brian. He gets on Report, and he got more than five crosses....
>
> *Mike:* ... and he gets let off.
>
> *Steve:* But if it's me or him (Mike) ...
>
> *Mike:* ... we get the cane or something.

Not all school work was seen by these boys as deficient in intrinsic rewards.

> *Mike:* I like all the work we do in Geography. We do things from a book about railways and other things like that. We have questions and that to answer.
>
> *KC:* Do you enjoy that?
>
> *Mike:* Yea.
>
> ... Music's alright, but we don't play no instruments or nothing. Just write from the board. We don't *do* nothing.

The most important cause of conflict in Steve and Mike's view, however, was the way they were treated by some teachers. Although the interview was characterized in the main by a cheerful good-humour and a willingness to make up teacher deficiencies in their own ways, attacks on their person or their rights clearly made them angry. Agreeing with Mike that the work in Geography was interesting:

Steve: But it's solid work. I don't mind solid work all the time, but he goes a bit too far.

Mike: And if you get it wrong he goes, 'You're so stupid!' It's not fair on us.

Most intolerable of all however was manhandling. One teacher in particular was accused of this. No doubt their words contained some bravado when they said:

Mike: One day we're going to give him a dig!

Steve: One day I'm going to pick up something and hit him back with it, cos I'm just about fed up with it.

Mike: One day I'm going to turn round and hit him.

The smouldering anger seemed real.

Nevertheless, taken as a whole and taken at face value Steve and Mike's descriptions of their motivation had much in common with the teachers' accounts. They said they found aspects of the curriculum boring, a fact which the teachers recognized too. They acknowledged their desire to have fun, regarding this, as some of their teachers had, as 'natural'. But they also declared their wish to learn especially as the fourth year approached. The single outstanding difference in the two accounts, therefore, was the fact that these boys claimed that much teacher behaviour was deliberately provocative. This clearly contradicted the teachers' views of themselves, at least as far as they had been prepared to divulge those views to me.

Brian, Dave and Frank

The attitude of these three boys to school, was rather different from that of Steve and Mike, in that they did not appear to find any value in it at all. Brian for example said 'All the teachers are bad'. Some small concessions were made later, so that Dave, for example, said 'Mr Foot — I like him. . . . He plays fair. He don't play by the rules but he plays fair'. However, the three boys seemed to be critical, overall. Asked to tell me any good things about school Frank said 'There aren't any good things, is there?'

Their major complaints centred round the curriculum and the attitude of teachers. They appeared to find little in the lessons which interested them. They complained of the amount of writing they had to do. The following interchange was typical.

Dave: When we have Mr Charles that's all we do; write and write all the time.

Frank: The same with Mr Greaves.

Dave: He says 'Open your book and copy from the blackboard', and there's a whole blackboard full of it!

KC: What sort of things would you rather do?

Frank: Well I wouldn't mind doing a bit of work, say for half the lesson, and then do what I want to do in the next half.

Dave: Tomorrow in music we're allowed to play records.

Frank: Cos if we do our work in one lesson then she gives us a treat.

It became apparent, however, that their rejection of school work was a rejection of an excessive amount of writing rather than of work *per se*.

Brian: Miss, I don't know why the girls have to do typing. Some of us would like to do typing.

KC: Can't the boys do typing?

Brian: No, we're not allowed to. I don't know why.

Frank: And we're not allowed to do cooking till we get our options. But in the other school, in the infants, we could do it.

KC: So why is that, do you think?

Frank: I dunno.

KC: When you say they should let you work for part of the lesson, and then do what you want to do, what sort of things would count as work?

Frank: Writing and copying.

KC: What about if you were allowed to make models and that sort of thing?

Dave: We only do that in Art.

KC: Would you count that as work?

Frank: No. That would be something that we would like to do.

The opposition to the official curriculum seemed, therefore, to be largely opposition to mechanical writing exercises. The boys seemed to think that they would enjoy lessons more if they were more active. For example, in another part of the interview Dave said that double science was 'alright' because they did experiments or had a film. Brian however had reservations.

Brian: But the teacher, the teacher's a bit bad. You're just talking to someone while he's talking, and he sends you out of the room, or puts you on report or something like that.

Dave: But the best part is that you do something ever so small and he gives you a house point for it!

Although Dave did seem to see some rewards in this situation the overall theme of these boys was that more free time would be the best way to relieve the boredom.

Frank: What they should do is have a limit of time for work, and then, say ... play the radio for ten minutes.

Dave: Cos like with Mr Charles, we've got a double lesson now, fourth and fifth lesson. We could do some work for one, and then for the other lesson do what we wanted.

These boys not only seemed more oppressed by the boredom of lessons than Steve and Mike, they also seemed more weighed down by the injustice of teachers, against whom they felt considerable resentment. Brian perceived the Home Economics teacher as deliberately attempting to prevent him taking that subject for one of his options. This injustice appeared to be keenly felt because here, at last, was a subject in which he could be interested.

Brian: Miss, on my option sheet for next year, the Home Economics Teacher — cos I want to do cooking — she, she won't even sign it now. She says, 'Come down on Monday' and she'll sign it, but she never did. She just took our names and that's it.

KC: Why do you think she did that?

Brian: I dunno.

Frank: She says it's too early.

Brian: Yea. Yea. But Mr Charles, right, he said if you want to do cooking you got to get it in fast, and by the time we've waited and other people have got theirs signed, we probably won't be able to do it in the end, because like — well we were like the first ones down, and she won't sign it! And we've not bothered to go down again. Cos we've been down a few times. And then other people go down, and they get signed straight away, and they go in the cooking group and we can't. Cos they say they're full with people before us. It's a bit bad isn't it?

KC: Well. Why do you think she does that?

Brian: I dunno.

Dave: I suppose it's cos she doesn't want us to do cooking.

KC: Well why? Why doesn't she?

Brian: Cos she'll sign some people but she won't sign others.

KC: Well why won't she sign yours?

Frank: I dunno.

Dave: Praps she's signing the girls and not the boys for cooking.

KC: Do many of the boys want to do cooking?

Dave: Yea, a lot do.

Brian: Yea. All of us in our class do.

This interchange was interesting, especially as it turned out that the boys' suspicions were unfounded and they were put in the Home Economics Option. Clearly it demonstrated a deep mistrust of the motives of teachers and, perhaps, a lack of understanding of the organizational constraints on them.

These three boys also complained that teachers were sarcastic, unfair, and violent. Like Steve and Mike they felt that when teachers behaved in this way their own behaviour got worse. Like Steve and Mike, they also seemed to think that mucking about was natural. Discussing an episode which had happened the previous lesson with Mr Charles, they said:

Frank: Someone put some books and pencils in Brian's bag and Mr Charles blamed him for it.

Brian: Yea. Just a minute ago. Just before we came down here. And someone put them in my bag I expect, cos I didn't. . . . But the ones who usually muck about he blames them doesn't he?

Dave: Well no. When you muck about he doesn't say, 'You're on detention tonight.'

Brian: Well he does.

Dave: Well, no! He, when he calls the register he makes you go out last, and when Mr Hardy comes along he says 'He's been naughty: she's been naughty'. And Mr Hardy puts you on detention. Cos he hardly ever puts you on detentions — Mr Charles. Mr Hardy comes along and does it.

KC: Why do you muck about? Do you muck about?

Dave: Yea.

Frank: Yea. But everyone mucks about at some time.

Brian: I know, but, Miss, they treat us wrong. Like with Mr Blake, he hits us over the head. And then he wonders why we muck about, when he hits us over the head!

Frank: Same with Mr Jones, too. If you get the slightest thing wrong, he gets hold of your neck and squeezes it for not getting it right.

Dave: Then he wonders why you answer back afterwards and are cheeky to him. Cos I was cheeky to him.

KC: What happened then?

Dave: He said 'What do you think you're going to do when you leave school, and in a job and are cheeky to your manager all the time?' I said, 'Well I've never been cheeky to my manager!' [Laughs] Because you know, if he gets hold of you by your neck and he pulls yer, and he wonders why you answer back afterwards!

Apart from illustrating the attitudes of these boys to mucking about and injustice, this extract illustrates their concern to get the account right,

with Brian and Dave disagreeing over which teacher put them on detention. They seemed to be concerned with accuracy as well as with arguing
their case.

Finally for these boys, school was made intolerable by a number of
organizational rules. These concerned eating and wearing coats in class,
smoking, and dinner times. Generally the rules relating to these were
seen as inhuman and unreasonable, and therefore a cause of trouble.

Brian: Miss — and you know at dinner times and playtimes, Miss,
after you've had your dinner, right? Right — the second
years and third years should have rooms where they can go
at dinner time cos it gets a bit boring outside.

Frank: It's cold.

Brian: They don't even, they don't even, Miss, let us into the
building, cos they go 'Oh you've got to have a pass!'

Frank: The only place you can go is the library, and if you haven't
got a pass you can't get in.

Dave: You have to stand outside.

KC: Why do you think they don't let you inside? I mean —
would you muck about if they let you inside?

Dave: That's one thing.

Brian: Some people do.

Dave: And things go missing.

KC: Well if people muck about, and things go missing, are they
right to keep people out, cos ...

Brian: Not *everyone!*

Dave: Yea — but if *one* person does something all the others —

Frank: — get punished for it!

Later, when the topic came up again:

Brian: I think, Miss, that the teachers at dinner time, they should
keep a look out and keep the fighting down. Like there's a
lot of fights and the teacher should patrol the playgrounds
and that.

KC: There's quite a bit of fighting is there?

Brian: Yea. And when you want to play in the goal nets, you're not
allowed. They take your ball away. And that's what they're
for, the goal nets. But they say 'Oh no. It's for the school,
the school team'.

Dave: They say to keep off the grass.

Frank: And they don't let you bring cards or nothing to play.

Dave: We got caught gambling.

Frank: Yea, but it's up to the children. If they want to gamble it's
their fault, isn't it?

Teachers, therefore, stood condemned for inhumanity, injustice and a petty interference in simple pleasures. These complaints were sophisticated in that they recognized that more liberty could bring problems. However, the boys believed that their teachers' approach could, and should, discriminate more carefully between pleasures which were disruptive and those which were not. It seemed to be this lack of subtlety which allowed the boys to argue that teachers were maliciously provocative.

Dave: There's only one good teacher. I reckon.... He lets you eat in class. Cos I don't see why other teachers don't. You don't do nothing when you eat in class. They should just not let you eat bubblegum.

Frank: Yea. That's fair on them.

Dave: But if you get caught eating a crisp you get done.

Brian: They take it away. They take your stuff away.

Frank: And you've paid money for it.

Dave: We wore our scarves once and they took our scarves away.

Frank: If you pay out money for the stuff you should have the right to get it back.

Brian: Miss, it's up to us if we wear our coats in class, if we want to or not. They say, 'Oh take it off'. And it's really cold. But *they* sit there in class with their coats on, some of them.

Dave: I don't see why we can't have a cigarette outside school. Cos we're outside school, on the football pitch.

KC: Well, why do you think they don't let you?

Dave: I dunno, really.

Frank: In school you might catch something alight, or something.

Dave: Not on the pitch you won't if you put it out.

Frank: But it's making sure you've put it out. My Mum's done that. Burned things cos she's not put it out properly.

KC: Why do you think they don't let you eat in class?

Dave: I dunno. I think they think that you make a mess in class with wrappers and that.

KC: And would you?

Frank: Yea. But you could put your papers in the bin.

KC: Would people do that though?

Dave: Well, we do eat in class but behind their back.

Like Steve and Mike, then, these three boys agreed with their teachers that an important cause of disruptive behaviour was boredom. They also agreed that trouble often stemmed from inter-pupil quarrels. However, they were even more explicit in their condemnation of teachers whom they regarded as unjust, unreasonable, lazy and bullying. It was these perceived qualities which in their view created teacher-pupil conflict. Importantly these qualities were ones which their teachers also condemned and the boys' behaviour cannot, therefore, be easily explained as the expression of alien values. Certainly there seemed to be no anti-school content in Dave's twin suggestions that teachers should: 'Give better lessons' and 'Be nice to children'.

Howard, Tony and Chris

Whereas Brian, Frank and Dave seemed to be weighed down by the injustice and boredom of school, these three boys seemed more like Steve and Mike, prepared to enjoy certain aspects of the official curriculum, though equally prepared to oppose teachers if they overstepped the mark. Perhaps even more than Steve and Mike they had difficulty in concentrating on the topic under discussion because there were other things of much greater interest to talk about. They told me of how they spent their weekends and evenings. Their activities were varied including breeding fish, 'skating round the streets', bingo, visiting relations (grandparents and uncles,) taking dogs out for walks (at six o'clock in the morning!) and vandalizing.

> *Howard:*   I go to the pictures, go to the ice-rink, or walk on the beaches, or fishing and all that. But mainly vandalizing.
> *KC:*   What do you vandalize?
> *Howard:*   This house what they're building up the road.
> *KC:*   Why?
> *Howard:*   Well they didn't ask, and where they put it, it's going to get in the way of our view, cos we've got a valley and that. So we just knock it down.

This directness of approach from moral principle to action seemed to underlie much of what they said. It also allowed them to have a more variegated picture of school than that held by the previous three boys. For example they were prepared to allow that other people might have different purposes which were valid and should be accommodated. Thus twice in the interview when they had strayed rather far from my original questions Howard brought them back to the subject by 'We're meant to be discussing school, not us!' And later, when they were planning a fight for later in the day 'That's enough of us! What would you like us to talk about now?'

The lessons of which they approved seemed to be those which reflected their active interests. Talking about their option choices, they said:

> *Chris:*   I'm doing Biology, cos in Biology you do cutting up things. And I'm doing Outdoor Education. In that — Outdoor Education — you go camping and all that. And you work down Parks and Gardens. And I'm doing Home Economics.

> *Howard*: Well you need Home Economics for a start. Cos if you don't get married you've got to cook things.
> *Chris*: Like for Outdoor Education I'll be going down Parks and Gardens and doing things like that. And you go camping at weekends.

He was clearly enthusiastic.[10]

Asked whether they would be taking CSEs.

> *Howard*: Yea. We most probably will get some.
> *Chris*: If you want to get certain jobs you have to have them.
> *Tony*: The job my uncle's doing, Miss, the job my uncle's doing, Miss, when he went for it they never asked him what CSEs he'd passed. They never asked him, so he was alright. But now they're making some redundant, they're making them say what exams they've had!
> *Howard*: At the moment hardly anyone's getting jobs. Everyone's coming out of jobs more than going in.
> *Chris*: Yea. That's Maggie Aggie! The bloke that stopped that bomb going to her house must have been the biggest burke going![11]

Apart from the fact that Chris's last comment might show further approval of direct action, in rhetoric at least, these boys demonstrated some awareness of the complexity of the relationship between qualifications and jobs. Howard's suggestion that they would probably get some CSEs was perhaps over-optimistic. He had been classed by his form tutor as an under-achiever, and Chris had been classed as the pupil in the form who had made least headway and could only read very slowly. Either they were not aware of how poor their achievement was or they did not want to admit it to me. Or perhaps, like Steve and Mike, they thought they could catch up in the fourth year, or that in the long run it wouldn't matter anyway.

Chris was one of the boys who attended the Special Class at regular intervals during the week. He seemed to enjoy going. He said 'You can do things in there and that. Like today, in Special, we'll probably do some plaster casts'. At another time he said 'I like woodwork, metalwork and Special — especially on Thursday cos we have a double film. And Science'.

Like David and Frank these boys confirmed the view I had been forming that for this class 'work' equalled 'writing' and that when they said they didn't like work it was this specific activity to which they were referring. Describing what he did in Special Classes:

> *Chris*: One day I do reading; this morning I done work [writing] and this afternoon I'll do, say, plaster casts.

Tony: Every time I get chucked out say of games, I go down to the Special Room. Miss Baker lets me in, don't she?

KC: What do you do there?

Tony: Work, or clean out the fish tanks.

The opportunities for enjoyable activities seemed to over-ride any possible negative effects from labelling for these boys.

KC: What sort of people go to Special?

Chris: People who are a bit behind.

KC: And does it help you catch up?

Chris: Yea.

Tony: Yea.

Their tone of voice was matter of fact, verging on enthusiastic.

There were disadvantages, however. Chris said he disliked Geography. It turned out that the main reason was that he had to catch up at home all the work he had missed while he was in the Special Class. Copying was seen as acceptable, if it wasn't all writing.

Dave: In some lessons I don't mind the writing.

KC: What lessons?

Howard: Geography.

Tony: Geography.

KC: Why do you like Geography?

Howard: Cos you're doing pictures. No, not even pictures. You're copying drawings like.

Tony: Maps.

Howard: And Power Stations and that.

KC: You like that?

Tony: Yea.

Howard: Yea.

The desire to do less writing however seemed to be behind these boys' desire, like that of their classmates, for 'free periods'.

Tony: Sometimes they let you do what you want, but half the time they don't let you.

KC: Do you think they ought to let you do what you want?

Tony: Yea. In some of the lessons. Say two lessons a day.

Chris: No. Say out of thirty five lessons a week we should have at least five lessons, right?

KC: What to do? What would you — would you be in the classroom in those five lessons?

Tony: Yea. You'd have to do something in a classroom, and got to do it quiet.

What seemed to set these boys aside from those earlier reported was that unless a teacher committed a serious outrage they judged what happened in school according to whether or not the activity was interesting. Teachers hardly featured in their discussion. The teacher who hit pupils was inevitably mentioned. As Tony said 'I don't like Mr Jones. Oo-err, he hits yer. He hits yer, don't he?' But this did not seem to bother Chris who said in response 'I like the work'. After that the subject of teachers was dropped, until well on into the interview when I re-introduced it. Its absence as a topic seemed interesting. I asked a direct question.

KC:	Does the teacher make any difference to the lessons?
Tony:	No.[12]
Howard:	Well Mr Jones —
Tony:	Yea. Mr Jones it does.

But that was all. Even when they reported outright conflict there did not seem to be the sense of grievance which Brian had demonstrated. Discussing why they were on report,

Howard:	I kicked at a teacher.
KC:	Which teacher?
Howard:	Mr Charles. I kept swearing and kicking at him.
KC:	Why did you do that?
Howard:	He kept having a go at me, so I had a go at him.
KC:	[To Tony] What did you do to get them? (The crosses on the report sheet)
Tony:	Well I hit Mr Blake. He had told me to go home so I went. And he went to see Mr Hardy about it. And I said, 'Well you told me to go home, so I went'. And he goes, 'Well, I'll see Mr Hardy about you'. So I says, 'Good'. So I went and had my dinner. And he called me back and he hit me, so I hit him.
KC:	How had it all started?
Tony:	Well he said 'Anyone who talks can go out'. And I never said nothing, and he says 'Go out'.
KC:	And you hadn't been talking?
Tony:	No.

The fact that I had to draw this information out of Howard and Tony, together with the matter of fact way in which it was communicated, suggested that such incidents did not colour their whole attitude to school. The interview was consistently cheerful. They claimed to find things in the school curriculum which they could enjoy and were looking forward to their options. Their attitude was optimistic and practical. Indeed, their most pressing complaints about school were that the toilets were locked at dinner time, that there was never any toilet paper, and that hot water came out of the cold water taps. This was hardly evidence of an oppositional culture. Rather when conflict occurred, it was seen as stemming from incidents where the teacher was transgressing fundamental moral principles: principles which the teachers also claimed to support.

These boys, also, corroborated their teachers' descriptions of pupils. They too gave evidence of the 'tribal squabbles' of which the deputy head had spoken, and of the consequent fights which often affected classroom behaviour. This evidence had also been confirmed by Brian, who had felt that the staff should do more to prevent such occurrences, especially during the dinner break. Finally, these boys gave evidence that they, at least, moved from insult straight into retaliatory action, a factor which had been noted by their teachers.

Barbara and Janet

These girls disliked school.

Janet: I hate school.
Barbara: Why do we have to come to school? It's stupid!

Their attitudes were, however, much more complex than these simple statements might indicate.

In the first place they had a number of grievances about the way teachers conducted themselves in general. This seemed to stem from a belief that if certain rules were necessary for the smooth running of an organization then teachers should obey them too. They complained, for example, that teachers broke the rule about staircases.

Barbara: Every morning in assembly they say 'Go up the "Up" stairs and not up the "Down" stairs'. But teachers go up them!
         [Pause]
KC: So what do you think about that?
Barbara: If they're going to tell us to do it, they should do it!
Janet: Yea. Cos they're not encouraging us to go up are they, if they go up and down them.
KC: Why do you think they do that?
Janet: I dunno.
Barbara: We only do it for a short cut and so do they. And when exams are on, we have to go up the 'Down' stairs; and when exams are finished they tell us to go up the other stairs, but *they* still go up them!

Teachers similarly were accused of abusing their position of power at dinner time. Pupils had to queue up as they arrived for dinner, and Barbara complained that sometimes there was no food left for those at the back of the queue. She also complained that those at the back got no free time. Teachers, on the other hand, ensured that they did not suffer in this way.

Janet:	The teachers all go in first.
Barbara:	Yes. They just walk straight in and get their dinner. Everyone's lining up, and they just walk straight in, in front of the lot of you, and get their dinner![13]
KC:	And do you think that's wrong?
Janet:	Yea.
KC:	Why do you think it's wrong?
Janet:	I think they should have their dinner in the staffroom.
Barbara:	Yea. Or they should wait in the queue. We've been working and so have they. They say, 'Oh, we've been working harder than you'. But we've been working haven't we? We've been writing it all!

In addition they pointed out that although pupils were punished for coming late to lessons, one teacher was regularly late.

Barbara:	... sometimes he don't come till about five to ten.
KC:	And what time does the lesson start?
Barbara:	Twenty-five past nine.
KC:	Why do you think that happens?
Barbara:	I dunno.

What appeared to be the final insult was when an outbreak of fleas occurred in the class.

Barbara:	All the people in our class they had flea bites. They kept coming up in bites; and we had to have medicals with matron. And we had to have our class fumigated.... The teacher had them as well. He had loads of them.
KC:	Did he?
Barbara:	And we all went for medicals, but he didn't.

This type of injustice seemed to be a serious source of grievance to these girls, but by far their strongest complaint was that school was a waste of time because they didn't learn anything. This they blamed partly on teachers and partly on the rest of the class. They also, however, seemed aware to some extent of the organizational pressures on teachers. After a long series of complaints about lessons:

KC:	Yea. So if I was a student now, right, and I came to you for advice cos I wanted to be a good teacher, what would you tell me I ought to do to make it better?
Janet:	I dunno.
	[Pause]
Barbara:	Yea. But the teachers can't do anything about it can they? It's the way the school's run.

KC:	Well, who does it? Whose fault is it?
Barbara:	I dunno. Whoever runs it.
KC:	Is that the teachers?
Barbara:	No. It isn't the teachers fault is it? [Pause] They . . . they have their orders don't they? [Pause] Do you have an order?
KC:	Do I have an order?
Barbara:	Yea. Like the teachers have to go to the lessons that they have to go to, haven't they?

Nevertheless within these perceived constraints it was clear that these girls felt that teachers might do more to improve the curriculum and discipline so that they could learn something. Talking about work they said:

Barbara:	It's easy at this school.
Janet:	We did harder work at our last school.
KC:	Do you think it's too easy?
Both:	Yea.
Janet:	We don't have to do much work. In English we read or do drawings.
Barbara:	And when we go to the Maths group he says 'Oh you're doing work which you should have been doing in the juniors'. And they're saying we're doing work which we should have done in the juniors! Well, if they say that to us, it's obvious we're not going to do it hard isn't it?
KC:	What. Because you think . . . ?
Barbara:	It's baby's work. Yea.

As with Steve, Maths was a source of complaint, although their view was slightly different. These girls were also in the lowest set, 'D'. Barbara seemed to agree with Steve that the groups had not been sorted out properly, and also cited Brian as an example. One of her major points, however, was that the groups did the same work anyway. She obviously monitored Brian's work, even though he was not in the same group. Her view was, therefore, backed up by evidence.

Barbara:	We all do the same thing in our Maths groups. Right? And everyone does the same thing in their Maths group. But they think they're higher. People in 'J' all do the same thing as people in 'D'. We all do the same work.
KC:	Do they do it better?
Barbara:	I dunno.
KC:	Do you think it's wrong that people are in different groups?
Barbara:	No, but we should do different work.
KC:	Why do you think that?

> *Barbara*: If some people are higher they should do harder work.
> *KC*: You don't think they do?
> *Barbara*: No. They do the same.
> *KC*: So why do you think that happens then?
> [Pause]
> *Barbara*: There's some thick people in the Maths group, and there's some others that ain't thick .... Like Brian — we've had three Maths books, right, and he's only had one, and he hasn't got to the middle of it yet!

She put Brian's lack of progress down to the fact that, typically, in lessons:

> *Barbara*: He sits there flicking a pea shooter all across the room, all the time, and other people do all their work.
> *KC*: What do you think about that? About Brian doing that?
> *Barbara*: He should get put on Report or something. He's so stupid! He is! He just sits there all the time.... He's on Report, and he got two crosses, and he thought it was funny!

These two girls also felt they didn't learn much in English. Once again they put the blame on both the teacher and their classmates.

> *Janet*: I think we should do more reading in our lesson. Mr Charles reads to us.
> *Barbara*: Yea. He reads to us. *We* should read to them, to him.
> *KC*: How would you organize a lesson like that?
> *Barbara*: Like starting at the front and work round. Like we used to do. Like we used to have 'A Hundred and One Dalmations' and we used to have a paragraph each — like that.
> *KC*: Why do you think they don't do it anymore?
> *Barbara*: Well, when some people are in our lessons, they go 'Oh well, I'm not reading'. And they don't have to. But the ones that read they don't listen to them. They just play motor car games under the desk and that. And throw paper. That's how thick they are!

Part of the problem was seen to lie in the fact that some of the class couldn't read:

> *Barbara*: They're so stupid though! Mr Charles tells them to read a book and they can't read! They can't write properly! They can't read a book, can they?
> *Janet*: No.

More important, however, seemed to be the view that many pupils didn't want to do the work and teachers didn't make them.

> *Barbara*: They can do the work. They don't want to do it. Cos if they think they don't have to do it they won't do it will they?

Janet: Cos if they know the teacher's soft they won't do it.
Barbara: Like Val. She says 'Oh we can't muck about with Mr Brown, but we can muck about with Mr Charles'. Like that. She goes along to the toilet and then she comes running in when he's in the cupboard and pretends she's been there all the time.

Discussing this problem in another part of the interview, Barbara said that teachers should 'Make them do it'.

KC: How?
Barbara: Scream at them. You know, put the book there and tell them they're not going out till they've done it. Then they'll do it.

It was the tendency of teachers to be too soft which, in their opinion, caused the trouble.

Barbara: Well, Mr Charles like, we do history, and there's this girl, Maureen, in our class, and she doesn't do it. She just sits there.
Janet: She just sits there. She gets away with blue murder she does.
Barbara: Yea. She don't do no work. She scribbles on her book so she don't have to do it. And he says, 'Oh, be like that then!' And she don't have to do it. But we have to do it.
Janet: He puts us on Report if we don't do it, and on detention.
KC: So why do you think he doesn't do it for her?
Barbara: Cos he feels sorry for her.
KC: Why do you think he feels sorry for her?
Barbara: Cos she's all scruffy. And she's always talking about how she hasn't got a mum, and her nan don't cook properly and that. And she just don't do it. But her brother's in our class, and he don't talk about that. He just does it. (The work)

Her brother was Howard. Barbara, also, felt that the special attention given to the less able was inappropriate.

Barbara: And the people who go to Special, they play draughts and things like that. They're supposed to go there to learn things. And while we're in the class doing work, they're going down to 'Special'. They do double lessons down the field, and single lessons they play chess. I don't know what they've got to learn things like that for!

The two girls were able to identify teachers of whom they approved. They appreciated teachers who made an effort to explain and make lessons interesting.

> *Barbara:* There's teachers in there now, in the Art, they're nice. (They were students on TP)
>
> *KC:* Do they make it better?
>
> *Barbara:* Instead of just saying, 'Oh, you've got to do this, you've got to do that' they show you how to do it. But most of the teachers in this school, they just say 'Oh it's on page 43. Get on with it. Hurry up!'
>
> *Janet:* And if you can't do it they make you stay in at break-time.
>
> *Barbara:* Yea. That's stupid. They should show you how to do it first shouldn't they?
>
> *KC:* Why do you think they don't?
>
> *Barbara:* Cos they don't. They can't be bothered.

They also approved of the probationary French teacher. Later in the interview the following exchange occurred.

> *KC:* Can you tell me what's good about her?
>
> *Barbara:* Well she's really nice.
>
> *Janet:* She explains it more, and she's a really nice teacher.
>
> *KC:* How is she nice? What's nice about her?
>
> *Barbara:* Well, if you don't know how to do it, she tells you how to do it. She shows you.
>
> *KC:* Does she get cross?
>
> *Janet:* Not all that much.
>
> *Barbara:* She does if you're being naughty. And like, at the end of term she tells you ghost stories.
>
> *KC:* Does she? And do people who muck about, work for her?
>
> *Barbara:* Yea.
>
> *Janet:* Yea. Cos they like her.
>
> *Barbara:* Yea. Cos she sorts it out, all her lessons — three lessons with her a week. One lesson we do geography, one lesson we have, like history of France, and the next lesson we have the TV programme. Like that.
>
> *Janet:* And sometimes we play games like French bingo.

Given the excessively conforming nature of many of these girls' comments in relation to the curriculum it perhaps seems difficult to characterize them as trouble makers. It is important, therefore, to note that Barbara was regarded by her teachers as loud-mouthed, and that it had been she who had boasted to me that, if I was to be their teacher, I wouldn't be able to control them. Her comments and those of Janet, however, give some indication of the basis of her disruptive behaviour. Although they both wanted to learn they were clearly resentful of teachers who were regarded as selfish in their interpretation of school rules and who did not teach efficiently. The girls, also, strongly condemned the behaviour of other members of the class, and it was easy to see how this, together with their outspokenness, and their belief that teachers were unjust and 'soft', could lead to the sort of classroom wrangles commented on by teachers. In this particular case it appeared that the girls' conformity to an idealized teacher culture, which no teacher actually espoused, was the cause of the trouble. Even this, however, is perhaps too simplistic. For in spite of the fact that Barbara and Janet wanted to learn, and condemned teachers for not teaching properly, they, like the teachers and their peers, found the curriculum boring. They seemed however to accept this as a necessity of life and certainly beyond the control of teachers.

Maureen, Liz and Val

Like Barbara and Janet these girls disliked school. They could see no purpose in it, considered it oppressive, and with one exception disliked all the teachers. Towards the end of the interview, after a depressing list of complaints from all three girls, I asked what might be considered a leading question, but which, given everything else that had been said, I was sure they would refuse to follow if they didn't want to.

KC:	Are *any* teachers nice?
Liz:	Miss Norman's nice.
Maureen:	Oh yes. She's very nice she is. The French teacher she is. (The probationary teacher again)
KC:	What's good about her? Do you work for her?
All:	Yea.
Maureen:	Yea. Well we play bingo sometimes.
KC:	You will work for her?
Val:	Yea. I like her.
KC:	Do you behave?
Maureen:	Yea.
Val:	Yea.
Liz:	She's the best teacher.
KC:	Tell me what she does that's good.
Liz:	Well she doesn't shout at us.
Maureen:	Yea. She sometimes lets us have bingo, doesn't she?
Val:	And when we've finished our work she lets us do what we want and that, as long as we don't make too much noise.

Given that this was the only favourable comment about school and teachers to come out of this interview it might be thought that here were girls who were entrenched in a different culture from that of their teachers. This view might be reinforced by the fact that the only teacher of whom they approved let them play bingo. The fact that it was French bingo does not really detract from its cultural overtones. Nevertheless, at the level of the values invoked to judge the school it is once again difficult to sustain an alien culture thesis, which would mean ignoring much more obvious interpretations.

Maureen was the girl identified by Barbara as having no mum, being all scruffy, and for whom Mr Charles felt sorry, thus letting her 'get away with blue murder'. Maureen did not share Barbara's opinion, feeling herself to be picked upon by both teachers and other pupils. Surprisingly, in spite of this, she laughed easily, making wry jokes against herself. Val had said she wanted to be a telephonist when she left school. I asked Maureen if she knew what she wanted to do.

> *Maureen:* No. Nothing would be good enough! [Laughing] No. I'm too naughty. You can ask her that. Aren't I Val?
> *Val:* Yea.

She seemed to delight in the absurdity of suggesting that nothing would be good enough for someone as naughty as she was. Later having complained that teachers 'picked on' her:

> *KC:* Why do you think they pick on you?
> *Maureen:* Cos they just like it! Specially if I've got some sweets! [Laughing] Cos they come round scrounging off yer. [Laughing]

There was no doubt that she was preoccupied with her home circumstances but this gentle humour cast doubt on any notion that her disruptive behaviour was a blind and irrational response to her problems. This impression was reinforced by the fact that she was prepared to distinguish between those times when she acted as she did because she was 'feeling like it', and those times when she blamed the teachers. Asked why she was naughty she said 'Well, I get restless sometimes, and teachers pick on you, and I just start losing my temper. And I don't do the work'. Some of this restlessness was without doubt a result of her total boredom with the curriculum offered by the school. This boredom as summed up in Liz's plaintive remark 'We always do nothing but write'.

> *Val:* I think school's a waste of time.
> *KC:* Do you?
> *Liz:* It wastes all the day.
> *Maureen:* Cos some of it, some of it I could learn at home. Reading and that.
> *Liz:* They give you too much to write down, and when you leave school they only tear it up. It's wasting the week.

One had the impression of precious life slipping by. They said,

> *Liz:* You ought to be able to choose what lessons you did.
> *Maureen:* That would be good.
> *KC:* What would you choose to do?

Liz:	Typewriting and woodwork.
Maureen:	Or sometimes have free lessons. That would be alright.
KC:	What would you like to do in your free lessons?
Maureen:	Oh, like, play games.
Liz:	Read comics.
Maureen:	And do handwriting and something like that. Cos I need handwriting practice don't I? [Addressed to the others]
KC:	Would you like to do better handwriting?
Maureen:	Yea.
KC:	Do you think it would be possible to have free lessons?
Maureen:	Yea. Some classes have free lessons don't they Val? And when I go to 'Special' sometimes I can have free lessons. Sometimes I do typewriting.
Liz:	Lucky.
KC:	What do you think the school ought to be doing for pupils? What ideally would you like to get out of school?
Liz:	[Sighing] Enjoyment.
KC:	Do you think school does anything for you?
Val:	Not really.

Asked if it could be improved they said they would like to paint more, and in History 'do models of castles and that'. They also said they would like to go out more.

Val:	Mr Charles says he's going to take us out on trips, and he never does. He just says it, but he don't do it. He just says it to tease us.
KC:	Would you like to go on trips?
Maureen:	Oh yea.
Liz:	Yea.
Maureen:	[Quickly] But not to *write* about them. Just *say* what we saw and that.
KC:	Do you think the writing you do is important? Do you think it's worth doing?
Maureen:	No.
Val:	Cos, sometimes, they just tear your books up.

If their view of the curriculum was depressing, their view of most teachers was perhaps worse.

Maureen:	They just nag and nag at you don't they? Nagging, nagging, nagging.
Val:	I don't think it's right the way they treat you. The way they push you about as well. Mr Baldwin, he started being funny didn't he, pushing me about and hitting me across the head.
Maureen:	And he swears and calls you sluts, whores and things like

> that. It's like this boy, he was going to come to this
> school, but he heard what the teachers said, and he
> wouldn't come to this school.
> *KC*: Do you think they do it for a joke?
> *Maureen*: I dunno.
> *Liz*: It's to annoy you.
> *Maureen*: They just think they can do what they want.

Unlike the other pupils interviewed, these three girls were not apparently so concerned with organizational rules. Only Maureen brought one up — wearing school uniform. She kept referring to it, but the others were not really interested, and it seemed only important to her because:

> Some of us can't afford it. Like I can't and that. I can't afford
> it.... See if you wear your own clothes you can get food in every
> day and that. And we have problems doing that.

Although she was given a note to carry round explaining why she was not wearing uniform, this singled her out in a way which she found unacceptable. She quoted other schools where pupils did not have to wear uniform. This, she said, was proof that it was not an essential trapping of Education. She also maintained that it was not fair that the staff and sixth form did not have to wear it. Asked what teachers should do when faced with someone in their class not wearing uniform, she said

> Well really, some of them, we wish like that some of them would
> go and see the headmaster and talk about it. But they just tell you
> off all the time.

The reasonableness of a demand to have the issue discussed, together with the perceived insensitivity of the teachers, gave force to Maureen's views. The picture which emerged from these three pupils was that they demanded nothing from school of a revolutionary nature. They merely wanted to be treated with respect, and to be offered activities which they could enjoy such as painting, making models, typing and woodwork. What they felt they got was writing and nagging. Their view of school was summed up by Liz. Asked what advice they would give to a student teacher, she suggested: 'Don't come here, or you must be mad'.

This outright rejection of their school experience does not detract, however, from the fact that these girls' descriptions of themselves corresponded in many ways to their teachers' descriptions. They found the curriculum boring and inadequate — as their teachers had suggested; and Maureen at least admitted to social problems which affected her behaviour and her relationship with other pupils. Once again, however, it was the perceived attitude of teachers to these factors which they regarded as the cause of conflict, a perception which appeared to be based on evidence rather than on preconceived ideas, in so far as they were able to make an exception of the young French teacher. Their blanket condemnation of other teachers seemed, therefore, to indicate that these teachers were claiming false motives for themselves, or that those motives were generally invisible.

Teachers' Views Versus Pupils' Views

Although any summary of the views expressed by 3Y and their teachers would divert attention from important individual differences, it is useful to make some comparisons in order to see where opinion agreed and where it diverged. For example there was agreement that:

1 The class often engaged in boisterous and disruptive behaviour.
2 This behaviour was a natural response to boredom and the difficulty of concentating on, and performing, academic tasks which were regarded as uncongenial and often inappropriate.
3 Teachers treated different pupils differently. (This is reflected in the pupils' accusation that teachers were discriminatory, and in the teachers' declaration that they took individual problems into account.)

However, there were discrepancies between the teachers' and the pupils' views on the subject of teacher motivation. For example:

1 As noted above, pupils interpreted the different ways in which different pupils were treated as discriminatory and unfair. Teachers claimed to work from an empathy with the problems of individual pupils.
2 Pupils claimed that much of the boredom of lessons was the teachers' fault, because they couldn't be bothered to teach and set them meaningless tasks. Teachers claimed that they were doing the best they could with limited resources and in the light of the fact that pupils found work difficult.
3 Pupils claimed, therefore, that much of their disruptive behaviour was the teachers' fault. It was a consequence of the teachers' lack of interest in their job, and their unjust behaviour. No teacher that I spoke to mentioned this as a possible source of misbehaviour. If they were being honest with themselves, and me, it seemed that they never considered this as a serious possibility, and some even appeared to pride themselves on the good, if turbulent, relationship they had with the class.

The evidence presented above, therefore, gives some support to the view that conflict was perpetuated by a misperception of the motives of the other. As Lacey[14] suggested it appeared to be the pupils who had most difficulty in perceiving their teachers' motives clearly. Nevertheless, the teachers' apparent failure to understand that it was their own behaviour which, being misinterpreted by pupils, caused much of the problem, meant that they too were unable to see clearly through the 'semi-permeable membrane'. They appeared to see the structural problems — an inadequate social and educational system — but failed to see the problem which was most immediate, the invisibility of their own motives.

Importantly, if the conclusions outlined above are correct, they corroborate the view that both teachers and pupils were acting intelligently and morally. Teachers claimed to be acting empathetically towards pupils in the light of the information which was available to them, which was the pupils' known social and learning problems, and the inadequacy of the system to meet those problems. Equally, pupils were acting intelligently. They quoted examples of teacher behaviour to support their views, and discriminated between teachers on the basis of available evidence. Without knowledge of the motivation which lay behind the behaviour of some teachers, it was not unintelligent to dismiss it as immoral. Their own responses, therefore, had the hallmark of moral indignation.

However, as intimated earlier, data drawn from personal accounts is notoriously suspect. In order to explore these conclusions further, therefore, evidence from an observation of lessons will be presented. This evidence is, of course, suspect too. I was the observer and my own bias has already been declared. I wanted to find evidence which demonstrated that both teachers and pupils were giving me a true account of their own motivation. With this caveat in mind, however, it is arguable that, whatever it was which my prejudice caused me not to see, I did find data which gave at least some support to the suggested analysis.

Evidence from an Observation of 3Y's Lessons

The school was understandably protective of its teachers, especially when my request was to observe them teaching this difficult class. Arrangements for me to visit lessons were made through a senior master who consulted with the teacher concerned. Unfortunately, it was not considered appropriate that I should observe the young probationary teacher of whom the class, without exception, had approved. Nor did I observe any craft lessons. However, I observed a wide spectrum of 3Y's timetable including lessons in English, History, Geography, Maths, Science, RE, Music and Drama. In addition Mr Charles, their form teacher, brought the class on a visit to the Polytechnic, enabling me to observe their behaviour out of school. Although these observations were limited (23 lessons in all) the patterns of behaviour I observed were consistent enough to suggest that they were typical. This impression was reinforced by the fact that the behaviour of 3Y and their teachers was similar to that reported in other research. Clearly my presence might have affected the behaviour of the participants, for example by eliminating some of the more aggressive aspects of teacher control. However, had such changes been too dramatic, I am sure that the pupils would have pointed this out to me afterwards.

The evidence from the observation of lessons is used to illustrate the argument that:

1　Both the pupils' and the teachers' views of their own behaviour could be corroborated by watching them in action.
2　Both the pupils' and the teachers' views of teacher motivation could be sustained by intelligent, but different, interpretations of concrete examples of teacher behaviour.
3　Teacher behaviour was particularly open to misinterpretation, as a result of their need to counteract disruptive pupil behaviour.
4　Teachers failed to communicate with pupils on a person to person basis.

The Pupils' Behaviour

The behaviour of 3Y corresponded not only with their own and their teachers' descriptions but with that of pupils in other research. As in the lessons observed by Willis, there was '. . . a continuous scraping of chairs . . . and a continuous fidgeting about which explore(d) every permutation of sitting or lying in a chair'.[15] In some lessons this was accompanied by banging desk lids or by an outburst of song, the favourite being 'Spurs are on their way to Wembley'. Sometimes this was sung under the breath, but at other times it blossomed into a full blown chorus with three or four pupils singing lustily. Pupils constantly shouted across the room to each other, to me, or to the teacher. They wandered about taking things from each others' desks, which sometimes resulted in an immediate skirmish, or else in a loud shout of 'Sir, Sir. He's nicked my pencil/biro/book!', followed by a shout of, 'I didn't' or 'It's mine' or, on being told by the teacher to return the article, by the pupil throwing it back across the room in exaggerated petulance.

Like Willis's 'lads', I observed 3Y reading comics, which they hid as the teacher approached. Boys played games with cars and coins and pencils. Girls sat doing each others' hair and talking about other things. At the beginning of one lesson I observed Steve and Mike taking a pile of new folders out of the stock-cupboard which had unwisely been left open. Other boys became accomplices by hiding the folders in desks around the room. When they realized I had seen them, they hissed 'You won't tell, Miss, will you? You won't tell!' The lesson which followed was largely taken up with a surreptitious game of passing folders from pupil to pupil.

Most of 3Y appeared to have developed to a high degree 'the core skill of being able to get out of any given class'.[16] Sometimes this consisted of disappearing for the whole lesson. I heard Tony and Howard discussing whether to go to geography (the next lesson). Tony never arrived. In addition I observed pupils walking in and out of lessons with either no reference to the teacher, or a shouted comment, such as: 'I've been (or got to go) to see Mr—'. Such appearances and disappearances created additional scope for disorder. Dave, for example, came in halfway through one lesson, banged the door, went to a desk in the middle of the room, dragged it noisily across to where two other boys were sitting, and shouted out 'What are we doing?' The teacher moved across to him and asked him to return the desk to its place. After much resistance Dave complied, only to edge it back into line with his friend's desk when the teacher's back was turned.

As with Willis's 'lads', sex was a constant topic of conversation. In one lesson for example, Steve wandered across to just within reach of the girls and made loud comments about the boys with whom they had been in the woods. Two of the girls pretended not to hear. Barbara lashed out. He skipped out of the way, with a shout 'Sir, I'm being attacked'.

That sex was not only a subject of burning interest, but also a means of having a laugh was brought home to me in a lesson where I substituted for a teacher who was away. I said we would have a discussion. Steve called out 'Can we talk about sex?' to a chorus of 'Yea, Yea' followed by direct and personal questions about my own sex life. The two finger gesture commented on by the deputy head was also prominent on some photographs I took when the class came to visit the Polytechnic.

The visit gave good scope for observing their behaviour. Willis commented of 'the lads':

> Outside visits are a nightmare for staff. . . . The lads are handling, pushing, pulling, trying, testing and mauling everything in sight.[17]

These pupils pushed and pulled and fought over expensive television equipment; fell upon the telephone in my study and started dialling numbers at random; engaged in a fight on the field; ran boisterously down a corridor, laughing loudly, and throwing open a line of windows; and mobbed an unsuspecting student who was sitting quietly in a common room. They fought to be on the photographs (Steve was on all of them bar one) pushing each other roughly out of the way.

The amount of work completed by these pupils in lessons and its quality was poor measured against the norm for the year group. This appeared in some cases to be due to the pupils having real difficulty, although some of the girls, especially Barbara and Janet, seemed to manage everything adequately. Nevertheless, in the midst of all this activity there did seem to be a willingness to engage in the subject matter of the lesson. Shouting was often in response to teacher questions or to demand help with a difficulty. Borrowing sometimes resulted in the equipment being used for work, as well as providing an opportunity for mucking about. Moreover, the pupils were in the habit of asking for house points and seemed pleased to get them. Perhaps most significantly, with two teachers (the geography teacher and a drama teacher whom they had for only one lesson a week) they abandoned their boisterous behaviour and seemed genuinely engaged in the subject matter of the lesson, rather than merely giving a minimal compliance.

From an observation of lessons then it seemed possible to conclude that the description given by both pupils and teachers of 3Y's behaviour was accurate. They did seem prepared to learn though they were often bored and as a consequene they took the task of entertaining themselves seriously. Although in this task they totally disrupted the work atmosphere it was clear from their mainly cheerful demeanour that they messed about 'for fun'. Sometimes they genuinely annoyed each other and the quarrel which ensued was real. More importantly, however, they appeared to fail to see the effects of their behaviour on their teachers and seemed genuinely surprised and offended if trouble ensued.

The Teachers' Behaviour

In a similar way the teachers' behaviour seemed to confirm both their own and their pupils' descriptions in all respects bar one. I saw no teacher engaging in violence, either physical or verbal, towards the pupils. I did not in fact observe a lesson by Mr Jones, the teacher about whom all the boys had complained. However their unanimity on this subject had left little doubt in my mind that what they had said about him was true. However, given that he was only one teacher among many, and given that he did not take the girls, he could not be blamed for the general level of dissatisfaction with teachers. The problems were clearly more widespread.

In all I observed over two thirds of the teachers who took 3Y. With two exceptions they fell most easily into Woods' categories of 'negotiators', 'fraternizers', and 'occupational therapists'.[18] The teachers had claimed that they:

> 'accepted outrageous behaviour'
> 'treated them friendly'
> 'encouraged and complimented them'
> 'didn't expect too much' and
> 'avoided "distance", "side" and "military discipline"'.

From the back of the class these descriptions appeared to be largely accurate. Their attempts to provide interesting material was also apparent. I observed a play reading, experiments in science, local history with Mr

Charles, and work on individual cards in Maths and RE. In music lessons they were sometimes allowed to choose their own songs.

Nevertheless, sitting at the back of the class it was also possible to see how the teachers' behaviour could be regarded as unsatisfactory. There was certainly some truth to Liz's complaint 'We always do nothing but write'. What happened was that any attempt by a teacher to do anything different was aborted by the behaviour of the pupils. Mr Charles had clearly been reluctant to bring 3Y to visit the Polytechnic. Their behaviour illustrated his reasons. In the classroom any attempt to break away from routine work seemed impossible because the pupils would not listen. Discussion at the beginning of lessons was characterized by pupils shouting out, wandering about, and not paying attention. As a result teachers quickly gave in and set them routine writing. When it became clear that they would not do even that they were allowed to draw a picture.

By far the largest type of teacher-pupil interaction which I observed might be described as 'teacher circling'. This occurred when teachers had set the class to work, and then moved round the room in an attempt to help them. As soon as the teacher's attention was given to one pupil, other pupils began to engage in non-curricular activities. The teacher, therefore, had to break off from her task to go and deal with these problems, leaving in her wake new activities which erupted as soon as her back was turned. Sometimes teachers circled round in this way for the whole lesson. At other times they stood back to address the whole class and bring them to order, only to be interrupted by a new request for help and the whole process started again. On one occasion a teacher became so exasperated that he ordered Maureen to leave. She refused angrily and in the end he was obliged to escort her from the room. On another occasion while attempting to read a story to the class there were so many interruptions that the teacher went into full retreat behind the desk, put the book away, and made no more attempt to impose his will on the lesson.

This type of interaction seemed utterly wearying to the teachers. At the end of one particularly disrupted lesson I approached the teacher and apologized for my presence saying I knew that having a stranger in the room often excited a class. She shrugged her shoulders and said dispiritedly 'That's alright. It's better having someone else here. They're usually worse than that'. Another teacher talking to me about the problem said, 'I don't know how one copes'. It was as if such teachers, having abandoned Woods' 'Dominance' strategies as a matter of principle and because they truly empathized with their pupils, were left rudderless.

The pattern in the geography lessons was different. Here the teacher was dominant and there was no messing about. As the pupils had described they were not allowed to sit next to each other, nor move out of their places. If they wished to speak they had to raise their hand. This teacher had been criticized by several pupils as too strict, and it was clear that some of the pupils both disliked and were afraid of him. Fear had certainly distorted Liz's views. On the way across to the first of his lessons which I observed, she advised me 'Don't come Miss. He's horrible. All old and wrinkled and horrible'. He turned out to be a pleasant looking man in his late twenties. I did not observe this teacher using any of the techniques of dominance described by Woods such as '... punching, handling, tweaking, clouting, slapping, hair-pulling, twisting, rulering and kicking'.[19] Nor had the pupils accused him of any of these. They had accused him of sarcasm and verbal aggression, but I did not detect any examples of this either. However, the pupils' behaviour gave credence on their claim that such techniques had been used in the past. They were totally subdued. As a result the teacher was able to sustain oral lessons based on exposition and 'question and answer' without it degenerating into chaos. Moreover, many members of the class seemed to be interested in the subject matter. Even if, as a person the geography master had disappeared, as a teacher he was clearly visible.

An outstanding feature of all these lessons was an absence of any communication on classroom issues. Except in geography, discussion even about the curriculum was minimal. Certainly I observed no teacher asking a pupil why they were engaging in a certain behaviour, nor explaining how they felt about it. Questions about behaviour typically took the form of: 'What are you doing?' followed by a 'Hurry up then' or 'Stop it'. Teachers appeared to be working on the assumption that they understood their pupils' motivation and that their pupils understood them. Given that Hargreaves *et al.*, in *Deviance in Classrooms*, found that:

> Teachers rarely state in any explicit way the rules which are broken by pupils. Rather pupils ... are required to fill in the rule or rules which are being invoked by teachers' utterances....[20]

It was not surprising that the teachers of 3Y were equally reticent about motives.

Nevertheless, their failure to discuss classroom issues did seem to be carried to extremes, and made it possible to argue that conflict might have been its consequence. This suggestion was supported by my observation of the play reading lesson. Here the atmosphere was quite different from any other lesson I observed. The pupils were calm, relaxed and cheerful, but clearly engaged in the teacher's purpose. She sat on a desk and the pupils sat where they chose and in any attitude they chose, but somehow the class had become a single unit. She was the only teacher who mentioned my presence. She conferred with the class saying that, as they had a visitor, would it be a good idea if they 'put me in the picture' about what they were doing. They agreed. I was then asked to share a book with Liz and given a part to read.

In contrast, no other teacher acknowledged my existence. Perhaps they intended to respect my observational status by pretending I wasn't there, although I had not requested this anonymity. Even if I had done so, it would have been a strange priority to put the request of an outsider above the legitimate curiosity of persons with whom one interacted on a regular basis. It seemed as if it did not occur to the teachers that my presence was something they should discuss with the class. This was all the more extraordinary because I was certainly a distraction, which a little discussion might have avoided. The first few lessons I observed were interrupted by pupils calling across the room to ask me who I was, what I was called, and what I was doing there. Later this changed to requests to know if I was going to the next lesson, with gratuitous advice as to whether or not it would be worth my while. Pupils would also walk across to engage me in non-curricular conversation. Throughout the teachers kept silence, except when they, too, came across to talk. It was embarrassing, but it was revealing. The pupils talked audibly to me about the teacher, and the teacher talked audibly to me about the pupils; and they did not seem to talk to each other about me.

Strangely, then, through an observation of teacher behaviour it was possible to understand how two contradictory accounts could be accepted without charging either party with a distortion of the facts as they knew them. Seen from one perspective teachers could be accurately accused of failing to teach, of setting mechanical tasks and of nagging. They could also be accused of injustice, of punishing indiscriminately so that some pupils 'got away with murder' and others were picked up for minor offences. However, given eighteen pupils avidly 'laffing' their way through the lessons, it was possible to agree that teachers were genuinely attempting to operate within a humanitarian framework, and to sympathize with them on those occasions when their patience snapped. Moreover, there was certainly no evidence from within the lessons themselves that the type of communication which would be necessary to dispel the pupils' inaccurate view of their teachers' motives, ever occurred.

This can be specifically illustrated by the instance when the teacher took Maureen to be disciplined by a senior member of staff. From my point of view as an observer her crime had been no greater than that of her pupil peers who had been challenging the teacher all lesson. Her crime was to be the last straw and she shouted abuse at the teacher, no doubt regarding his action as discriminatory, which in one sense it was. Unfortunately, by taking offenders to a senior member of staff, there seemed a likelihood that the pupils' sense of injustice would be compounded. For example they felt that it earned them a public reputation against which it was impossible to fight. Tim said:

> If people get into trouble like we have, and we are there at the time and haven't done it, they blame us. Cos they know we're in trouble so they blame us all the time. And we can't do nuffink about it.

Moreover, it was not always possible for the senior member of staff to find a satisfactory solution to the conflict which had occurred. The senior mistress, to whom girls such as Maureen were taken, explained that she talked to such pupils:

> ... about how we behave to people; why they think the situation has occurred; don't they think they have a duty; don't they see the problems the staff have; and we're all trying to help each other.

Although this approach bears a resemblance to the one being advocated by this research it was always likely to fail. In the ten to fifteen minutes which the senior mistress said she might have available to sort out such a problem, it would not be possible to work through even part of this agenda. Moreover, the questions she raised were inevitably 'closed', because, as she said, she felt obliged 'to have a way out for the teacher in the end'. This did not appear to stem from a simple closing of cultural ranks, but from a knowledge that teachers did not send pupils to senior staff without good reason, and from an understanding of the stress caused by disruptive behaviour which, as she said '. . . some teachers have to put up with all the time'. Whatever the teacher had done, therefore, was already forgiven by this senior mistress, due to her understanding of the mitigating circumstances and knowledge of the teacher's goodwill.

However, the evidence suggests that it would be just those mitigating circumstances and motives which would be invisible to the pupil. The senior teacher's inevitably rushed attempts to persuade pupils like Maureen that the matter should be closed, even when the pupil felt the teacher was seriously at fault, would be another cause of resentment to take back into the classroom. The pupil would not know that later the senior mistress might go to the member of staff in question, and say, 'Look — it wasn't easy. You shouldn't really have done that'.

The ultimate weakness of looking to senior members of staff to resolve classroom conflict, however, would lie in the fact that personal relationships can neither be forged, nor mended, vicariously. The senior mistress recognized this, admitting that in really difficult cases she had to appeal to her own relationship with the pupil and say 'Do it for me'. Sending pupils out of class might be a useful way of gaining time to let anger subside, but finally, if the analysis above is correct, the solution to classroom conflict would need to be found in the classroom itself.

Conclusions

This chapter had two major aims. The first was to explore the feasibility of the theory described in Chapter Two, and in so doing explore the links between a person centred approach and sociological approaches. The second, which was closely linked with the first, was to demonstrate that 3Y behaved in ways which were typical of intransigent pupils in other studies, and to introduce some of the characters who would be involved in the experimental lessons. Although it is clearly important to resist making extravagant claims for the type of evidence presented in this chapter, there are important conclusions which can be drawn.

In the first place it seems entirely reasonable to suggest that 3Y were typical members of the anti-school subculture identified in other research. They said, and did, and believed the same things as the intransigent pupils studied by Lacey, Hargreaves, Willis and Woods. In addition, their teachers, who were engaged in various degrees and ways in the survival strategies described by Woods, were providing the class with a similar type of experience. Secondly, whatever one's preferred sociological perspective — structural-functionalist, marxist, or phenomenological — it would be possible to identify aspects of the evidence presented to support one's view. 'Working-class' values could be illustrated by the pupils' enjoyment of bingo, Steve's view of books as useful missiles, and Howard's vandalism of property. The theft of school folders might (just) be cited as evidence of anti-middle-class values.[21] The desire of some pupils to 'learn' might be used as evidence of false consciousness, and disruptive behaviour could be interpreted as a revolutionary tendency.

Equally if one's preferred perspective was psychological or social-psychological it would be possible to identify evidence to confirm it. Teachers and pupils could be characterized as suffering from psychological set. Alternatively it could be suggested that 3Y were deprived (and, therefore, disturbed) or even that they were unable to understand their teachers because they were intellectually immature. Labelling theorists could point out the effects of the Maths Groupings on Barbara and Steve, and the anger of Maureen and Val at the suggestion that they were 'sluts and whores'.

However, the evidence presented in this chapter demonstrates that none of the conceptual categories employed by such theories can adequately explain the behaviour of an individual pupil. Indeed, once attention is focused directly on such individuals the degree of categorical deviancy is such that a new type of explanation is required. Thus, although many of the pupils' preferred activities could be linked with working class or anti-school subcultural norms, others could not. For example, all the pupils liked the French teacher who clearly took her job seriously, and was strict. Barbara, a key intransigent, wanted more difficult work in English. Maureen, who hated school, wanted to improve her handwriting. Liz wanted to do woodwork and Brian, typing. All the boys wanted to do cookery. Steve declared that the 'good thing about school is the education', and Mike that it was '. . . coming time to sit down and study it all now'. Chris was looking forward to his fourth year options, and all the pupils discriminated carefully between teachers, sometimes disagreeing with each other about the meaning of teacher behaviour. There was little in all this to which middle-class teachers, Rhodes Boyson or even feminists could object — none of whom are traditionally regarded as the cultural companions of the likes of 3Y.

Moreover those things which the pupils claimed as their right — such as to spend their free time in a warm place and to eat when they were hungry, were rights claimed by teachers. It was not unusual to see teachers in the staffroom wearing coats and eating and smoking as they worked. What pupils were demanding was to share in their teachers' cultural norms, not to change them. Alternatively, they demanded that if such behaviour were truly inappropriate in an educational institution, teachers should mend their own ways and act in accordance with the rules they imposed on pupils. What is clear is that, although the sociological category of a 'counter-school culture' can be portrayed as 'alien', 'self-sufficient', and 'entrenched' in 'opposition to authority', such labels do not adequately describe its members, whose behaviour can be more directly understood as an expression of human rather than cultural concerns. Both 3Y and their teachers invoked human rights as the criteria against which the school should be judged. Their differences derived from differences in their knowledge of schooling; and although one's knowledge is affected by one's cultural milieu, it is a commodity which can transcend cultural locations if the actors are prepared to enter into an open exchange of ideas — that is, if they are prepared to take the concept of Education seriously.

The theoretical perspective taken by this research predicts disagreements on the issue of justice where persons interact in heavily constrained situations. However, it suggests that the result can either be the creation of a new way of being together, resulting from the dissipation of differences in the revelation of a fundamental unity, or the hardening of boundaries round the self and groups, and the production and maintenance of conflict. The evidence from the discussions with and observations of 3Y and their teachers suggests both their fundamental agreement about existential moral principles and a failure, particularly in the case of the pupils, to recognize this agreement. This failure, however, could not be represented as mindless prejudice. Rather it appeared to be the consequence of the fact that teachers did not communicate the reasons for their behaviour. Thus, Barbara excused some teachers with the argument 'It isn't (their) fault is it? They have their orders, don't they?' and Robert found some reason for the amount of writing which Mr Charles asked them to do, saying:

> It would be a bit hard on him to keep talking to us. He'd get a sore throat. Cos if he talked to every lesson through the day, he'd get a bit worn out.

Such insights were rare. All too often the reply to the question 'Why do you think the teacher did that?' was 'I dunno', or, 'Cos they can't be bothered'. If progress was to be made, the morality of teacher behaviour would need to be made plain. The evidence from which 3Y were currently operating was too open to misinterpretation.

Notes

1 Quoted in Young M.F.D. (1971) frontispiece.
2 Willis, P. (1977) p. 11.
3 Woods, P. (1979) pp. 202 to 203.
4 Woods, P. (1979) pp. 144–5 uses this concept in his discussion of the teachers at Lowfield. Thus if a teacher involved herself in the development of a new course, she would be betting not only on the effectiveness of the course, but that the time she spent going to meetings would be worthwhile — perhaps by bringing her to the notice of the head, or by promising a reduction in disruptive behaviour once the course began.
5 Woods, P. (1979) A 'committed' teacher is one who has become so involved in the system that extrication from it would involve considerable personal loss — perhaps financial as well as psychological. 'As a price of membership' however 'members give up something, make sacrifices, which in turn *increases* commitment' (p. 143). Commitment also makes it difficult to criticize the system, so that 'The deeper the commitment ... the more extensive the rhetoric' (p. 165) necessary to sustain it.
6 Although it was called the 'third' year, it was in fact only the second year that the pupils had been in the school, due to the recent introduction of middle schools and entry at 12+.
7 Willis, P. (1977) makes a similar point, arguing that consciousness contains, at different moments, different aspects of a much more complex unconscious understanding (p. 122). Personal accounts can, therefore, seem contradictory if an integrated, but unconscious, explanation is not assumed.
8 See Chapter Two, Section 5.
9 Woods, P. (1979) pp. 265 to 266.
10 This desire for out of school activities was also mentioned by Tim whose interview is not included. He complained that teachers said they would organize trips but then broke their promise. He saw this as a way of bribing pupils into doing more school work, and spoke longingly of excursions to 'mountains and big hills'.
11 This was a reference to a postal bomb discovered in 1980, not the 1984 Brighton bomb.
12 This contrasted with Robert's view. (Robert's interview is not included) When asked 'Do you like Science?' he replied, 'Yea. But he doesn't like us a bit, does he?' KC 'Does it make a difference? Do you feel it matters whether the teacher likes you or not?' *Robert* 'Yea. Yea it does. Cos they keep picking on you. You say you haven't done something and he says you have. And then you get put on report.'
13 Robert and Jim confirmed this. *Jim* 'When we go into dinner the teachers should queue up with us. ... They just get their ticket and go straight up, forward of us — go past us, and just get their dinner.' *KC* 'Do you know why they do that? Do they give any reasons?' *Robert* 'They're too lazy ...' *Jim* '... to line up. They should just line up with us.'
14 Lacey, C. (1970) p. 175.
15 Willis, P. (1977) p. 13.

16   WILLIS, P. (1977) p. 27.
17   WILLIS, P. (1977) p. 31.
18   WOODS, P. (1979) Briefly, Woods describes 'negotiator' as those who try to reach compromises on the 'You play ball with me, and I'll play ball with you' principle (p. 153); 'fraternizers' work on the principle 'If you can't beat them, join them' (p. 155); and 'occupational therapists' on the principle that 'bodily involvement, accompanied frequently by dulling of the senses passes the time' (p. 163).
19   WOODS, P. (1979) p. 150.
20   HARGREAVES, D. (1975) p. 106.
21   Although there is, of course, plenty of evidence of middle class appropriation of institutional property, for example through the mechanism of expense accounts.

4   Experimental Design

A short series of experimental lessons was carried out with 3Y in the last term of their third year. The aim of these lessons was to explore what would happen when a teacher, working within all the normal constraints, attempted to elevate into pupil consciousness her good intentions and her problems. The method was to replace survival strategies with discussion. Conflict would not be ignored, nor would it be avoided. Instead, pupils would be invited to say why they were behaving disruptively and the effects of their behaviour on the teacher would be explained. They would be asked to discuss what should be done. At the same time they would be encouraged to evaluate teacher behaviour, to challenge anything of which they disapproved, and to require an explanation. If the theory outlined in Chapter Two was correct, this process should result in a reduction of conflict, even if the interests of the different parties were diametrically opposed.

Although the lessons were experimental they were not characterized by rigidly laid down procedures and objectives. There was no detailed research plan,[1] no trained research team, and no clear idea of what a positive result would look like. Moreover, the decision that I would take the lessons[2] meant that there was not even an independent observer. This apparent lack of rigour, however, was necessary if the aim of the lessons was to be fulfilled. For example, the intention to work with all the normal constraints operating on teachers precluded the introduction of expert help such as was used in the NCHE experiments.[3] In that research, which worked from a similar theoretical position to the one taken here, lessons were monitored, and teachers were given substantial support and in-service training so that they could improve their performance in specific interpersonal skills. Changes in pupil behaviour were then measured and tested for their statistical significance. The results were impressive, demonstrating that where teachers increased their scores on personal attitudes to pupils, not only was disruptive behaviour reduced but academic performance improved.

While acknowledging the value and importance of such work, a repetition of the methods used would have been inappropriate here. Any participation in the lessons by an 'expert', whether by providing guidance or ongoing evaluation, would have made the proposed method more expensive than the typical constraints on teachers would allow.[4] Moreover, a non-participant observer, even had he been able to resist the ploys of 3Y to engage him in classroom interaction, would have been able to add little which could not be deduced by an analysis of taped recordings of the lessons. More fundamentally, the use of 'expert' others would have been to undermine the theoretical basis of this research. If, as has been suggested, human nature is an expression of Bohm's holomovement, then the wealth and diversity of the ways it can be validly expressed negates the notion that there are 'experts' who 'know better' than others how to be persons. Indeed, as was argued in Chapter Three, it was not skills which 3Y and their teachers lacked so much as a faith in each other's personhood.[5] In short, in spite of the obvious dangers of a lack of objectivity, the aims and theoretical basis of this research demanded that 3Y and I should be both the subjects of the experiment and the research team. If we could not solve our problems together by monitoring, evaluating and planning in the untidy way which typifies real life and, if we could not work with whatever skills we had and develop new and perhaps more useful ones as we proceeded, then the theory would fall and classrooms would become sites where 'experts' were needed to tell uninitiated persons how to be.

For the same reasons, it would have been entirely inappropriate for me, as teacher, to have developed a detailed methodology and specific objectives. Working to develop the 'sense of oneness' advocated by Bohm, the lessons had to be allowed to unfold in essentially unpredictable ways, because they would be the product of creative persons, choosing the present and opening up new possibilities for the future. Indeed, had I predicted the future, or even worked towards specific long-term behavioural objectives, I would have fallen into the trap of working with a 'model of oneness'. Such a model might predict, or hope, that the pupils of 3Y and myself would come to agree about this or that, in this or that sort of way; which would have been to put a mortgage on creativity, and to render the invitation to 3Y to dispute the present and create the future, meaningless. It would, in effect, have promoted me as researcher/teacher out of the status of 'human-person' into the status of 'expert-person' — a nonsense.[6]

Logically, therefore, the lessons had to be conducted in the light of general principles rather than in accordance with rigidly laid down procedures, devised to reach specific outcomes. Nevertheless, these principles were stringent and amounted to a system of beliefs which would sustain me against the inevitable challenges from 3Y, especially once they became aware that I did not intend to use control techniques. The lessons were, therefore, an open-ended experiment in which I attempted to act upon the following articles of faith:

1   that all those involved in classroom interaction were persons motivated by the twin existential and moral principles of creativity and unity, informed by intelligence;

2   that throught the revelation of this fundamental unity, order, not chaos, would ensue;

3   that although the possible ways of expressing of this moral order were limited by real constraints, there would be sufficient alternatives to provide real choices for the participants; that the future, although not infinitely open, was open enough to allow a solution with which all involved could agree;

4   that because any solution to classroom problems would be creatively achieved, its exact nature could not be predicted, nor pre-planned;

5   that what could be predicted was that a solution would be found;

6   that what could be pre-planned would be one means of achieving the necessary interpersonal understanding, and that this would be by replacing survival techniques with a free exchange of information through discussion of the motives, feelings and problems of all involved;

7   that the road to a solution would not be easy, requiring that everyone reassess their beliefs in the light of the beliefs of the others;

8   that within the inevitable time lag, it would be easy, and tempting, to dismiss the other as unintelligent, or immoral, or amoral objects, who were incapable of empathetic understanding; that this temptation would need to be resisted;

9   that it would be necessary, therefore, in the time needed for persons to reassess their beliefs, to forgive unacceptable behaviour;

10   that even after time had elapsed and a full exchange of ideas had been achieved, those involved might still disagree as to the best way of operating within the given constraints; but that if this situation occurred compromises and bargains could be forged in which persons, relating to clearly visible other persons, would be prepared to give and take; so that the rights of none would totally supercede the rights of the other; and so that communication could continue on an open basis, in the hope of discovering a solution which everyone found more rewarding;

11   that no special skills over and above those generally available to teacher and pupil-persons would be required to instigate this process; that the skills required would be those of listening empathetically and communicating honestly: neither dismissing

the other's viewpoint, nor too easily relinquishing deeply held beliefs of one's own: inviting criticism while maintaining a view of oneself as person; and giving criticism while making explicit one's view of the other as person; and

12 that the development of such skills would be the natural consequence of knowledge of the other as person.

My actions as teacher-researcher were based on these beliefs in-so-far as I was able to maintain them. In this way the link between theory, aims and methodology was forged. Nevertheless, this did leave some serious problems relating to the validity of any results, or conclusions, which might be drawn. The lack of an independent observer and the unusual requirement that, as the teacher, I had to believe in the theory which, as researcher, I was setting out to test, could clearly interfere with objectivity. When presenting examples of person-centred interaction, Rogers, with supreme courage and immaculate logic, challenges person-readers to look into themselves to assess the truth of his arguments.[7] This is, perhaps, ultimately the only way to determine the validity of analyses of subjective evidence. Nevertheless, in the present instance other props to credibility are provided. For example, tape recordings were made of all the lessons and discussions, and verbatim reporting of both my contributions to interaction and those of the pupils has been liberally used in order that the reader can judge the validity of the conclusions, The multi-subjective nature of the evidence thus guarded against one-eyed vision, especially as the majority of the actors — the pupils — were deeply sceptical about both the theory and the method. If, in the end, they agreed that a result had occurred, there seemed good grounds for arguing that it had.

There were, however, two other problems which could affect the validity of any results. The first was that because 3Y already knew me in my interviewing role they might not regard me as a typical teacher. The second was the difficulty of promoting a non-punitive ethos which was necessary, not only to facilitate open discussion, but also to demonstrate that any reduction in disruptive behaviour was not a consequence of fear. Clearly I could make statements that I did not intend to punish pupils and, as far as it was within my power, I could stand by such promises. Nevertheless, any suggestion that the relationship which 3Y and I developed could be separated from institutional reality would be naive. At the most obvious level 3Y would know that, if they behaved in my lessons in an excessively disruptive manner, the classroom door could be opened to admit another teacher demanding vengeance. Moreover, I would be closely linked with the school punishment system via Report Sheets. Finally, even within a person-to-person relationship the intention not to use punishment is clearly questionable. At the point where persons interrelate, disapproval, which is inevitable at times in an honest relationship, becomes a punishment in itself.

Nevertheless, it was felt that neither of these difficulties — the impossibility of totally eradicating fear of reprisals and the fact that I was not 'really' 3Y's teacher — was overwhelming. For example, all the teachers I had observed had been enmeshed in the school punishment system, but this had not prevented 3Y from seriously disrupting some of their lessons. And the fact that both 3Y and I would be encouraged to make our disapproval of each other's behaviour explicit, so that it could be discussed, and either understood and accepted, or retracted and forgiven, would arguably divest it of threat — at least in the long run. Equally it seemed likely that my change of role from interviewer and observer to teacher would be a convincing one. As 3Y's teacher I would be interacting with them for a different purpose. I would no longer be a sympathetic listener, but a teacher whose intention it was to get pupils to work and behave in ways of which I approved. Given that I had found most of the classroom behaviour that I had observed unacceptable, my emergence into the role of teacher promised to be traumatic and would quickly dispel any romantic elements in our relationship. Moreover, my transformation would be encouraged by the different constraints within which I would be working. Interviewing pupils I could give my full attention to a small group. As teacher I would have to contend with the whole class. Interviewing I could end interaction when it no longer seemed profitable. As teacher I would have to wait for the bell. Observing I had no responsibility for what occurred. As teacher I could be called to account. Perhaps most importantly, however, I felt my change of role would be real and convincing because of my past experience. Sixteen years of teaching pupils such as 3Y had provided me with a repertoire of opting out and control techniques upon which it would be only too easy to fall back if things got difficult. The problem of resisting such techniques would be as great for me as for anyone else and I suspected that I would often fail. It, therefore, seemed highly probable that once I stood up in front of 3Y they would have little difficulty in recognizing me as a teacher.

In spite of the fact that the theory underlying these experimental lessons demanded that they should be approached in a spirit of openness, it was necessary to make some preparation. This did not detract from the theoretical base of the lessons for it would be intelligent for a teacher-person to make plans based on known information. What was important about the plans which were made was that they reflected my understanding at the commencement of the experiment and could, if new information emerged and the constraints under which I was working allowed, be changed. For example, I drew up two sets of rules relating to classroom behaviour, one set which applied to the teacher and the other to pupils. I did this first of all to clarify for myself what I believed appropriate behaviour would look like, and secondly, so that I could present the rules to pupils at an early opportunity for discussion. This I felt would be a useful way of checking whether 3Y agreed with my understanding of their attitude to teachers, and it would give them a clearer view of my own beliefs. The rules for teachers were based on the views which 3Y had expressed in their interviews.

The *Rules for Teachers* read:

The teacher must not:

1 Pick on pupils
2 Shout at pupils
3 Nag
4 Hit pupils
5 Call pupils names.

The teachers must:

6 Be fair
7 Keep order
8 Have a sense of humour
9 Keep promises
10 Listen to pupils
11 Make lessons interesting
12 Teach something worthwhile
13 Make reasonable work demands.

3Y were to be invited to consider and revise these rules as they felt appropriate, after which they would be asked to point out and discuss with me those times when, in their view, my performance was less than satisfactory.

The *Rules for Pupils* derived directly from my observations of 3Y's lessons and reflected my feeling about the sort of behaviour a teacher had the right to expect. They read:

A. Work
(Work = thinking, discussing, writing, drawing, making models)
1 Do as much work as you can.
2 When *you* are not working *do not disturb* other people.

B. Noise
(You are making too much noise when you disturb people in the room, and worse in other classrooms)
1 Do not shout.
2 Do not bang about (desks, chairs, rulers, books or anything else).
3 Do not sing.

C. General Behaviour
(Main idea — be nice to people. Do not annoy people)
1 Do not push, punch, wrestle, etc.
2 Try to help other people.
3 Say 'Please' and 'Thankyou' if you want something.
4 Listen to people, including the teacher.

5 If *you* do not want to work, do not make work difficult for other people.

D. Equipment
1 Do not waste paper.
2 Take care of books.
3 Do not steal pens/felt tips/glue, etc., provided by the teacher.
4 Do not mess about with the tape recorder.

These two last rules (D3 and 4) were added as a consequence of the events of lessons three and four. All the rules, however, were open for discussion and revision.

My plans about how and when discussion would occur were equally open. If possible I intended to attempt a class discussion of the rules, but in the light of my observations of 3Y's behaviour I was not optimistic that I could maintain such a discussion without the use of control techniques. I intended, therefore, to initiate discussion as and when I could and especially after conflict had occurred. If necessary I would take time outside the lessons to talk to pupils, but in order to remain within the constraints normally operating on teachers, this would be kept to minimum.

It was arranged that I should take 3Y for the last two lessons every Wednesday morning for one term. They had History at that time and they were studying the late nineteenth century. In the event, owing to the usual disruptions caused by examinations and other summer term activities, we had only twelve lessons together. At the time of planning the curriculum this was not foreseeable. Nevertheless, I was aware of other constraints: the need for the lessons to be classroom based and moderately resourced; the frequent absenteeism of pupils which made continuity from one lesson to the next difficult; the differing levels of pupil skills; differing pupil interests; and 3Y's intolerance of, and joy in finding ways to counteract, boredom. In addition, there was the research demand that I should find time in lessons to discuss problems with pupils. A consideration of these constraints led to the decision to do topic work centred round the years 1870 to 1910. This would free me from a didactic role so that I could interact with pupils on an individual basis, and it would give pupils some autonomy in the choice of subject matter and the speed at which they worked.

Because Mr Charles (whose lessons I was taking) generally worked from a class text, a set of project books was borrowed from a local teachers' library. I prepared an information card for each book which gave page numbers where information on different topics could be found. This was intended to help but not restrict pupils. Similarly, a workcard was prepared for each book indicating the sort of questions it could help them answer. Once again the use of these workcards was to be optional. Pupils were to be invited to do writing, drawings and models to illustrate their chosen topic. The work was then to be mounted on large sheets of paper

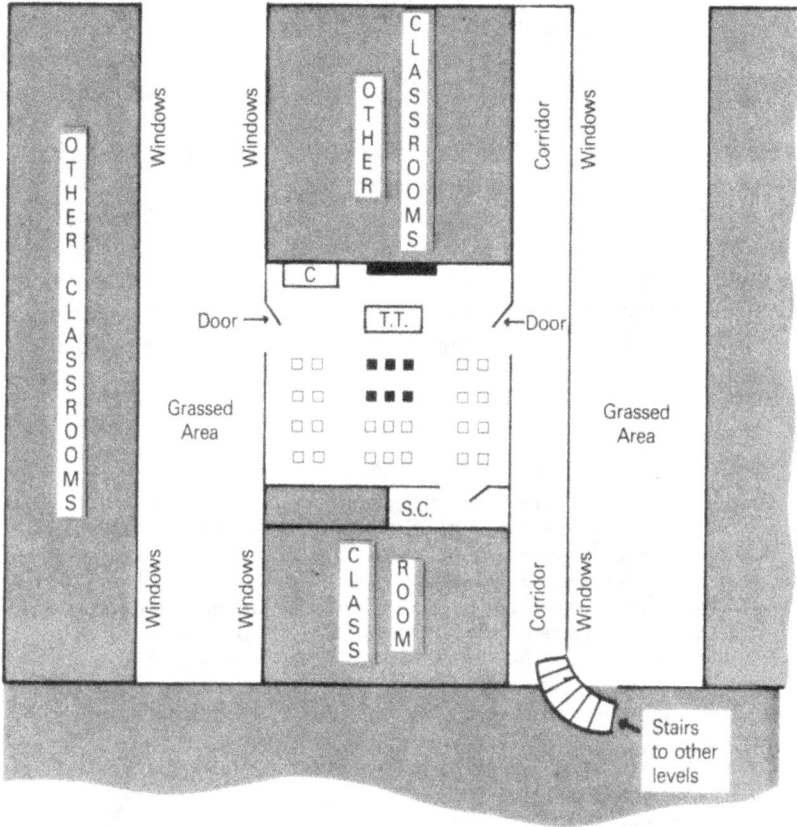

	Other parts of the school building
C	Cupboard
▬	Blackboard
T.T.	Teacher's table
■	Desks on which the books and tape recorder were placed
S.C.	Stock Cupboard

and put on display at the end of term. Finally, I decided that 3Y should have free access to all equipment and be responsible for its return. I believed that teacher-persons had the right to expect pupil-persons to be honest and careful about this. From an observation of 3Y's lessons, however, I predicted that unless, or until, this right could be agreed, my rejection of the role of guardian of property would lead to loss and damage. I, therefore, asked Mr Charles to lock away his stock (pencils, biros, rubbers, rulers, colours, glue and paper) and took in my own.

The evidence from the experimental lessons is presented in three chapters, each of which has a different focus. Chapter Five looks at the way in which the events of lessons one to four appeared to me as teacher. Chapter Six describes the effects on general classroom behaviour of discussion with three key disruptive pupils, and Chapter Seven considers the relationship between the curriculum and classroom behaviour. The diagram gives details of the setting in which the lessons took place.

Notes

1 There was, however, a detailed curriculum plan (outlined later in this chapter).
2 There were two major reasons why I decided to take the lessons myself. The first was that it would have been unethical to ask a teacher to engage in an experiment which, if it failed, would leave them with severe survival problems. The second reason was that an important set of data would be the inner thoughts and feelings of the teachers involved. While it might have been possible to develop a relationship with a teacher in which there was enough trust for him to divulge such feelings and thoughts to me as researcher, there was always the possibility of omissions and misinterpretations, and the process would have been very costly in teacher time. I could take my own feelings and thoughts home with me to study at leisure, so that although I might be mistaken about myself, the margin of error would arguably be reduced.
3 These experiments are reported in ROGERS, C. (1983) pp. 197 to 221.
4 This was acknowledged by those conducting the experiments, as demonstrated by the description given of the way the computer was used: '... the NCHE conducted sophisticated studies that gave computer feedback to teachers about their interpersonal functioning in the classrooms. At the same time, the computer could tell those same teachers about their students' performance on a variety of indexes *they normally would not be able to follow because of time and personal* constraints.' (My emphasis) (In ROGERS, C. 1983, p. 202)
5 There is some doubt in my mind about whether personal skills, as distinct from survival or communication skills, can ever be taught. Indeed, I am not even sure what such skills would be or whether they exist. Perhaps the ability to laugh might be one of them, but this ability is one which resists training programs and is, therefore, a continual problem for actors, (and politicians). Geschwind, (in MILLER, J. 1983) says, 'When someone gives you the command to laugh, you try to control the many muscles of the face from the so-called "face area" of the motor cortex on both sides of the brain. You have, in fact, never acquired the program for controlling these regions in the act of laughing, and you behave as you do whenever you attempt a poorly learned skill. As a result, the individual muscles do not participate to the proper extent and with the proper timing. The effect is a very poor laugh.

On the other hand, an amusing event or a funny story leads to stimulation of structures deep in the brain in the so-called limbic system which is very important for emotional responses.... That group of nerve cells has built into it the whole program for laughing which is exactly right — you now produce a normal laugh. Yet you cannot directly stimulate that region in the depths from the part of the cortex which understands language, and thus language cannot trip off the response of laughing.' (pp. 125 to 126) It is because such emotional responses cannot be trained, and because persons learn very quickly to distinguish between a false and a true laugh or smile, that I am sceptical about the concept of personal skills (and incidentally less fearful about the attempts of unscrupulous behaviour modifiers to fool their potential victims). One's performance as a person seems to have more to do with one's understanding of the situation than anything else. If you like someone you will smile properly; if you think the story is funny you will laugh from the depths of your limbic system. I am irresistably reminded of Mr Potter, the Principal of the College of Lifemanship in School for Scoundrels, who proclaimed mournfully 'Once sincerity raises its ugly head lifemanship flies out of the window'.

6   This argument refers back to the discussion in Chapter Two about the necessary indivisibility of persons if they are to be regarded as free and moral. While it is clear that I can become an expert in a field of knowledge, or a skill, as I learn more and might even become an expert in *knowing about* persons as I meet and study more of them. I can't become more expert at *being* a person and still be free. Such expertise would imply growth or change in my nature and, therefore, the determinism of divisibility and more primitive causation.

7   Rogers does, of course, also produce 'harder' types of evidence such as the results of the NCHE experiments mentioned above. Nevertheless his appeal transcends objective data. In *Freedom to Learn* (1983) under headings such as 'The Challenge' (p. 40) and 'Do We Dare?' (p. 297) he asks teachers to consider the evidence in the light of the totality of their own knowledge of what it is to be themselves, to be human.

5   *Lessons One to Four*

The first four lessons are treated in this chapter as a single unit, with lesson four marking an important watershed in my interaction as teacher with 3Y. That lesson was characterized by the total disintegration of my teacher role, and by anger. Although theory, common sense and past experience had led me to expect such conflict, this knowledge did not assuage the unpleasantness of what occurred.

One purpose of this chapter is to chart as honestly as possible the changing state of my thoughts and feelings as the four lessons progressed, in order to demonstrate the difficulty of maintaining a belief in pupils as moral persons. A second purpose is to demonstrate the way in which the constraints upon me (and especially the constraints of the pupils' own behaviour and my perception of the expectations of professional others) made communication difficult and how, as a consequence, my actions were based on inadequate information. This chapter is, therefore, an exploration of the way in which the belief that disruptive pupils are immoral and need to be controlled can be recreated even in the mind of a teacher who is determined to resist it, and of the way in which her actions could create a parallel false belief in the minds of her pupils.

In order to illustrate the effects of the first four lessons on my actions and beliefs, the evidence which follows is a combination of (1) fairly substantial transcripts from the recordings to give 'objective' glimpses of what was being said and done in different parts of the classroom; and (2) my thoughts and feelings as these happenings occurred. Although the pupils' voices are heard, my failure to engage them in discussion meant that there was little way of knowing what their contributions meant.

Although a clear picture has already been drawn of my beliefs and and objectives in my capacity as researcher, it is important to clarify briefly the way in which, as teacher, I evaluated 3Y's behaviour. This is necessary if my own behaviour in the lessons is to be understood. As teacher my ultimate objective was to encourage 3Y to learn some History. I believed that such learning was valuable not only as a way of understanding persons in other times and cultures, but as a way of understanding one's own culture more fully. I also believed that through the medium of project work I could help pupils with study skills. These beliefs are not unusual, and in any case need not be substantiated here. They are stated merely as items in the rationale from which I began, and the need to justify them would only occur if they were challenged by pupils. My curriculum plan had, therefore, been divised in the belief that the area of study was educationally worthwhile and potentially interesting. Moreover, within the constraints of a fixed syllabus and limited resources, I believed I was meeting 3Y's earlier criticisms as far as I was able. Nevertheless, given the literary nature of many of the tasks, and given the length of a double lesson (an hour and twenty minutes) I did not expect the pupils to concentrate all the time. I was not, in principle, opposed to 'time out'.

However, a prior objective as 3Y's teacher was the eradication of disruptive behaviour. This objective had priority for two reasons. Firstly, as already described, an observation of 3Y's lessons had convinced me that their behaviour seriously detracted from their teachers' ability to help them with their work. If my curriculum objective was not to be jeopardized, 3Y's behaviour had to change. The *Rules for Pupils* outlined the changes which I felt were necessary. The second reason for making the eradication of disruptive behaviour my first objective, however, was a moral one. Disruption, especially in the form of excessive noise, is a form of pollution which teachers have always understood. It has real consequences for physical well-being and seriously encroaches on the personal space of others. Indeed, by definition, disruptive behaviour interferes with others without their consent and, therefore, has moral implications. There are times, of course, when physical disruption is the only defence available when one's own rights are being transgressed, as 3Y had pointed out. However, they also claimed that much of their messing about was done 'for fun', appearing ignorant of its consequences. I believed that those consequences were far reaching, affecting not only teachers but innocent peers and also, in the long run, the interests of the disruptives themselves and that, therefore, such behaviour should be challenged on moral grounds.

Denscombe in an article on teacher attitudes to noise commented that:

> ... where teachers operate in closed classrooms they appear to experience a social pressure to minimize noise, and may in practice exhibit a fundamental preoccupation with maintaining quiet orderliness in the classroom, irrespective of its pedagogic implications.[1]

This statement almost exactly reflected my position. For although I believed that quiet orderliness was in most cases educationally beneficial, in those few cases where I could see that some noisy disorder might contribute to the learning of a few, its effects on others (for example on the class next door) would put it morally out of bounds. It was the paramouncy of the moral over pedagogical implications which led me to a position where, although I would be willing to compromise quite drastically on my curriculum objections, I felt I could not compromise on this more fundamental issue. Moreover, like the teachers observed by Denscombe, I experienced this as a social pressure as well as a personal belief. My teaching experience had taught me that other teachers in the school would judge my competence, less by whether 3Y learned anything than by whether I prevented them from disturbing the rest of the school. Importantly, however, I cared what other teachers thought because I agreed with them. Equally importantly, for present purposes, whether or not I was right to agree and care is not at issue. This is merely a statement of my beliefs as I began the experimental lessons with 3Y and, as such, it provides data which can help to explain my behaviour.

Lessons One and Two

I began this first double lesson in a state of strong and conflicting emotions. Specifically I was torn between hope and fear — hope that the method would work, and fear that in the attempt I would be exposed as inadequate. The anxiety thus produced centred, at the beginning of these lessons, on the immediate problem of how to get 3Y to listen for long enough to understand both the research plan and the curriculum task.

I had some initial advantages and I hoped, but did not know, that these would be enough to let me communicate sufficient information for the experiment to begin. For example, 3Y were not expecting me. It seemed likely that my unexpected appearance would momentarily stay their hand. Secondly, I hoped that the unusual nature of what I had to communicate might extend their normal listening time. Thirdly, in this initial period I could use some control techniques (body postures, eye contact, use of voice and expectant pauses) which, because my intentions would not yet be fully understood, might carry enough of an element of warning to preserve order temporarily.

All these advantages, however, would be short-lived. The use of control techniques had to be abandoned very quickly if they were not to interfere with the message that I intended to take 3Y into partnership. Moreover, once the element of surprise had passed, it seemed likely that 3Y might interpret my appearance as an opportunity for messing about, whether in order to test me or just for the fun of it. The following detailed extracts from the opening stages of lesson one illustrate the way in which I performed under these circumstances and my perceptions of 3Y's response.

The pupils entered the classroom in their usual boisterous manner.

On seeing me standing at the front of the room they demanded to know where Mr Charles was. I responded to individuals by saying that I would be taking the lesson and by asking them to sit down so that I could explain. When I felt reasonably sure that everyone had arrived, and having achieved a precarious silence, I began:

KC: I asked, actually, if I could come and take these lessons with you ...

Steve: [Calling out] Miss. Have you got the photos? (These were the photographs taken on the visit to the Polytechnic the previous term and which Steve had not yet seen)

KC: Could you listen first of all to what I have to say, and then there will be time to say what you have to say. What I want to do — if you remember, last term I came along and we had interviews. I asked you to come along and talk to me. And the reason I wanted you to talk to me was because I want to know how to tell students who are learning to be teachers, to teach. You remember that was the question I asked you. Well, if I've got to tell students what a good teacher is like, you probably are the best people to be able to tell me, and you actually gave me a lot of information.

[Dave put his hand up.]

KC: Yes Dave?

Dave: Me and Tim went up to the University last night.

[General conversation began round this topic]

KC: Alright. Let me, let me finish first of all what I want to say, and then.... You gave me lots of good ideas, but it seemed to me — Tim — [He was talking] ... that if I ... [Further interruption] ... if I just told people the ideas without trying them out, then that wasn't really a very good idea. And so what I want us to do this term, and it depends on you sort of helping me, what I'd like to happen is — I'll do some teaching with you, and then through the lessons, and perhaps a bit at the end of the lessons you tell me (not talking about other teachers) you tell me what *I've* done wrong, and you tell me what you've liked about it; you tell me whether it could have been improved in any way. And we'll try and see if we can get something organized. Now that's my idea right? And we can forget about that for the moment. [Murmuring.] But one of the things that I did think would be useful to help me, so that I know and can remember what people have said, is if we have a tape recorder playing. So that we can talk into the tape recorder and I don't have to be worrying trying to remember. Cos I've not got a very good memory for remembering exactly what people said. So what I said to Mr

> Charles was 'Can I come and take some History lessons?',
> and he said 'Yes that would be O.K.' So I'm going to take this
> Wednesday morning lesson now until the end of term.
> Alright? The double lesson.

Throughout the whole of this explanation I felt tense. I was aware
that my speech was disjointed and over-emphatic. I had been fairly
successful in aborting alternative subjects for discussion but was becoming
increasingly aware of signs that 3Y would not be prepared to take much
more. I was anxious to get them working, but knew that this necessitated
a considerable amount of further explanation. I, therefore, denied them
the chance to discuss what I had said preferring to move on to a description
of the curriculum. I continued:

KC:	What I thought we could do is to take a time in History when your great-grandparents were alive. I thought we could have the dates 1870 to 1910. And what I thought we could do — I've brought along some sheets of paper.... Are you listening Barbara?
Barbara:	Yea.
KC:	What I thought we could do is ...
Pupil 1:	[Calling out] Our great-grandfathers?
KC:	That's right.
Pupil 2:	[Calling out] We weren't alive.
KC:	That's right.
Pupil 3:	How will we know?
KC:	Well I've brought lots of books along. What I thought we could do — I've brought these sheets along and I'd like everybody to have a sheet of paper.... Barbara. [She was talking] I would like you to collect lots of information of those years and what life was like in those years. Now I've brought lots of books along — books on costumes, books on ships, books on trains, books on schools,
Dave:	On football?
KC:	I can get one on football but I couldn't get it for this week, but I can get it for another time. And I thought if we all took a sheet (and at the end you could take the sheets home, with the work that you've done) if you all have a sheet and have pieces of paper — we've got plain paper here and writing paper, and do pictures on the plain paper ... and gradually build up a sheet, each person doing one of their own ...
Barbara:	Can we share?
KC:	Well yes, you can share. I thought about sharing. But the only trouble with sharing is who would take it home at the end?

Janet: I don't mind.

KC: Well alright. If you want to work together you can do. That's alright.

            [The pupils began noisily pushing desks together to form new groups. One large group of seven was being formed]

KC: Now one of the things we're going to have to ...

            [Pupils continued pushing desks about, and talking loudly]

KC: One of the things we're going to have to.... Dave can you just listen a moment, you'll have chance to talk, a bit later. One of the things we're going to have to think about is having enough space to have a sheet of paper. I don't mind you sitting together, and you can sit together in groups. That's fine you know. I doesn't make any difference. But I think you'll have to be reasonably sensible, and make sure that you've got enough space to do the sort of work that you're doing.... There's just one other thing I need to tell you about these books. In these books you'll find ...

            [Holding up a book]

Pupil: *The Clipper Ship?* [Reading out the title]

KC: *The Clipper Ship.* In these books you'll find a piece of card like this, and on the piece of card there's the title of the book — it says here *The Clipper Ship* right? And then it gives you some things that are inside that book and some page numbers. That's just to help you if you want to go straight to a page, to the sort of thing that we might use. Not all the contents — a lot of the things in these books aren't to do with those years that we're going to be doing. Yes Dave? [He had put his hand up]

Dave: Can we take the books home?

KC: We'll have to talk about that won't we? It might be possible.

Pupil: [Made a suggestion about what they could do but inaudible on tape due to other noise].

KC: That would be great. Yes. The other thing is there are lots of ideas that we could use. What I'd like to do, I'd like to cover that wall, and perhaps even that one there, with things that are about life in England between 1870 and 1910.

Pupil: [Calling out] They all got pulled down last time.

KC: Well, we'll make sure that they don't this time, because what we'll do, we'll collect them together, and we won't put them up until they're all ready.

Pupil: [Calling out] But ...

KC: [Fixing eye on pupil] ... and we'll make a super display and perhaps invite somebody in to see it.

Pupil:	[Calling out] ... they pulled them down last time.
KC:	Well, yes, I *know* that. [Beginning to feel irritated] [Other pupils called out on the subject]
KC:	Yes ... yes ... Well, we'll get started fairly quickly I think. But what I'll do, I'll come round an talk to you, because I'm sure people will have different ideas as well.

My major objective by the end of this interchange was to get 3Y working as quickly as possible. Although they had taken less than a minute to move their desks into new groups, the episode had been noisy and seemed to me to contain a high element of mucking about. I did not experience this as opposition to what I was saying, however, so much as an indication that they wanted to stop listening and do something. This interpretation was reinforced by the fact that by the end of the interchange pupils were beginning to come out to the front to look through the books. This I took as a willingness to become engaged in the curriculum I was proposing. I, therefore, abandoned any further attempts at talking to the whole class in order to begin discussion with individuals and small groups.

Most of the class chose books and were supplied with equipment fairly quickly. I was relieved that they appeared willing to engage in the work and began to relax. The large group which consisted of Barbara, Janet, Liz, Jean, Dave, Tony and Frank were chatting as they worked. Only when their voices threatened to seriously disrupt the work of others did I intervene. On those occasions I tried to make my views clear. At one point when loud cries of delight and laughter followed a declaration by Dave that Margaret, a girl in another class, 'fancied' Frank, I said 'One of the things we're going to have to think about is whether you can work quietly in a large group like this'. On another occasion:

KC:	Let's try an experiment where instead of using voices like this [Normal teacher voice] we use voices like this [Spoken in a hushed voice]
Tony:	What — use little voices?
KC:	Yes.

Later still, after a further outburst I said:

KC:	Now then. This is one of the things that goes wrong isn't it? Now what have I done for that to happen? Have I done something wrong to make you as noisy as that?
Janet:	Yes. You should shout at them Miss.
KC:	You think I should shout at them? I don't really think I need to shout at them because I think they know.
Barbara:	Shout at us, and we'll shout back!

KC: I think it would be better if we all just decided ourselves, without shouting. Cos if I shout it's as bad as you shouting isn't it? Let's just see if we can.

Tony: I'll go mad if you shout at me!

Complete silence fell at the end of this interchange broken only by Howard who was tapping the desk with his ruler in an apparently absent-minded fashion.

Steve: Be quiet, Howard. You're just making me annoyed!

The effect of these mini-discussions was, however, short-lived. In particular I felt that the large group of seven pupils generated too much non-curricular entertainment and consequent noise. Towards the end of the lesson I approached them again.

KC: Now I'm wondering whether you're going to be able to do your best work ...

Dave: [Cutting in] I am. I'm just ...

KC: Are you?

Tony: [Showing me his work] How about that then Miss?

KC: Yes. That's very good. But one of the things we're going to have to think about is whether you're sitting in the right place to do good work. That's something that you can decide.

Barbara: [Sounding aggrieved] We've done all that!

KC: You've worked.... Yes that's very good. I'm not criticizing you. I'm just saying it's one of the things you'll have to think about.

Apart from these occasions on which I attempted to begin an exchange of ideas on the subject of noise there were other short-lived outbursts which died away naturally. These included Howard banging on the desk from time to time, pupils calling out to ask for something, one whistle, and one flurry from Steve of 'Spurs are on their way to Wembley'. None of these outbursts were sustained, however, and I perceived them as absent-mindedness.

In general I did not feel threatened by 3Y's behaviour during this period, and felt that I could afford to spend a large part of my time discussing the curriculum with individual pupils and groups. I encouraged the pupils to go and help themselves to equipment and books when they wanted them rather than calling out. I was aware that some of them — particularly Dave, Tony and Mike made frequent visits to the tape recorder, but as they did not appear to be touching it, I did not intervene. Their behaviour was not disruptive so I preferred to continue with curriculum discussions which had a high priority if I was to convince pupils that I was trying to give worthwhile lessons.

Because most of the pupils had quickly found a subject which they were prepared to do I was able to talk more intensively with Steve, Robert and Jim. Steve, who was sitting next to Robert and Jim had begun to draw a modern car. I pointed out that this was outside the dates which I had specified, but he said he wanted to do it anyway. I sat down in front of the three boys and tried a different approach.

> KC: Do you think there are any books, or subjects, that you think we ought to do, that I don't seem to have thought of?
> Steve: I know. Sex — about men and women.

I perceived this suggestion as a challenge, but took it at face value.

> KC: We had a discussion about that before, didn't we? A long time ago now.
> [I was referring to the lesson at the beginning of the year when I had stood in for a teacher who was away]
> Steve: We didn't.
> KC: We did, love. Anyway, alright, Steve, I'll see what I can find. Presumably — er — what you would be interested in would be how men and women were different with each other then and now. They didn't have the same contraceptives as we have now, and they had very large families, didn't they? They didn't know how to prevent themselves from having large families. So that sort of thing would be interesting.

Robert and Jim joined in the conversation which then ranged over problems of population control, poverty, housing and public health. The total conversation lasted over fifteen minutes. At the end I made a note that Steve had decided to do work on Sex, but that although Robert and Jim might do public health, they would also like to see some books on 'Cowboys' and 'War'. My belief that Steve's choice was a case of 'mucking about' was reinforced when he picked up the note and showed it to Tony.

> Steve: Look. Robert — 'Cowboys'; Jim — 'War'; Steve — 'Sex'!

Tony laughed and took the note across to his group. He read it to them quietly, but there was little response.

> Steve: [calling out] Read it out again, Tony.
> Tony: [loudly] Robert's got 'Cowboys', Jim's got 'War and Steve's got 'Sex'.

Once again, however, there was little response from the rest of the class.

Although from time to time I helped several pupils to find suitable books for their chosen topic, on only two other occasions was I able to begin an exchange of ideas about how the curriculum had been received. One of these discussions was with Frank. He was a member of the large group of pupils, but unlike the rest who worked steadily as they chatted, I observed him coming to the table to change his book a number of times. He had chosen to do the early development of flight, but appeared to be dissatisfied. Eventually he approached me.

Frank: Miss, I can't ... I don't know what else to do. [He had drawn a picture which he showed me]

KC: Right. Have you got a book?

Frank: Here, Miss. But it's a bit too late (ie. after the date 1910).

KC: There *is* one in there.
[I opened the book and started looking through]

Frank: What about that?
[Pointing at a picture of a balloon]

KC: That one's a bit before — oh no, wait a minute, it isn't. Yes, that's alright. It's 1891.

Frank: [Pointing at another picture] What about that?

KC: That's not a proper aeroplane. [It was a diagram showing the effect of air currents] That shows you. . . .

Dave: [Standing by and listening] That just shows you how the wind comes off the wings.

Frank: I don't want to do that.

KC: Don't you? Which do you want to do?

Frank: None of them really?

KC: Would you just like to look at a book now, till the end of the lesson?
[There were about ten minutes left]

Frank: No. I want to do somthing, but I can't find nothing *to* do.

At this point I was interrupted and the problem was not solved. Frank looked through the books for a few more minutes and then returned with one to his desk. It was clear to me, however, that I would need to spend more time with him discussing what he might do.

My conversation with Howard, on the other hand, led me to believe he was satisfied with the curriculum. Alone among the class he had rejected the idea of sticking pieces of writing and drawing onto a chart, and had asked instead if he might enlarge a typical industrial street scene onto one of the large sheets of paper. He sat by himself, painstakingly drawing it out. From time to time he took 'time out' for a walk round the class, but on these occasions he caused no disturbance and after a minute or two returned to his work. Like his ruler tapping, these breaks seemed to me to stem from a need to do something active rather than from boredom. Once he came to show me what he had done.

KC: That's coming on nicely.

Howard: The building's alright. It's the people I've got to worry about!

KC: Yes. That's where the trouble will start.

He took himself off to his desk an re-applied himself to the task. About five minutes before the end of the lesson he approached me again.

Howard: Shall I stop this now until next time?
KC: Yes, if you like. You can just look at a book quietly. You've worked hard.
Howard: [Sounding pleased] Have I?
KC: Yes.

By the end of the lesson I, too, was feeling pleased. I felt relaxed as pupils brought their work to show me and returned their books and equipment. There was no formal discussion at the end of the lesson, but nor was the ending disorderly. When the bell went I told pupils they could leave as soon as they had given everything in.

My Feelings at the End of Lessons One and Two

My assessment of this first double lesson was that it had been minimally successful. This assessment was based not only on the subjective knowledge that as the lesson progressed I began to feel less anxious, but also on the more objective evidence of work which the class had produced and the recordings. Listening to the tapes confirmed my impression that by 3Y's standards the lessons had been quiet and orderly. They also corroborated my view that however imperfectly I had performed, I had given the class enough information for the experiment to begin.

Nevertheless, I was also aware of the limitations of what had occurred. Although I had introduced a number of issues which would need to be discussed and had given some of my views, I came away from the lesson with little more than circumstantial evidence about the pupils' reaction to this. At the end of the lessons I was inclined to think that the pupils might be prepared to engage in the curriculum I had suggested. After listening to the tapes I was no longer sure. Specifically, it became apparent that the actual curriculum which most of the pupils had been following had not been History 1870 to 1910 but sex. Steve had made this explicit, but the conversation of the large group of pupils had also centred continuously round this topic, and the recorder in the classroom had been persistently, though surreptitiously, used to record salacious comments about other members of the class. At the time I had been only minimally aware of this alternative curriculum. It was as if 3Y and myself had been living in two different planes of reality which merely touched at their boundaries. Perhaps it was because I did not violate their curriculum space that they had been prepared to go through the motions of conforming to my wishes.

My final assessment of these lessons, therefore, was that although I had gained in confidence and had had some practice in communicating my views, I had no proof that my communications had been received, nor that I was perceived as a person, rather than as an object who could be easily manipulated or ignored.

Lessons Three and Four

My second meeting with 3Y occurred after a break of two weeks, because in the intervening week the lessons had been cancelled. The school had been involved in examinations and the timetable had been completely taken over for this purpose. In addition to the difficulty which pupils might have in remembering what had taken place in our first two lessons, the situation was complicated by the presence of two pupils who had been absent at that time. One of these pupils, Brian, had been away because he had been cut badly when Steve pushed him through a plate glass window. He had only just that day returned to school.

In order to try to elicit 3Y's views of the lessons more systematically than I had managed at our previous meeting, I had decided to present the class with the list of *Rules for Teachers* which I had derived from their interviews with me. First, however, I needed to remind pupils of the task in hand. The lesson began noisily. Pupils talked loudly as they entered the room and desk were pushed across into new groups. Brian and Steve scuffled roughly with each other near the door. It was almost ten minutes after the bell before everyone had arrived and the class was sitting ready to listen. I briefly explained again the curriculum task and then reminded them of the research objectives.

KC: We're going on from the conversations we had last term, and you're going to try and help me to do what you think a good teacher ought to do. And one of the things I've done in preparation for this lesson, I listened again very carefully to the tapes we made, and I made a list of rules. These are rules for teachers, right? I'll put them on here shall I ... [Pinning them on the wall] ... and then you can see them. And what I'm going to ask you to do at the end of the lesson is to score me — give me a mark.

Pupil: All of us? Wow ... !

KC: So we're going to have to discuss it and see how it goes, because remember, I'm wanting to learn.

[A general buzz of conversation began]

KC: Let's just have a look at this shall we, because the other thing I want you to do — I might have left something off which you think should go on the list, that ought to be another rule for teachers.

I began to read through the list of rules asking them if they thought I had got them right. For example when I got to number seven I said,

> KC: I've got to keep order. A lot of pupils said they liked teachers to keep order. But you said you wanted them to be strict but not *too* strict. So that's a very difficult thing for me to know just precisely what you mean. So you're going to have to help me with that one.
>
> Steve: Sir — Miss — Can we listen — can we play the tape now for one lesson and listen in the . . . .
>
> Tony: [Interrupting but inaudible]
>
> Steve: [Shouting] Shut up Tony! Play the tape for one lesson and listen in the next?
>
> Pupil: Yea. So I'll put it on now. Yea. It's on.
>
> Pupil: Can we have a spare lesson?
>
> KC: Let's have a look at the rest of these first.
>
> Steve: [Shouting] Does it say not to annoy people?
>
> KC: It says the teacher should be fair.
>
> Steve: Oi. Miss. What about. . . . Oh, forget it! You say. . . . You've missed one out.
>
> Pupil: Eh?
>
> Steve: She's missed one out.
>
> Brian: What's she missed out?
>
> Steve: Do not annoy people.
>   [General noise and argument broke out]
>
> KC: Can I just say something straight away? Steve! Dave! [they were arguing loudly]
>
> Steve: Miss. Have you got my sex books?
>
> KC: Just listen will you first of all. Just listen. One of the things that people said when they talked to me last term, was that teachers don't listen. Now I think it might be useful if, next week, I bring in another set of rules. Because it seems to me that pupils don't listen to teachers! So if you want me to listen to you, then it's only fair that it goes the other way, and that pupils listen to the teacher. Now you're going to have a lot of time to talk, but I just want to make sure that we all understand what I've written. [Silence fell, and I began to go through the rules again]
>
> KC: Number nine — that I must keep promises. Now I promised to get you some books Steve, so you'll be able to judge me at the end of the lesson won't you?
>
> Steve: You've missed out number thirteen.
>
> KC: What would you put there?
>
> Steve: Do not annoy people.
>
> KC: I'll put it on for next lesson.
>
> Dave: Better Options.

> *KC*: Well, what I've tried to do is to provide some choice for you haven't I? So — let's get ourselves organized.
>
> *Steve*: Have you got my sex books?

It is easy to see the change in my attitude as this interaction progressed. I began with a wish to discuss the rules for teachers, and finished with a desire to get 3Y working as quickly as possible. My insistence on doing most of the talking myself, and my cursory acknowledgement of pupil contributions were a response to an impression that some pupils were messing about, and thus to the fear of disorder. For example I perceived Steve's request to listen to the tape in the second lesson as a threat. The comments which had been inserted onto the tapes in lessons one and two were offensive, and I believed that if I allowed the current tape to be played it would be filled with similar inflammatory material. I was not prepared to risk the personal affront to pupils abused on the tape, nor the potential chaos which such abuse might bring.

Moreover, although I wanted the rules for teachers to be discussed, I was not prepared to allow an unruly debate at this stage if I could avoid it. My appeal that they should be fair and listen to what I had to say had been an attempt to indicate how I felt about this. I did not perceive much positive response. My teacher persona, therefore, overrode my research commitment and I opted out. Nevertheless, I felt something had been achieved. I had given notice that at the end of the lesson pupils would be invited to criticize my performance, and I felt sure that what I had said had been heard.

The rest of the lesson passed for me in a blur of noise from which now sullen, now maliciously grinning faces emerged. As an observer I had identified the outward form of teacher circling. In lessons three and four I experienced the phenomenon from within. It left me with a few vivid pictures of isolated events, but mainly with a memory of being helplessly buffetted by 3Y's activities. Steve rejected as uninteresting the books on sex which I had provided. He, Brian and Mike systematically devoted their time to disruption. They inserted themselves roughly into established groups of pupils creating angry scenes. They fell off chairs, shouted across the room to each other, and sang. They made no attempt to work. Brian responded to my suggestion that he might like to make a model by producing and throwing paper aeroplanes. Later he decided to explore the potential of the books on sex. He shouted:

> *Brian*: I want to read the sex books.
>
> *KC*: Don't shout, Brian.
>
> *Brian*: [Loudly] Where are the sex books?
>
> *KC*: Brian. Don't shout. Will you not shout! Now if you want to look at these come and sit with me and I'll tell you about them.
>
> *Brian*: I want to sit with Mike.

KC:	Come here and sit down. I want to tell you about them first. [He snatched at the books to take them from me]
KC:	Brian — don't snatch. Now let me tell you about them first.
Brian:	What about them?
KC:	This one ...
Brian:	[Sounding bored] Yea.
KC:	... is written by a woman who lived in the nineteenth century....
Brian:	Yea.
KC:	... and she was very concerned that girls were out on the streets as prostitutes.
Brian:	Yea.
KC:	She thought that they were very badly treated and that they should be treated properly.
Brian:	What about this one?
KC:	Now this is a book which was actually written in 1929, so it was a bit later.
Brian:	What's it about?
KC:	It's a book for women about how they should behave with their husbands when they're married.
Brian:	Yea.
KC:	Now listen, Brian. They are my two books, so be very careful with them.

This was the longest interaction I managed to achieve with Brian, and this was matched by a similar failure to discuss problems with other pupils. A brief interchange with Steve about playing with the tape recorder was the only other example of an exchange of ideas. I had asked him several times to stop turning it on and off. On one occasion, during a brief respite, I continued by asking him what work he was going to do.

Steve:	I ain't doing no work. I don't want to do nuffing. I want to annoy Howard. You keep nagging on.
KC:	I keep nagging on?
Steve:	You keep nagging on. I ain't going to do nothing if you nag on at me.
KC:	Why ... What ... When did I nag you?
Steve:	You nag on at me.
KC:	Well you'd asked hadn't you that we could tape for one lesson and then listen to it afterwards. If you keep stopping it we wouldn't have anything to listen to. Isn't that sensible? [Silence]
KC:	What should I have done?
Steve:	I don't know.
KC:	Now if you don't tell me what I should have done, Steve, I shan't learn, shall I?

At this point I was interrupted by another pupil asking for glue and Steve temporarily disappeared from my consciousness.

Approximately fifteen minutes before the end of the lesson I asked 3Y to begin packing up so that we could discuss my performance. I was feeling in part humiliated, in part angry. I perceived myself as having acted patiently and reasonably and was beginning to find descriptions of the pupils as disturbed, inadequate, even wicked, increasingly appealing. It took no less than twenty-three requests that Brian, Steve and Mike should sit down before anything resembling silence had been achieved, and discussion could begin. My response was to go into an attack.

KC:	I said to the teachers that all that was needed for a group of people like you, was that they should be treated sensibly and properly, and that they would then behave sensibly and properly. Now I've been seeing all this lesson behaviour which I know, and which you know, is not appropriate to a classroom. Brian! I'm still waiting for you to listen! Now I don't know where to go from here, because you see, what you have done this lesson — a lot of you have not worked ...
	[I began to notice some indignant expressions, and hastily added]
	... a lot of you have worked ...
Brian:	I've worked!
KC:	Well you see, Brian, you're being silly now aren't you? Because you know perfectly well what I'm talking about, and you're just being silly.
Pupil:	I've worked!
KC:	Yes. You've worked.
Barbara:	Can we go?
KC:	No, Barbara. It's not time yet.
	[Other pupils began to call out to say that they had worked]
KC:	Now I'm of the opinion that this lesson was very bad.
Tim:	Miss. Can you sign this please?
	[His Report Sheet]
KC:	I can sign yours, yes.
Dave:	Miss. Am I getting crosses? Am I getting crosses?
KC:	You were quite good.
Steve:	Miss Cronk. Miss Cronk. Am I getting crosses?
Pupil:	He's apologized.
KC:	An apology isn't ...
Steve:	Oh — I don't get a cross do I?
KC:	We'll see. We'll talk about it in a minute. Now I want you to think about your own behaviour this lesson.

Mike:	If you give us ticks, we'll behave.
KC:	I'm not open to bribery, because I don't think that's really the root of the problem is it?
	[General mumbling broke out]
KC:	I don't think you people give yourself a chance. I'm convinced that the people in this class are capable — as I've seen from a lot of you — of good work. But some of you are not trying to show what they can do. So that when I go back and say that there are people in this class who can do good work, and other people say 'Let me see what they've done', from some people I can show nothing!
Pupil:	I don't like this class.
KC:	Well I don't see any reason why you don't like this class . . .
Pupil:	I want to transfer.
KC:	. . . because, in fact, the people in this class are all, on their own, very nice . . .
Pupil:	Yea.
KC:	. . . like when I talked to you in ones and twos. And there's no reason at all why people in this class can't be as good as anybody else in their work, and can't enjoy school like other people do. You see, what has happened in this lesson, you've made me feel, inside, very cross. And that means I can't do my job properly.
Barbara:	Are we going to mark you on the chart then, Miss?
KC:	Well, I know how I'd mark myself!
Pupil:	Ten out of ten!
KC:	No, I wouldn't. Because for example on Number Five: 'Keep Order'. I think I don't get *any* out of ten!
	[Pupils called out suggestions of what mark I should be given]
KC:	Another thing. If you look at Number Ten: 'Do not nag'. I feel you've made me nag this lesson. I know I've nagged some people.
	[Suggestions were made that I should get five out of ten, or seven out of ten]
KC:	Then you need to ask the question if I have nagged, and if I have shouted, why have I had to?
Pupil:	Because of us.
KC:	Do you think that's right? Do you think that's the case?
Pupil:	Yea.

At this point a loud and physical argument broke out between Steve and Barbara about who should write my marks on the sheet. Mercifully, it seemed to me, the bell went. A sort of discussion had been achieved, but it was a discussion without order, carried out against a background of scuffling and tomfoolery, often with everyone shouting out at once. All I wanted to do was get away.

The final episode of the lesson concerned the signing of report sheets. I kept Steve and Mike to the last.

Steve:	Miss, we don't get a cross do we? Miss? Eh? I don't want a cross, Miss.
KC:	I didn't want somebody being noisy all lesson.
Steve:	I'm sorry. I was just in one of those bad moods, cos of yesterday. (His mother had been brought up to the school) That's why I haven't done no work.
KC:	And what had that got to do with me?
Steve:	Well I've been taking it out on all the teachers. But I'm going to settle down now Miss. I'm just about settling down. I'm going to get a transfer from this class.
Listening pupil:	Creepy!
Steve:	Go away.
KC:	You see I think this is a good class. I mean I honestly think — well I wouldn't come along here when I didn't have to if I didn't think that, would I?
Steve:	So can I have ticks for this lesson?

I began to be tempted to give in for the sake of peace but I felt that if I did, Steve might see me as an object which could be manipulated, rather than a person with rights and responsibilities.

KC:	I can't put ticks for this lesson.
	[I put crosses on his form, and signed it]
KC:	[To Mike] I don't think I can give you ticks for your behaviour either, can I?
Mike:	Come, on Miss.
	[I put crosses on his form too]
Mike:	For Christ's sake!
KC:	Well, it's not me that's done it. You know that perfectly well.

They stormed angrily out of the room.

Evaluation of Lessons Three and Four

My immediate evaluation of these lessons was very negative. This in itself is important evidence. For many teachers it would form the basis of their next lesson with 3Y. My perception was that although I had tried to be reasonable and fair I had been met with systematic opposition. I would have preferred not to have met 3Y again. Alternatively, I would have enjoyed battering them into submission. My belief in them as creative, intelligent and moral persons was deeply threatened. So negative were my feelings that I did not even want to listen to the tapes, and indeed it was three days before I replayed them. When I did so, thus confirming my decision to continue with the lessons, it felt like an act of will. One more abandoned piece of research would have been unremarkable; and I could have excused myself to the school under the pretext of unexpected commitments elsewhere. Teachers do not have this choice and must protect themselves as best they can. Back in the staffroom I joked about the experience. The mortification and sense of insult, identified also in the research of Willis and Woods, was too acute to be revealed publicly.

As I listened to the tapes, however, my evaluation changed in important ways.

1 It was clear that I had dominated attempts at discussion with my talk. Although it was important that I should reveal myself as a person to pupils, part of this process had to be a demonstration that I was prepared to listen. From the pupils' point of view my performance could have been seen as an attempt to dominate them.

2 The fear of disorder which was, in part, the reason for my excessive talking had perhaps made me over-sceptical about the pupils' contributions. Listening to some of Steve's suggestions again, it seemed possible that they represented a real point of view rather than a simple attempt to disrupt my efforts. I had perhaps confused a lack of agreement about the ground rules for discussion, with more serious opposition, at least on some occasions.

3 It seemed possible that my concern for the preservation of order had led to a failure to discriminate between the few pupils who were being disruptive and those who were being disrupted. I had seen the whole lesson and the whole class in terms of the behaviour of a minority. It was possible, therefore, that my generalized criticism at the end of the lesson would have been seen by many as unjust. Moreover, it had taken a reminder from a pupil to bring me back to my declared agenda — the discussion of my own behaviour.

4 In spite of my strong feeling of failure at the end of the lessons, the tapes revealed that I had communicated important pieces of information about myself and my views to 3Y. They knew that I disliked noise and disruption. They knew that I would accept criticism and publicly criticize myself. They had heard me say, even though they might not believe, that I respected them in spite of my disapproval of their behaviour. They also had some evidence about my attitude to punishment. Although I had given Steve and Mike crosses on their report sheet, which might have

felt like punishment or even revenge, they had been disruptive throughout the lesson without new punishment occurring.

As a result of this new evaluation I come to see lessons three and four as a move forward. The theoretical perspective of the experiment had predicted a period of chaos, while those involved considered old information in the light of new. Importantly, lessons three and four had provided a shared experience of conflict and, therefore, a good basis for discussion. In addition, they had highlighted the manner in which the professional demand for an orderly classroom operated in opposition to the research demand for open discussion. I decided, therefore, that in order to open up discussion, I must modify the crippling effects of my need to keep order. Clearly I could not simply decide not to bother any more about how 3Y behaved. This would have been to remove a real constraint upon teachers and to create an artificial situation. More importantly, perhaps, it would have been to present a false image of myself, for the behaviour of the pupils did bother me. Even if I could have acted out such a pretence, which I doubted, I would not be helping 3Y to see me as the person I was. I, therefore, decided to discuss the events of lessons three and four privately with the three most disruptive pupils, Steve, Mike and Brian. By reducing the numbers involved I hoped to reduce opportunities for disruption. By making the discussion private, I hoped to reduce the pressure of being publicly observed. For even if the three boys refused to cooperate, with luck, nobody else would know. In these circumstances I hoped to be sufficiently relaxed to stop talking and start listening. I, therefore, arranged to withdraw Steve, Brian and Mike from Mr Charles' lesson on the following Monday morning.

Conclusions

The aims of this chapter were to describe the experience of teaching 3Y from the teacher's point of view, and to identify the problems in meeting disruptive behaviour with discussion. Clearly my feelings and perceptions cannot be over-generalized. Another teacher might have been more, or less, concerned with order. Another class might have been (or have been perceived as) more, or less, disruptive. Nevertheless, it is possible to identify factors in my experience which would be reproduced in other situations.

My feelings as the lessons progressed and the immediate problems I perceived, have already been sufficiently described. They highlighted, however, a much more fundamental problem and one which lends support to the theoretical argument of this research. This was the need for me to make quick summations and evaluations of incoming data in order to act. The evidence from the tapes indicated that my ongoing interpretations of pupil behaviour may have been wrong, yet I acted upon those interpretations, thus possibly reinforcing the pupils' negative views of me. In reviewing these first four lessons I found that, in spite of my efforts to promote discussion, I was in the end ignorant of a number of crucial facts, and that I had been acting upon unverified assumptions. For example, when I attempted to engage 3Y in discussion, they responded by shouting and reinforcing their points against each other with physical blows. I did not know whether they did this for fun; as a challenge to me; because they lacked the skills of discussion; or from a mixture of all these factors. When I gave information about my intentions I did not know whether they heard me; whether they believed me; whether they suspended belief until they had tested me; whether they believed me but couldn't care less; or whether they believed me and concluded I would be easy to manage. When I criticized their behaviour I did not know whether they thought I was unfair; whether they thought I was right, but had no intention of admitting it; whether they thought I was right but didn't care; or whether they disagreed with the rules I was invoking.

Although I had some indications of possible answers to these questions in certain instances, I clearly had not succeeded in gaining sufficient information upon which to base appropriate action. My attempts to gain clarification were hindered by a desire for 'quiet orderliness' which prevented me from sustaining a conversation when noise broke out elsewhere; by the physical difficulty of sustaining a conversation in a noisy atmosphere and in the face of interruptions for help; by the personal barriers I erected in response to perceived insult and threat; and by a conviction, at the time, that I knew the answer anyway. These factors led me to make hasty decisions about the meaning of pupil behaviour, and in lessons three and four they led to teacher circling and ineffectiveness.

This analysis does not allow a naive conclusion that I should have 'tried harder'. As a matter of fact I tried very hard. Rather the conclusion must be that teachers need to be aware of the limitations of the contents of their consciousness. Their information about, and view of, classroom interaction is almost inevitably partial. This is not due to the fact that they are unaware either of the constraints upon their actions, or of the unfortunate effects of competitive capitalist schooling. It is because in classroom interaction they are one person among many; and because, being a teacher-person, they must often act before it is possible to collect all the relevant information. Importantly, this conclusion should not be allowed to undermine a teacher's ability to act, and act quickly if they perceive the need. But teachers, however experienced, should act in the knowledge that they may be wrong and they should be anxious to explore this possibility.

The evidence from lessons one and two indicates that this is especially important when things appear to be going well. The taped recordings of those lessons indicated that my interpretation of 3Y's behaviour had been at least partially incorrect. I had thought that the lack of disruptive behaviour had been a consequence of the willingness of 3Y to conform to my curriculum objectives, whereas the tapes indicated that it was more probably a consequence of the fact that they were able to follow their own alternative activities. Without this later interpretation it would have been easy to dismiss their changed behaviour in lessons three and four as a consequence of psychological instability. A senior mistress had said:

> The other thing I have never understood (and this happens with poor ability children) is that you can meet them one day and they're OK, and the next morning they're not. You think 'Great. Thank God! I've got the right relationship.' And you meet them the next day and they're completely different.

If the 'right relationship' was merely a mirage produced by a temporary compatibility of two differing sets of objectives, then it becomes easy to see how it could disappear overnight. The evidence from lessons one to four, therefore, warns against an extrapolation from superficial appearances to the more fundamental aspects of inter-personal relationships. It suggests that teachers need to be constantly sensitive to a variety of possible interpretations of conformity, if sudden non-conformity is not to appear senseless.

Note

1   In Woods, P. (1980(b)) p. 79.

6 The Effect of Teacher-Pupil Discussion on General Classroom Behaviour

The major aim of this chapter is to demonstrate the degree to which 3Y were prepared to reduce their disruptive behaviour as a consequence of discussing the problems which it had created for me as their teacher. Equally, it demonstrates the degree to which I was prepared to negotiate a change in my objectives in the face of 3Y's arguments. It is, therefore, an exploration of the morality of our behaviour, that is of the degree to which we were prepared to take each other's problems and interests into account, once they were fully known.

At the end of lesson four our interests had seemed totally incompatible. As researcher I was anxious to demonstrate that 3Y would reduce their disruptive behaviour in the face of my personal stance towards them. As teacher I was equally anxious to reduce their disruptiveness because it threatened my professional persona. I also wanted to persuade them to learn some history. The pupils, on the other hand, were concerned with the joy of living; and disruption, rather than a study of history, seemed to provide the best opportunity for this. The test of our morality was, therefore, severe and could only be demonstrated by our willingness to compromise. Moreover, the nature of any compromise would be pertinent to a demonstration of our morality. If it was too easily achieved with one party too readily denying their previously held position, it might appear to be a consequence of fear rather than an empathetic balancing of rights. If it was won with too much difficulty, it could cast doubt on our empathetic understanding of the other. Equally, however, because the moral problem we faced was a difficult one to which there was no obvious answer, creative persons would be likely to suggest and prefer different solutions, so that the final outcome might need to be a compromise between compromises.

By the end of lesson four I had been able to express some of my views to the pupils, but, as was suggested in Chapter Five, 3Y had, as yet, few grounds for taking what I said seriously. Not only did my actions often belie my words but both were incomplete and, therefore, inexact expressions of my beliefs. I needed to communicate my position more fully. Equally I needed to listen carefully to the pupils' perceptions of the lessons. This chapter describes two discussions with Steve, Brian and Mike between lessons four and five in which I attempted to instigate person-to-person discussion of my problem. This is followed by an analysis of the events of lessons five to ten, inclusive.

The multi-subjective nature of the evidence presented in this chapter also allows a consideration of the coherence of the pupils' rationales. For example, it allows a comparison of the explanations of their disruptive behaviour with other teachers (which they had given me earlier in the year) with the reasons they now gave for disrupting my lessons. Moreover, because they were now asked to plan their future behaviour on the basis of these explanations, the degree to which they had conscious access to their motivation, or to which their rationales were more than justificatory rhetoric, could be explored. Finally this chapter highlights some of the professional problems and consequences of responding to disruptive behaviour with discussion.

In presenting the evidence a loosely chronological and thematic approach have been combined. An impression of the sequence of events was necessary to demonstrate the unfolding effects of discussion, but some categorization was helpful in making the data more manageable. The chapter is, therefore, divided into four sections:

1 The content of two discussions with Steve, Mike and Brian.
2 Problems in carrying out the discussions.
3 The effects of the discussions on classroom behaviour in lessons five to ten, inclusive.
4 Conclusions.

1 The Content of My Discussions with Steve, Mike and Brian

I had two discussions with Steve, Mike and Brian between lessons four and five. The first took place during the last period on the Monday morning, but it left so much unfinished business that I asked Mr Charles if I could meet the boys again during his lesson at the same time on the following day. He agreed. We met in a small room which was sometimes used by the Remedial Department for individual work.

I explained that I wanted them to talk to me about our previous history lesson. Initially, I needed to check whether the boys' evaluation of their behaviour agreed with mine. In their earlier interviews these boys had said that they regarded messing about as a natural and justifiable response to boredom. Steve had further claimed that it did not affect his work output, that it was a technique to make work bearable. As far as I had been concerned their behaviour in lessons three and four had resulted in no work from them, and had interfered with my work and the work of other pupils. If they disagreed with my evaluation I would need to discuss with them the basis of their alternative perception.

In the event there seemed to be no disagreement. Having got their agreement that the discussion could be recorded, I said:

> KC: ... what I wanted to talk about was our History lesson. I want you to talk about me, and us, and what happened in that lesson.
>
> Steve: Oh yea. We were messing about.

They quickly claimed, however, that they were not alone in this type of behaviour, and Steve reiterated the point that messing about did not necessarily mean that no work was done. They accused Barbara of being equally noisy.

> KC: One of the differences between Barbara and yourselves is that Barbara's done a lot of work.
>
> Brian: Yea — but she's got a big mouth.
>
> Steve: Yea — but we could do a lot of work, and we can mess about still. That don't mean nothing.
>
> KC: A lot of the noise was coming from you three on Wednesday.
>
> Mike: [To the others] Yea. We did you know.

At no point in the discussions did the boys deny that they had been disruptive in lessons three and four. Nor did they claim they had done any work. It was therefore possible to move on fairly quickly to a discussion of their reasons for their behaviour. Mike argued a disengagement from the curriculum 'I didn't feel like it. I didn't feel like working.' Steve explained his behaviour as a reaction to the fact that he was already in serious trouble.

> Steve: Well, for one, just that Wednesday, I'd had enough with people, because my mum had to come down to school, and you know, I didn't like that too much. And I hadn't behaved myself in school. So I have to behave myself, and I didn't have to mess about no more. And I do my best, but then, as I realized, I just got angry with all the teachers. I got five crosses that day. (On his Report Sheet)
>
> KC: Did you?
>
> Mike: Yea. I got four.

Brian gave reasons which, he claimed, explained why the behaviour of everyone in the class was poor.

> Brian: Miss, anyway, you know when you had us on Wednesday —
>
> KC: Last two lessons in the morning wasn't it? Yea?
>
> Brian: You had us at a bad time then, Miss. Cos we'd just had a bad

lesson didn't we? [Addressed to the others] And anyway, Miss, everyone wants to go to dinner and break time and that, so they're just trying to get out.

These responses were consistent with the views expressed by the boys in earlier interviews. At that time Mike had indicated a willingness to engage in some school work but had clearly preferred active to literary pursuits. He had also expressed anger at the way he was treated by teachers. If, as Brian claimed, they had just come from a bad lesson (by their definition characterized by excessive writing and/or teacher vindictiveness) this would be consistent with him not feeling like work in my lesson. Steve in the earlier interviews had also complained about the overbearing attitude of some teachers. He had, however, also declared himself to be positively in favour of Education, and expressed a wish to do well. This duality of concern was again apparent '. . . I do my best, but then, as I realized, I just got angry with all the teachers'. Brian, on the other hand, in the earlier interviews, had been unable to find anything good to say about school. He had complained about bad lessons, bad teachers, and an inhuman organizational set up. His present explanation of the behaviour of 3Y was once again consistent. They had misbehaved because they had come from an unpleasant lesson, and because a five lesson morning was too long.

What was interesting about all three explanations was that none of the boys named anything which I had done, as a cause of their behaviour. Thus, although during lesson four Steve had accused me of 'nagging on', he now, while not retracting the accusation, identified his anger about another event as a major source of the trouble. In effect I seemed to have been invisible except as an object upon which to vent their feelings. I needed, therefore, to present myself as a person who had views about my rights and to discover how far they agreed with me.

In order to achieve this I asked them to discuss the *Rules for Pupils* which I had drawn up earlier. They each had a copy, and Steve read them out. I said 'What I want to do is to decide whether these are good rules; and whether any of them ought to go, or whether there are any I have missed out'. The only rule which was directly challenged was the one about shouting:

KC: What about this one — 'Do not shout'? Is that sensible?
Steve: Yea.
Mike: No. No — cos you shout across the room for a rubber or something.

Apart from this objection, all the rules were accepted. Interestingly the one on stealing was hotly supported. As I had expected, free access to equipment had led to some disappearances.

KC: I lost two glues last week . . .

> *Steve:* I bet I know who nicked them!
>
> *KC:* ... about ten colours, and some biros.
>
> *Steve:* You chipped out of your own pocket for that didn't you? [He had established this fact in the first lesson]
>
> *KC:* Yes. But I mean, in one way that's not the point.
>
> *Mike:* Here you are, Miss. You can have this pencil, Miss. I don't need it.
>
> *KC:* Whose pencil is it?
>
> *Mike:* Mine, Miss.
>
> *KC:* Well, won't you need it today?
>
> *Mike:* No, Miss. You can have it, Miss.

Mike's offer, in spite of my doubts about who owned the pencil seemed like an act of empathy. It was not accompanied by an exchange of smiles or glances with the others, nor by an exaggerated air of self-righteousness typical of 'taking the mick'. All three boys seemed genuinely concerned and kept coming back to the problem. They had a keen sense of property rights, which often led to fights between them over the ownership of a biro or pencil. The discrepancy between their attitude in this discussion and Steve's earlier theft of school folders seemed to be based on a distinction between institutional property and private property. In a later part of the discussion, Steve said:

> You're dishing it out of your own pocket. I wouldn't mind if it was out of school stuff, but you're dishing it out of your own pocket.

As the discussion about the *Rules for Pupils* progressed, it became clear that the problem was not that the boys disputed my definition of the sort of classroom behaviour I had a right to expect, but rather that they regarded my rights as incompatible with theirs. In particular they felt that they had the right to enjoy themselves, and that this was something which neither they, nor the other pupils in the class, would give up easily. At one point we were discussing the rules about noise:

> *KC:* 'Do not bang about — books, pencils, rulers or anything else.' Is that possible? I mean, am I right to ask that?
>
> *Mike:* Yea.
>
> *Brian:* Everyone bangs on the desk and that!
>
> *KC:* Well, I mean could we stop it? These are rules for everyone.
>
> *Brian:* Yea. But you never will, Miss. You'll never stop it, cos it happens in every class, doesn't it? [To the others]
>
> *KC:* Well, if people agreed it was a good idea, then everybody could agree not to do it, couldn't they?
>
> *Brian:* Yea. But they wouldn't would they? If you went up to Howard and told him not to bang on the desk no more, he'd do his nut or something: throw chairs at yer.

Brian's assessment of the central problem in teacher-pupil interaction was shared by Steve and Mike. Moreover the clash of interests between pupils and teachers appeared to be so obvious to them, that they were not interested in discussing it. They brushed aside discussion of whether I had a right to expect pupils to obey the rules because that was not at issue. What mattered to them, and what they were prepared to discuss at length, were possible ways of resolving the clash between my rights and theirs.

Steve argued that if I wanted to protect my rights I would have to use punishment. The pupils' rights would be protected by making that punishment scrupulously fair. I argued that this should not be necessary, that we could 'just agree' not to annoy each other. Brian dismissed both these possibilities, suggesting that many of the difficulties could be overcome by tighter classroom management and, finally, Mike suggested that if I wanted improved classroom behaviour I would have to give something in return. This suggestion was taken up by Brian and Steve and became the basis of an uneasy agreement. The arguments for and against these different solutions were strongly expressed and reflected not only the differing perspectives of the participants but also an increasing empathy with my problem and involvement in finding a solution which would work.

It was clear from the start that the boys did not believe that there was any way in which I could make the history lessons more interesting for them. Given the constraints under which I was working, including the constraint of 3Y's behaviour, I, too, felt that I had done as much as I could in the short term. This ideal solution to the difficulty, therefore, was not one which was open to us. Early in the discussion I had said:

KC: What I really wanted to know is what happened in the lesson, and why it was all messing about: and, you know, what can be done by someone like me to make the lessons better for you.

Mike: Nothing.

KC: You reckon nothing?

Mike: No.

It was this constraint, which the boys perceived as immovable, which was behind Steve's recommendation that I would have to punish.

Steve: What you want to do, you want to be strict, Miss. You know you don't want to let us run away with what we want to do.... At first you let them run away with it. Send them out if they mess about. Send them out and send them to Mr Hardy (a senior member of staff). Just like that. And then they won't do it again. If you have backchat, don't give them any more chances, right? To Hardy! No excuse. Just send them straight away. It's a bit stupid to let them off the hook.

This became the constant theme of Steve's contributions. Thus he argued later:

> *Steve*: Now in my point of view, you should have said to him and me and him: 'Mr Hardy'. That's the danger!

Clearly I could not accept Steve's suggestion. The use of such a threat would have interfered with the research results which required evidence of a change of behaviour which was not imposed. As importantly it would also have created enormous operational problems. The type of justice which Steve envisaged was exact and would allow for no mistakes. For example, at one point he said,

> *Steve*: And don't go for the boys; go for the girls.
> *Mike*: Yes. The girls mess about just as much as us, and they get away with it.
> *Steve*: [Almost incoherent in his vehemence] And if Barbara, if Barbara shouts her mouth off, and she gets away with it all the time, and you say to us, 'Right. Hardy!' Now, don't mess about, Miss. Cos if we get tooken up if we mess about and shout, and you say, 'Hardy!' and we say 'No' and Barbara gets away with it, and we get up there ...

He trailed off, overcome by the indignation generated by this imagined piece of sexist discrimination.

I saw his point. I also saw intractable operational problems. Barbara was loud-voiced, but she also accomplished a great deal of work (a point I had made to the boys). The difficulty of weighing the appropriate punishment for a piece of behaviour which might in one case infringe only one rule — noise, and in another case two rules — those relating to noise and work, would have made the immediate and exact justice which Steve was demanding difficult to achieve. It would require an exact agreement on what actions were to be considered as rule-breaking and in what situations. All this seemed to be beyond my competence, and I clearly foresaw accusations of injustice.

I attempted to communicate my theoretical and professional dislike of Steve's suggestions. For example, I said 'But why do I need to send them to somebody else?' Steve had a ready answer:

> *Steve*: Well, if they're messing about it's no good going 'Yea. I'll let you off if you don't do it again'. Everyone does it, so you might as well just stand out and say 'Right. We'll go to Mr Hardy'. And you can send one of us with the person to make sure he goes to Mr Hardy. It's no good giving chances. That's stupid!

At another point I said,

> KC: Isn't there any way I can do it without punishing people? You see I think it ought to be possible.

And later,

> KC: I still don't know what to do on Wednesday. Have I *really* got to come in and punish you if you misbehave?

As I made these pleas I felt that Steve was in danger of writing me off not as 'teacher-object' but as 'stupid-object'! At best I must have appeared to be a slow learner. I felt in great need of support. Brian and Mike had been silent as Steve gave his advice. They appeared to dislike it as much as I did, though for different reasons. I, therefore, attempted to find out what they were thinking.

> KC: Do you agree with Steve?
> Brian: I dunno.
> Mike: [Reluctantly] Yea. I do.

I pushed them harder.

> KC: Well, you can think of yourself last Wednesday. You can think what happened last Wednesday ...
> Mike: No I don't agree! It's a load of bullshit!
> KC: What do you think then, Mike?
> Mike: Nothing. I just hate school.

This sounded more promising, but Steve interposed again with his view that if I wanted pupils to behave in the way I had outlined, I would have to use punishment. Unwilling to lose sight of Mike's contribution, I said:

> KC: Alright then. Supposing, come this Wednesday, you're misbehaving, and I say, 'Steve, Brian, Mike — Mr Hardy!' Now what are you going to think then?
> Steve: I'll think 'That fucking bitch!'
> Mike: I shan't like you no more.

A few minutes later, however, unable to think of an alternative solution, Mike finally agreed with Steve.

> Steve: Well listen here. The best thing what you've got to do luv
> ...
> Mike: [Laughing] Luv!
> Steve: ... is to send them to Mr Hardy.
> Mike: Just get hold of them and drag them up. I would!
> KC: So if you misbehave on Wednesday, that's what I have to do with you is it?
> Mike: [Glumly] Yea.

Mike clearly hated the course of action to which he was now agreeing. His agreement could only derive from an ability to empathize with my difficulties, and to put my rights alongside his own. His stance towards me at this point seemed to be a personal one.

However, although Mike's contribution was theoretically significant and personally rewarding it increased my problem. Now, two out of the three boys were suggesting that punishment was the only solution and this was something to which I could not agree. It was, therefore, fortunate that Brian was present. Like Mike, he hated every aspect of school. Unlike Mike, he was not prepared to agree that punishment was the answer. Like me he saw intractable difficulties. In his view it was bound to be a discriminatory and an unjust method of resolving our clash of interests. He, therefore, suggested that I should improve my classroom management and, thus, prevent disruptive behaviour. For example, discussing ways in which I could avoid losing any more equipment Steve had suggested 'The best thing you want to do, you want to let everyone stay behind until you get the same equipment what you've brung . . .' But Brian objected to the indiscriminatory nature of this punishment.

> *Brian*: I know — but there's people what have done nothing staying in as well!

He suggested that I should keep a tighter control over the equipment in the first place, and then it wouldn't go missing.

> *Brian*: I'll tell you what you should do if they want stuff, Miss. You should go and do it for them. Say like they want to glue something. You should do it for them. You should say 'Bring the work up' and then you do it.

His idea about how I could prevent salacious remarks being inserted onto the tape recorder was similar.

> *KC*: What about 'Not messing about with the tape recorder'. Is that a fair rule?
> *Mike*: Yea.
> *KC*: Is it fair that I ask you not to mess about with it?
> *Brian*: Miss. You should stand by the tape, and everybody who wants to say something, they should come up one by one.

Steve was clearly sceptical about whether Brian's suggestions would work, and I did not like them much either. Although the role of guardian of property was marginally more acceptable to me than the role of judge and executioner, which Steve had suggested, I foresaw that it would waste too much of my time in an unproductive activity; time which would have been better used talking to pupils about their work.

Mike was the first to suggest that if I wanted them to give up messing about in the lessons voluntarily, I would have to give something in return.

KC: But is there no way I can get you to enjoy the work for its own sake, or to do it for me rather than for Mr Hardy?

Mike: Bring us down here every week, Miss.

However, it was Brian, who eventually introduced the compromise to which we all, though with some reservations, could agree.

Brian: Miss, no, I tell you what Miss. You have us for a double lesson don't you?

KC: That's right. Yes.

Brian: You should have one lesson when we can do what we like, and another lesson for work.

Mike: Yea.

KC: What sort of things would you want to do if you were doing what you liked?

Mike: Play cards.

Brian: We'd just play cards and that.

Steve: What you want to do, Miss, is something else as well. Do one lesson, do the first lesson reading, let us all read and work and all that, and we have to bring it to you and all that; and the second lesson we just mess about. Not mess about *mess about*, but . . .

KC: Yes. Just do your own thing.

Mike: Play cards and that.

KC: But one of the things that worries me would be the amount of noise. Because if people in other classrooms . . .

Steve: But if they make a lot of noise, say, 'Out!'

Mike: Yea. Send them out of the class.

This was a solution which involved everyone giving up something and everyone gaining something. The boys would give up their right to take free time in their first lesson and gain the right to do what they wanted in the second. However, they would also agree to give up totally their right to be disruptive. Steve's distinction between messing about ie. engaging in enjoyable activities, and *messing about* ie. being disruptive, was an important one. If the boys were excessively noisy I would be given the right to punish.

I would gain at least one lesson of work from them and a release from the need to impose discipline. If the bargain were kept it would prevent the need for confrontation and the danger of teacher-circling. Time out would not be won from minute to minute through on-the-spot interaction, but would be an explicit concession with defined temporal and behavioural limits. Moreover, with the teacher-time thus gained, there was nothing within the rules of the agreement which precluded me from using it to continue to look for some curriculum activity which might be attractive enough to tempt the boys away from card playing. In return for these gains, however, I was asked to give up, publicly and explicitly, my role as teacher during the second lesson. The sort of smokescreen which teachers set up to make it difficult for a passing onlooker to distinguish between work activities and time-out activities, could not be invoked. Any teacher, looking into the room and seeing the boys, and perhaps even the whole class, playing cards, however quietly, would have no difficulty in deciding that no work was going on. Nevertheless, the bargain would allow me to achieve my prime objective — the prevention of disruptive behaviour, while leaving me space to pursue my teaching role.

Importantly, the bargain was a useful indicator of the coherence of the boys' rationales. It was entirely consistent with the recommendations which they had made in the earlier interviews when they were asked how the school might avoid conflict while still getting the pupils to do work. Brian at that time had suggested free lessons, and Steve had described his favourite teacher as one who made them work but put time aside at the end of the lesson for having a laugh. Moreover, as we were due to have a history lesson the following day, the bargain could be used to test the degree to which the boys could plan and control their future behaviour.

Neither I, nor the boys, expected the bargain to be an easy solution to the problem. We were all agreeing to work uncomfortably close to the constraints upon us. The boys would have to conform in the face of pressure from peers to be disruptive. In allowing card playing in class, I was running the risk of interference from the school authorities and objections from parents. If any of these members of our role set made it impossible for us to comply with the agreement, it would have to be re-negotiated.

Similarly we were all only just within the limits of what we, as persons, could tolerate, so that we experienced an element of self-doubt. Steve put this in words at the end of the second discussion.

> *Steve*: Knowing us, knowing us, Miss, and what we've discussed for the past two days; knowing us, now, we'll mess about in the classroom tomorrow, and get done. And we'll be the only ones what did it most probably!
>
> *KC*: Well, why do it? Why not decide not to?
>
> *Steve*: I know.

But the tone of his voice indicated that he knew that the future was never as easy as that.

2 Problems in Carrying Out the Discussions

There were two major problems in carrying out these discussions. The first related to the way in which they were conducted, and the second to the shortage of time.

The major difficulty lay in the fact that I could not force my agenda on the boys. As part of the experiment the discussions were an example of negotiated interaction, as well as producing a negotiated agreement about the future. Woods experienced similar problems when talking with pupils at Lowfield Comprehensive. He commented 'Many of the discussions ... were "laughs" in their own right.... The discussions ... became part of school life, rather than a pause in it'.[1] Thus I constantly had to ward off the challenge of other topics of conversation introduced by the boys.

Being now a participant-actor rather than an observer, I had some advantages. For example, Woods described having to listen to 'time-absorbing, tedious, and discomforting ...' accounts of the pupils' exploits. However, when Steve and Brian began to 'wander off into peripheral monologues' about how they had been chased by a boxer dog, or how Steve had pushed Brian through a plate glass window, 'He's called "glarss arse" now, Miss', I could bring them back to the subject by saying 'But I still don't know what I ought to do this Wednesday'.

Nevertheless the agenda was constantly threatened. There were consistent and insistent demands to 'listen to the tape'. This was difficult to refuse as I felt it was a reasonable request and it could have been productive. Because time was short, however, I resisted for as long as I could. On other occasions the boys introduced a topic which was too important to reject. For example, Mike produced some cigarettes out of his pocket into which he had inserted bangers. The purpose, he told me, was to 'play a joke' on people who accepted one, 'See, Miss, you light it and it blows up'. This seemed such a dangerous form of entertainment that I continued to discuss it for a while.

The threat to my agenda was therefore real and was increased by the boys' determination to be in control. Sometimes they exerted their power in support of my objectives. For example, on one occasion when Brian was fiddling with the tape recorder Steve said:

Steve: Leave it alone!
Brian: No! I can do what I want!
Steve: Pick that up and I'll pick you up!
Brian: You don't own me do yer?

Later all three boys turned their attention on an unsuspecting pupil who had been sent to get the room keys.

Pupil: Miss Green says can she have the keys back, please?
Mike: [Shouting] No, she can't. Get out.
Steve: [Shouting] Get out!
Brian: Get out.
Steve: Get away from the tape.

> *Mike*: [Shouting] Get away from the tape. It's on!
> [The pupil was not near the tape]
> *Mike*: And don't say nothing.
> *Steve*: Don't say nothing.
> [The pupil left the room after I had given him the keys]
> *Steve*: Right! That told him didn't we, Mike?
> *Mike*: Yea.

Given such forceful control techniques, and given my repudiation of the threat, or use, of formal power, the only way I could ensure that my agenda, rather than an alternative one, was followed was through persuasion. This took two forms — a simple repetition of my request, and reward. Thus I managed to win some more time at the end of the following exchange in the first lesson.

> *Mike*: Can we play the tape back now, Miss?
> *KC*: Can we just finish going through this? (The *Rules for Pupils*)
> *Mike*: Can we play it now, Miss?
> *KC*: Well, can we just ...
> *Mike*: Cos we haven't got long now, Miss.
> *KC*: Let's just discuss this — ever so quick.

One form of reward which Steve and Mike valued was house points. In the second discussion I had said that I viewed our talks as a form of work. Steve asked if he could have a house point if he did it well. Part of his concern was to extricate himself from the trouble he was in school.

> *Steve*: I want to get a good report, and perhaps another house point.
> I tell you what, Miss. How's this? I'll have an excellent
> tomorrow and a house point today, and I'll promise to be
> good.
> *Mike*: Yes. We'll be good.

Although I was not prepared to make such an agreement about the following day's history lesson, I did say they could have a house point if they discussed the problem without messing about. This had some effect. For example, at one point Brian and Steve began a noisy and physical dispute about the ownership of a biro. Mike intervened 'Come on! Stop arguing! Now you've lost your house point!' The dispute ended immediately.

Perhaps the major reason that the discussions achieved so much, however, was that the boys seemed to enjoy them. They were a reward in themselves. Before the first discussion I had been afraid that they would perceive me so negatively after the anger which had been generated on the previous Wednesday, that they would not want to come. In the event they came readily and cheerfully. This was partly due to the fact that it allowed them to get out of other lessons. At the beginning of the second discussion I said:

KC: Right. Well now, the reason I wanted to come again — you'll be getting fed up with me!

Steve: No we're not. We're enjoying it. We don't do no work.

KC: Well, this is work isn't it? Talking about things.

Mike: Yes it is.

Steve: I don't know. We enjoy it. You can come again tomorrow.

Mike: Yea.

Again at the end of the discussion, when it had become impossible to keep them to my agenda, and the demand to replay the tape had become irresistible, I said:

KC: Have you had enough of this really? Have you done as much thinking as you can?

Mike: [Yawning] Yea.

Steve: Yea.

KC: [Laughing] Are you tired? Poor old Mike!

Steve: You see, the reason we like coming with you, Miss, the simple reason is — we do no work.

KC: Well, I think you see that this is . . . .

Steve: [Cutting in] Well this may be work for you, but it's better than writing, all writing!

These comments together with Mike's repeated requests to know when they would be coming down to talk to me again, and his suggestion that I could solve my problem by bringing '. . . us in here every week, Miss', probably explained why, in spite of interruptions and the fact that for much of the time the boys were in control, the discussions were so fruitful.

The Constraint of Time

An important constraint on holding discussions such as those outlined above is the shortage of teacher time. In using two lessons I attempted to stay within the limits of what might be possible. Most teachers in secondary schools have at least two free periods a week, and may well be convinced that their sacrifice would be worthwhile in exchange for improved behaviour from a class such as 3Y. Moreover, it would be unlikely that other teachers would object to pupils such as Brian, Steve and Mike being taken out of their lessons. As Mr Charles said 'They wouldn't do any work, anyway'. Nevertheless it could be argued that the time taken for my discussions with the boys was unrealistic. Free periods do not always materialize, and teachers have other pressing jobs. Moreover, I was fortunate in the fact that I was not timetabled to take 3Y again for a week. Another teacher may have had to meet the class the following day before any discussion could take place and before their anger had cooled. My failure, therefore, to engage in fruitful class discussion in lessons three and four, thus generating a need for out of class time, raises important questions about the viability of the method being proposed. This will be discussed more fully in Chapter Eight. For the moment it has to be recognized that my access to time, and my ability to control timing, did not reflect the position in which many teachers find themselves. That said, however, the identification of an hour of teacher time to talk with a group of disruptive pupils did not seem to be an impossible constraint to overcome. Whether or not such time should be found would depend largely on whether using time in this way would be effective. The next section discusses this.

3   The Effects of the Discussions on Classroom Behaviour

The evidence from these lessons, like that from the discussions, is presented in a way which combines a chronological account with a thematic approach. Because Steve, Mike and Brian had become such central characters, my interaction with them will be considered first. This will be followed by an account of my interaction with the rest of the class.

Steve, Brian and Mike

At the beginning of lesson five the class came into the room and became noisily engaged in finding their work. Steve sat at a desk and called out to Frank.

> Steve: Give us a pencil, ruler and pen.
> KC: [To Steve] Now what would you like a book on? Trains? Cricket? Air Travel? Food and Cooking?
> Steve: Food and cooking, please.
> KC: Food and Cooking. Do you want to do drawing, or do you want to do writing?
> Steve: Writing.

I showed him some books and gave him some paper.

Meanwhile an argument had broken out between Brian and Frank over a pen.

> Brian: [Loudly] I want that!
> Frank: [Shouting] I want a pen.
> Steve: [Calling out] I want a pen. Frank — will you give me a pen, for the last time!
> Frank: There isn't one there.

KC: There isn't one love, cos we're short of them aren't we? (This was a reference to the thefts)

Brian: I want a pen!

Frank: [Shouting] There isn't one!

KC: There are pencils there.

Brian: [Loudly] I want one. (a pen)

Mike: Don't shout!

Steve: You'll have to go to Hardy.

Brian: Well, tell him (Frank) then.
        [He took the pen]

Frank: What am I going to use?

Steve: A pencil.

Frank: Well. . . .

Steve: You've got a pen. You've got a pen of your own!

Brian: Yea.

Frank gave up the unequal struggle and turned his attention to other things.

Frank: [Calling out to Mike] What you doing yours on? What you doing it on Mike? [No response] [Louder still], Mike — what you doing it on? What you doing it on? What topic?

Mike still did not reply.

Meanwhile, apart from giving the information that we were short of pens, I had been engaged with other pupils. Nevertheless, I had been very aware of what the boys were doing because of the amount of noise which was generated. It seemed clear, however, that they were remembering our discussions. The noise seemed to be a by-product of the difficulty caused by the lack of equipment, partly due to the thefts of the previous lesson. Mike was clearly sensitive to the problem of noise, telling the others not to shout and refusing to be drawn into a noisy interchange with Frank. Steve was also clearly remembering his advice to me that if they were noisy I should send them to Mr Hardy.

I did not remind them of our agreement and after getting what they needed they sat down without any prompting and worked almost silently for the first lesson. At the end of that time Brian came up to me and gave me his work.

Brian: There you are, Miss. Are we allowed to play cards, Miss?

KC: Have you finished?

Mike: I have.

KC: Well, you know the rules. You must sit very quietly and not disturb other people.

Brian: Can we play cards then, Miss?

KC: Well, wouldn't you like to do a bit more?

Brian: We've done loads!

> *Mike*: We have done some, Miss. And we'll be quiet.
> *Brian*: At least we've done some, Miss.
> *KC*: You have. You're right.
> *Steve*: Miss?
> *Mike*: [To Steve] You're still doing your work.
> *Steve*: I've just finished.

My words, as well as my tone of voice expressed my dislike of the situation. Brian picked this up unerringly. After I had repeated that part of the bargain which was to my benefit — 'Sit very quietly' and don't 'disturb other people', he pushed me harder — 'Can we play cards then, Miss?' I stalled. 'Well, wouldn't you like to do a bit more?' Brian, no doubt beginning to feel some indignation with the growing suspicion that I was about to welch on the deal overstated his case. They had not done 'loads', but as Mike with more accuracy said, they had produced a page of writing and a picture which was 'something' and they had worked quietly for a whole lesson. I agreed that they could play cards.

This interchange with Brian and Mike illustrates the effect of the discussions of the two previous days on my behaviour. One of the complaints which the pupils of 3Y had made in their interviews with me, was that teachers made promises which they did not keep. Had our bargain been less explicit and less fully worked out I have no doubt that I would have refused the permission to play cards, which would have led to resentment, and perhaps to confrontation and punishment. Had, for example, the boys come in at the beginning of the lesson and suggested a similar bargain, without the discussions, I may well have been non-committal or even mildly encouraging — 'We'll see' — in the hope that the half-promise would encourage them to do more work.

Nevertheless, within the terms of the bargain, I was still at liberty to persuade the boys to abandon their card game. As they were settling down I went across to them.

> *KC*: One of the things, actually, one of the things I'll need doing is a big chart with the title of the display on it. Saying, HISTORY 1870 to 1910. Praps you'd like to do that?

I got no response, and went to attend to someone else. A few minutes later, Steve approached me and said he would do the title sheet. He took a large piece of paper and went to sit by himself at the back of the room, where he meticulously began to sketch out the words. He worked quietly on it for the rest of the lesson. At the end he brought what he had done to show me saying 'I'll do it next week'.

Meanwhile Brian and Mike quietly played cards. In a lesson which was generally characterized by quiet talking, their voices registered on the classroom tape recorder only twice. Once, when they started their game Mike said 'Is this a full pack of cards?' The answer was not loud enough to be distinguishable, in spite of the fact that the passage of a train a quarter of a mile away could clearly be heard. Towards the end of the lesson, Mike forgot himself and started to sing. I said 'Mike, love' and the singing stopped immediately.

This with some variation was typical of the behaviour of the three boys in lessons seven to ten. In lessons seven and eight Steve worked straight through. Brian and Mike worked for one lesson and played cards quietly for the second. They were joined by Val who occasionally raised her voice, but who was affected enough by the prevailing ethos to reduce the volume if I said 'Val. Voice'. Five minutes before the end of lesson eight Steve brought his work up and fell back on his old habit of annoying the girls. I said 'Steve, please don't spoil it at the end'. He moderated his activities though it was clearly an effort.

In lessons nine and ten the same pattern emerged although it appeared that Steve had hoped to finish the chart and join the card playing group which this time consisted of Brian, Mike, Val and Frank. At the end of lesson nine Brian said

Brian: I'm playing cards now.
Steve: Not yet.
Brian: I can.
Steve: I've not finished. Can I have a pen please, Miss?

He continued to work at the chart through the lesson.

These results had both theoretical and professional implications. There seemed little doubt that the discussions and explicit agreement reached between the boys and myself affected their behaviour and mine. There were, of course, other factors at work. For all four of us the agreement was set within a constellation of other concrete realities and social meanings. I was concerned not only to open up potentially educational channels with the boys, but also with my professional image. Steve was affected by a wish to do well and a desire to clear up the trouble he was in in school. Brian and Mike were affected by their dislike of the curriculum. Nevertheless, given these different existential starting posts, we all behaved in ways which were different from our behaviour in lessons three and four. In each case the change was consistent with what had been agreed. I still did not like letting the boys play cards, but I allowed it. Brian and Mike still did not like doing any work, but they did it. And Steve, while perhaps still believing that I might take his advice and send him to Mr Hardy, moved far beyond the letter of our agreement in his efforts to conform.

The most important consequence of the new behaviour deriving from our discussion was its effect on the rest of 3Y. At the most obvious level the boys were no longer interfering with other members of the class and, thus, were no longer the cause of part serious, and part mock, quarrels. They even took it upon themselves to monitor each other's behaviour and sometimes rebuked other pupils. This had the effect of creating space for me to engage other pupils in discussion. The space was not merely temporal, a result of the fact that with the reduction of disruptive incidents I did not need to spend time attempting to keep order. It was also psychological. As it became clear that the three boys intended to abide by our agreement, from whatever motives, I was able to stop worrying about the problem of order and talk more constructively with other pupils.

The Behaviour of the Rest of the Class

The vast majority of the interaction between myself and the rest of 3Y involved curriculum issues and will, therefore, be discussed in Chapter Seven. However, there was some interesting evidence relating to general classroom behaviour which is worth recording.

The type of interaction in which I engaged reflected the phase of the lesson. Hargreaves *et al.*, in *Deviance in Classrooms*, identify five such phases: the 'entry' phase; the 'settling down' or 'preparation' phase; the 'lesson-proper' phase; the 'clearing-up' phase; and the 'exit' phase.[2]

My lessons with 3Y were less complex than this, with the 'entry' and the 'exit' phase being largely outside my control. Pupils occasionally arrived at the classroom before me, and even when I was there came in without being given formal permission. Similarly, once the final bell had gone they were allowed to leave as soon as they had returned their work and equipment. The pattern was similar to that described by Hargreaves for older children:

> With older children teachers generally do not impose any further rules for the exit phase, except that pupils are not expected to push or run during exit. Typically in these cases the teacher will say, if the bell has gone 'You can go when you're ready' or, if the bell has not yet rung, 'You can go when the bell goes'.[3]

This left only three phases in the lessons with 3Y in which I was actively involved. These were the settling-down phase, the work phase and the clearing-up phase. There was also, of course, 'time out', which was negotiable. The evidence from the lessons will be presented phase by phase rather than lesson by lesson.

The settling-down phase　The settling-down phase was inevitably noisier than the other phases, with pupils legitimately moving about and asking me for help to find a book. It also contained more opportunities for disruptive noise as the pupils competed for scarce equipment. There were sometimes unfinished conversations to be completed, too, before the work phase began. In the main, however, any noise was generated by curriculum concerns.

The following extract from lesson five illustrates the type of interaction which took place in the settling-down phase. It also demonstrates (a) how two pupils were prepared to refrain from disruptive behaviour in spite of my inefficiency; (b) the manner in which I communicated with these pupils on the problem of behaviour; and (c) an apparent consensus on this issue. The extract spans thirteen minutes soon after the beginning of lesson five. It centres round two boys Robert and Jim, who could not find the book from which they had been working the previous week. They were standing by the table on which the books had been spread and next to the classroom tape recorder. Other pupils were round the table, too, looking for books.

Robert:	[Singing quietly on to the tape] We're a couple of yo-hobs.
Dave:	[Into the tape quietly] Robert wanked himself last night, and he enjoyed it!
Frank:	[Calling across] Miss, can I have a ruler?
Robert:	Mind, Miss. [About to throw a ruler to Frank] Airmail!
KC:	Don't throw it, please. [He didn't]
Robert:	[Still looking for his book] No. It's not here.
KC:	Now, Jim love. What were you doing last time?
Robert:	Oh. It's gone. Miss, that book's gone.
KC:	Which one?
Robert:	That one on, er . . .
KC:	The Cowboy book?
Robert:	No. . . . Er . . .
KC:	What subject were you doing?
Robert:	[To Jim] Oh — what's that book called?
Jim:	I can't remember.
	[Dave started messing about with the tape]
KC:	Don't rub it off.
Robert:	Medicine! That's it! It's not here.
Howard:	Miss, will you help me with my picture?
KC:	Yes, as soon as I've got these people settled. That's the best thing.
Robert:	Have you got one on health? Have you got one on health, Miss? [To Jim] Shall we do one on health?

I began to look for a book on health at the same time giving quick advice to other pupils. Robert and Jim started to talk about death.

Jim:	How are you doing to get out of the grave then when you're dead?
Robert:	Well, if you're like me you're psychic. And all the earth on top of you, you can get out of it.
KC:	[Coming back to them after a detour to another pupil] Jim, love, now what is it you were doing?

159

Jim:	Medicine.
Robert:	All these Jewish people they have money at the bottom of the grave.
Janet:	Miss. Have you got some colours?
KC:	You know where they are.
Janet:	Pardon?
KC:	You know — they're in the bag. [To Jim and Robert] It looks as if someone has taken them (the books) already.
Robert:	No. No-one else has got it.
KC:	Well, I certainly brought it, love.

They went round the class quietly looking for the book, but came back without it.

KC:	That's a nuisance isn't it?
Robert:	[Continuing to look through the books] There's a bit on health here.
KC:	Yes. [I moved away to look for the book in my bag]
Jim:	We could buy a tent and go canoeing.
Robert:	[Into the tape] There was this boy once, and he had a problem. His name was Howard. He'd escaped from the nuthouse. We're sure cos we traced him back, you see. I've got to go, now, cos he's coming!
KC:	I've got something to say about that (the tape). Let me see what you did last week. [They showed me their work]
KC:	Well, I can only think that I made a mistake, cos I had all the books out last night. [I went to another pupil]
Robert:	[Softly into the tape] La-la-la. . . . La-la-la. [Heavy breathing into the tape] Look out, Jim. He's giving it a wank! [I came back]
KC:	Er . . . What was the other thing you said? Wasn't it cowboys?
Robert:	[Looking at a book] What about the development of explosives? That's good.
KC:	The Chinese were the first to use them weren't they?
Robert:	Yea. But that was only gunpowder. Then they made dynamite and TNT.
Jim:	Where d'you get the books from, Miss?
KC:	From the Polytechnic Library.
Jim:	Shall we go over there and have a look?
KC:	I got all the ones out that were useful. [Laughing] I absolutely raided the shelves. I can't understand why I've not got it here.

Jim: You probably left it over there.

KC: Well. Can you do something else this week? I can only apologize, love, for this. Cos I really, I really did sort it out for you and I thought I'd brought it along. It's my fault that I didn't bring it. We did have it last week here, and I can only think that I thought you weren't using it. Could you do this today, and then I'll make absolutely certain that the health book comes next week.

Jim: Shall I bunk this then? (the work he had started the previous week)

KC: Oh no. Don't throw it away, cos we can finish it next week. What about doing something on housing cos that's to do with health isn't it?

I went away for a few seconds to help someone else in difficulty.

Robert: [Into the tape recorder] Howard loves Liz. He shagged her last night.
            [Silence]

Robert: This is wasting tape, you know, on us, Shall we turn it off? [He contemplated the tape recorder]

Robert: You can hypnotize yourself watching that. [Pause for a few seconds] Look at both of them (the spools) at the same time, right, and you'll see three. Right? [Pause] Both of them at the same time ... [Pause] Did you see it? Went into three, didn't it?

KC: [Coming back] One of the things that we've been talking about, and decided, is that we won't have people playing with the tape recorder. See if we can stop that, because we've had people playing with it rather a lot.

Robert: I'm only looking at it.

KC: Yes. OK.

I suggested that they might like to do some work on better housing conditions. Jim changed the subject.

Jim: When did cowboys die out then, Miss?

KC: Well in those days they were just managing to defeat the Indians. You know, the Battle of Little Big Horn, that was in 1869 I think, just a year before this. And after that.... [Dave came up and pressed the counter-meter on the tape recorder]

Robert: Now you've mucked it up!

Dave: No. It's alright. It still works.

Robert: Yea. I know. But now you don't know how far the tape's gone, do yer?

Dave: Yes you do. That's nothing.

> KC: I was just saying to them that we'd agreed we're not going to play with the tape any more.
>
> *Dave*: No. I know. Just leave it on....
>
> KC: ... just leave it on. And then we'll see and be able to play it back.
>
> *Dave*: Yea. Right. Have you got anything else on aeroplanes Miss?
>
> KC: There might be something in *The Machine Makers*.
>
> *Dave*: Oh. Can I do two? Aeroplanes and trains. Railways.
>
> KC: Yes. That would be good.
>
> [Dave, Robert and Jim went to their seats furnished with books]

This rather lengthy extract from the settling-down phase of lesson five is interesting in a number of ways. Firstly, it illustrates the way in which teacher inefficiency wastes pupil time. Because of my oversight Robert and Jim had lost a third of a lesson. Given the weight which pupils had put on teacher inefficiency as a cause of pupil boredom and, therefore, of misbehaviour, I was fortunate that Robert and Jim did not fill this time with disruptive activities.

Secondly, the episode gives some insight into the attitude of these boys to the curriculum. This will be discussed in more detail in Chapter Eight, but the interchange quoted above demonstrates that Robert and Jim were prepared to be involved. They had looked for their book once and were prepared to go round the class looking for it again without causing any disturbance. They were prepared to suggest and discuss alternative topics, and finally to do some work on housing which was related to their original choice. At the same time Jim's willingness to throw away the writing he had done the previous week illustrated the low value which he put on written work. Most importantly, perhaps, their conversation illustrates their activity of mind. While they were waiting they turned their attention to other interests. These included recording comments about other pupils, but also included subjects such as rising from the dead, canoeing and the effect on vision of watching revolving spools. Thus, in a lesson when these boys had both an excuse for, and an opportunity to engage in, oppositional behaviour, their main concern seemed to be not to waste precious living time.

Thirdly, the extract gives some indication of the way in which I mediated to other pupils the contents of the discussions of the previous two days. Because the behaviour about which I needed to communicate, ie. playing with the tape recorder, was not disruptive, it took second place to discussion about the curriculum, illustrating in action my hierarchy of objectives. For example, when Robert had been talking into the tape I said 'I've got something to say about that'. But I postponed saying it until after further curriculum discussion. When I did talk to the boys about their behaviour with the tape recorder, it was in the form of a communique: that is, I neither issued a command nor invited a discussion. Thus,

KC: One of the things we've been talking about, and decided, is that we won't have people playing with the tape recorder ...

I was not specific about who 'we' were, though I meant to convey that pupils were involved and thus to imply that they could comment on the decision if they disagreed with it. Nevertheless, my words could have been mistaken for a command, and perhaps gave grounds for Brian's warning the previous day that whatever the four of us agreed in discussion, other pupils would object if I 'told' them what to do.

In this specific instance neither Jim, Robert nor Dave appeared to object. Robert in response to my comment justified himself within the framework of the rule 'I'm only looking at it' — by implication expressing acceptance of the rule. This acceptance was also implied in his criticism of Dave for pressing the counter-meter. Dave also seemed to accept the rule. He claimed to know about the agreement, approving it in a matter of fact way, before moving on to more interesting things — 'Yea. Right. Have you got anything on aeroplanes, Miss?' Because like Steve, Mike and Brian the boys seemed to think that the rule was reasonable, no further discussion was necessary.

Finally, the extended extract from lesson five gives an indication of the type of activity which characterized the settling, down phase of the lessons. Two thirds of the way through the reported interaction the majority of the class were sitting down and working quietly. There was thus no marked break between the settling-down phase and the work phase. As pupils were engaged in individual or small group work they made the switch from one phase to the next automatically once they had furnished themselves with what they needed. In none of the three double lessons being considered did I need to remind them to get down to work through the use of a switch signal.[4] It was taken for granted, and individually accomplished. There were, therefore, before the end of the reported interaction periods of silence, broken only by my voice or the voice of Robert and Jim. Thus at the end of this episode I was able to move straight across to Howard who was still waiting for help, and sit down to work with him on his picture, without further reference to the class.

The settling-down phase of lessons seven and eight, and nine and ten followed the same pattern with silence quickly falling. This was especially significant in lesson seven which began in a frenzy of excitement. Mr Charles had asked to come in at the start of the lesson to return their English exam papers on which their marks were written. This was accompanied by loud shouts of:

'Sir! Sir!'
'What d'yer get?'

> 'Thirty-six I got.'
> 'Oi. What d'yer get?'
> 'I got eighty-two.'
> 'Who got less than fifty-seven?'

and so on. There were also loud outbursts of song. After five minutes Mr Charles asked for the papers back. After eight minutes he left.

This episode was interesting, reflecting at least superficially the behaviour of pupils belonging to street gangs in San Francisco who were observed by Carl Werthman. He wrote,

> As soon as the grade is handed down, gang members behave like good social scientists. They draw a sample, ask it questions, and compare the results with those predicted under alternative hypotheses. The unit of analysis is a *set* of relevant grades. The one received by a particular student is only a single member. No interpretation of a grade can be made before others are looked at.[5]

3Y could certainly have been engaged in a similar enterprise. Alternative interpretations, for example, that the pupils were merely competitive and (taking the teacher's grade at face value) wanted to know where they stood, are weakened by the interview comments of Steve, Mike, Barbara and Janet on the injustice of the Maths grouping.

Given then that the interaction with Mr Charles not only created excessive noise and excitement, but was also arguably an important exercise in the evaluation of school justice, it was significant that four minutes after Mr Charles' departure the class had settled down to work in near silence. During that time I had given one reminder about noise:

> *KC:* . . . Can we remember that we're using small voices to talk to each other.

but there was no immediate response. Indeed my words were almost inaudible due to Janet's simultaneous shout of:

> *Janet:* Miss. I lost this. [Holding up a piece of her work] Now I've found it in the book!

The silence, therefore, seemed to be self-imposed rather than a consequence of my request.

The work phase The work phase of lessons five to ten were characterized by long periods of silence, or near silence. They were also notable for an almost total absence of comments spoken into the tape recorder. This did not appear to be due to a waning interest, but to an acceptance that it was not an appropriate activity when 'work' was being done. For example, Mike, while refraining totally from talking into the tape recorder during the lessons, could not refrain from switching it on again after the end of lesson eight to record 'Howard is a queer'. Moreover, in lessons eleven and twelve which will be discussed separately, the tape recorder once again came into its own.

Part of the reduction in noise may have been due to the break-up of the large working groups which characterized lessons one to four. This occurred through pupil choice. The subject was never mentioned again, but a group of four girls was the largest which occurred.

Nevertheless, although the work phase of the lessons was characterized by long periods of quiet or even silence, it would be inaccurate to give the impression that there were no interruptions. On only two occasions, however, did noise reach a level where I felt it necessary to make a general comment. In lesson six there was an outburst which led me to say 'Now — we're not having any silliness in this lesson. You've probably noticed that'. And in lesson ten I commented 'Could I just remind people, some of whom have forgotten, that we're using small voices'.

Most of the other interruptions were from individual pupils and were work related. They seemed to stem from a long habit of shouting out for things which they needed. Thus:

Barbara: [Shouting] Who's got the glue?
KC: Ask quietly dear.

Increasingly pupils began to move quietly to find what they needed. There seemed to be no basic disagreement with, or opposition to, my request. The difficulty lay in remembering. For example, in the midst of one period of silence the recorder picked up someone whistling under their breath, but it appeared to be the whistle of a person physically expressing concentration, and died away in a few seconds without intervention. On another occasion a pupil noised 'Wer-um, Wer-er, Wer-um, Wer-er'. Once again the noise appeared to be more a release for pent-up energy than any form of opposition, and it, too, quickly petered out.

On two further occasions the interruption took the form of a pupil asking me non-work-related questions. In one period of silence Robert suddenly asked:

Robert: What school did you go to Miss?
KC: Pardon?
Robert: What school did you go to?

I told him and silence was re-established. On another occasion Steve asked, across the room,

Steve: Miss, do you live at the Poly?
KC: No dear.

The conversation closed.

Once again neither of these questions appeared to be either 'alien' or 'oppositional'. They appeared to be the products of persons who, while engaged on fairly mechanical tasks, were pondering on my human existence. They were not the questions which one would address to a 'teacher object', unless it was to annoy or offend, and there seemed to be no element of this intention in the way they were delivered. They were straight questions such as one might ask of a 'teacher-person', demanding straight answers such as one might give to a 'pupil-person'; and such answers having been given no behavioural problems were created.

Inevitably noises were recorded of chairs moving on the composite floor of the classroom, but this was not excessive. On one occasion, after ten minutes of almost complete silence, when all that could be heard on the classroom tape was the faint droning of my voice as I talked to a pupil, one short comment from Barbara, and a pencil falling on the floor, Howard suddenly stood up and dragged his chair noisily across to another desk. It was Steve and Tony who reprimanded him.

Steve: Howard! Go back to the Infants!
Tony: Howard! Go back to your nutty school!

This episode seemed to indicate that the pupils actually valued the quieter atmosphere and wanted it to be preserved. This would account for the lack of any necessity for discussion on this subject during these lessons. No-one challenged or seemed to want to challenge my reminders that we should try to be quiet. Even Howard, in lesson six, came up to me and said with approval

Howard: We've been quiet today, haven't we Miss?
KC: Very good, love, yes.

The clearing-up phase Just as the work phase emerged naturally out of the settling-down phase, so there was no specific break when pupils began to pack up. Different pupils stopped work at different times, and this was a matter for individual decision and negotiation. Thus Brian and Mike had negotiated the right to pack up halfway through each double lesson. In lesson eight Val negotiated the same agreement and, in lesson ten, Frank did the same. The other pupils worked through the bell and variously began to pack up towards the end of the second lesson. They gave as their reasons that they had had enough or had just finished off a piece of work. On such occasions I accepted their decisions saying only that they must not make a noise. Thus for example, ten minutes before the end of one lesson Barbara asked for some glue.

KC: We haven't got any.
Barbara: Why?
KC: There isn't any left. We'll have to stick it next week.

Janet was listening and started to pack up.

Janet: Miss, I've put the pictures on there, and everything.

KC:	Aren't you going to do any more?
Liz:	No. Cos we ain't got no glue.
Janet:	[Showing me the work] Does that look alright, Miss?

In lesson ten there was a lengthier negotiation with these three girls, who asked to go out of the classroom. This was a challenge to normal practice and, as no prior agreement had been reached, needed to be discussed. It occurred about twenty five minutes before the final bell.

Janet:	Miss. Can I sit out on the radiator for a minute?
KC:	Why do you want to go out there?
Janet:	[Laughing] Cos I want to.
KC:	Is there someone you want to see?
Janet:	No. I've seen everyone I want to see.
KC:	I don't think you're supposed to.
Janet:	Oh, Miss ... [Pleadingly]

But she went back to her seat. Five minutes later she returned with Barbara and Liz.

Barbara:	Miss. Can we sit out there? (on the grass)
KC:	Er ...
Liz:	They're playing cards.
	[Pointing to Brian and Co]
KC:	Er ...
Liz:	Oh please.
Janet:	We'll sit down, and we won't muck about.
KC:	Well, I'm afraid I'll get into trouble if you go out.
Janet:	Well, can we go on an errand for you Miss?
Dave:	[Listening] They just want to get out of work.
Janet:	Well, we've done more than you!

This argument was so true that I felt I could not, in justice, totally deny their request. I suggested that they could go for a short walk in the corridors but asked them not to make a noise. Then I crossed my fingers. There were no repercussions in the classroom. No-one made any further comment, perhaps, like me, recognizing the justice of Janet's argument, for the girls had produced a large quantity of good quality work for the display. Silence fell. Two minutes later the girls came back quietly and went back to their desks.

This was a curious and revealing piece of negotiation. Clearly the girls' objective was to go out of the classroom. I was not sure why they wanted to go out, although it seemed as if going out was the end in itself, not the means to a further end. This could be deduced from the fact that it did not matter to them where they went. The radiator on which Janet originally said she wanted to sit was in the corridor just outside the classroom door[6] and in full view. She could, conceivably, have sneaked off somewhere, or have arranged to meet someone out there. However, the second request to sit on the grass made this unlikely. The grass was directly outside the second classroom door and even more publicly open to view, as all the classroom windows looked out onto it. Moreover it was totally cut off from the corridor where other pupils might have been lurking, and in addition was a totally unsuitable place for a smoke. The most plausible explanation of why the girls want to go out was Janet's own 'Cos I want to'.

I did not find either the request or the reason given objectionable. The girls had worked hard and a break with a change of scene for a few minutes arguably improves concentration.[7] My hesitation had been due to a fear that the girls would be disruptive when they left the class, or that other members of staff would disapprove of the fact that I had let them go. This resulted in some interesting responses from the girls. While prepared to argue the justice of their case they, also, seemed to see my problem.

When I first said 'I don't think you're supposed to', Janet, while still not happy, appeared to think there was some justification in what I said and dropped her request. When I seemed uneasy about the new request to sit on the grass, something which classes sometimes did on fine summer days, Janet, attempting to read my thoughts, said 'We won't muck about'. When I then said 'Well, I'm afraid I'll get into trouble' Janet appeared to see the whole of my problem. Her suggestion that I could send them on an errand, which would be official, would not only get them out of the classroom, but save my face.

It was my perception of their empathy with my position which won my agreement that they should go for a walk. Given Barbara's comments in the earlier interview, when she explicitly recognized the constraints upon teachers 'They have their orders, don't they?' it was not surprising that these girls quickly perceived the nature of my problem. What is equally theoretically important was their willingness to take my difficulties into account.

The packing-up phase of the lesson was therefore characterized by an increase in movement and increase in conversation as more people finished. This resulted in the last ten minutes of the lessons being marked by an increase in noise, but it was not the noise of loud voices and boisterous activities which threaten order. During this period my role changed from one of discussing work, to receiving it. Most of the pupils brought their work to show me before putting it on the pile ready for me to take away. They seemed to want approval.

There were two other issues which were important in the packing-up stage. One was the state of the room. The pupils were grossly untidy, dropping screwed up bits of paper onto the floor if they made a mistake on them. I did not make a class issue out of this, preferring to spend the time I had for discussion on the twin priorities of noise and the curriculum. The success achieved in getting the class to moderate noise, however, was an indication that at a later date they could be persuaded to tackle the problem of the state of the room. The litter appeared to be the result of thoughtlessness about the work that was being created for others. Thus five minutes before the end of lesson six I went round the room picking up bits of paper. As I did this I met Robert sweeping bits of paper off the desks onto the floor.

> KC: [Laughing] Oh, Robert love! I'm going round picking it up, and you're going round shoving it on the floor again!

He joined me in my task. There seemed, therefore, nothing which an explicit identification of the problem would not overcome.

The other issue was that of recovering all my equipment. At the end of lesson four Howard had appointed himself as monitor by collecting pencils, biros and rulers from other people and bringing them to me. I had said 'Thanks, Howard. That's kind'. On that occasion, however, as already noted, a considerable amount of equipment had gone astray. News of this seemed to have percolated round the class, and in the rest of the lessons Howard applied himself to checking the equipment more rigorously. He asked me how many of each article I had brought, and on being told that there was a list in the bag, he got it out and went round the class ensuring that everything was collected. He bemoaned, as if they were his own, the speed at which the glue sticks were used, checking the waste paper bin for 'empties' to ensure that none had been 'nicked'. In this way, and without any further effort on my part, I lost no more equipment.

4 Conclusions

The clearest conclusion which can be drawn from the evidence presented in this chapter was that the discussions with Steve, Mike and Brian were followed by a reduction rather than a continuation, or escalation, of disruptive behaviour. This claim is substantiated by objective and multi-subjective data. Not only did the tape record long periods of silence and quiet movement and talk; not only did I cease to fear that 3Y would be noisy; but the pupils themselves commented on the phenomenon. Moreover, this was achieved within the normal constraints operating upon teachers, and without the interests of any party being discounted. The formalization of 'time out' which carried its own agreed rules meant that it no longer had to be won by pupils in minute to minute interaction. It promoted rather than reduced my educational role by allowing me to avoid dominance techniques and teacher circling.

The evidence also supports the theoretical claim that the behaviour of at least the three most disruptive pupils (Brian, Mike and Steve) was intelligent, that is based on an evaluation of data. Their discussion of the problem of order indicated a sophisticated understanding of the factors involved in its maintenance. They demonstrated that they were capable of weighing my interests against their own, of evaluating the differential effects of reward and punishment, and of interpreting institutional reality. Their differing views showed an independence of thought arising from their own experience and objectives. However, they were also prepared to work out ways in which these differences could be satisfactorily resolved. Moreover, having reached a possible solution they were prepared to try it out in practice. In addition, the evidence demonstrates that what the pupils said and did with me as their teacher, was consistent with what they had said to me in my interviewing role. Thus, not only did their behaviour appear to stem from intelligent evaluations of their situation, but they appeared to have conscious access to these evaluations, which allowed them to make bargains about their future behaviour. Perhaps classroom interaction was of such great importance, that Dennett's backroom boys of the unconscious[8] felt the need to keep the conscious mind well informed.

The theoretical hypothesis, that the pupils' improved behaviour derived from a moral stance towards me as a person, is less easy to demonstrate. The reduction in conflict can be explained in at least three ways. In the first place there was some indication that the pupils did empathize with me as a person, and were prepared to moderate their behaviour on this account. Steve's willingness to allow me to punish him if he misbehaved, Mike's grudging support for this view, and Janet, Barbara and Liz's understanding of my difficulty in allowing them to leave the room were examples of this. However, the pupils' conformity can only be described as empathy if it can be shown that it was not motivated by other considerations. The evidence cannot demonstrate this. For example a second possible explanation would be that, in spite of my protestations that I would not use punishment, it was ultimately this fear which moderated the pupils' behaviour. Thirdly, it is possible to argue from the evidence that the pupils conformed not out of consideration for me, but because it suited their own purposes. This last possibility is interesting, for it would rest on the assumption that the pupils valued for themselves the sort of behaviour which I was advocating. There did seem to be some indication of this, and if this interpretation is correct it would weaken any simplistic theory of culture clash.

This ambiguity over the pupils' motivation will be investigated further in Chapter Seven. However, it is worth raising two related points here. In order to demonstrate that the pupils' behaviour was altruistic, as well as intelligent, it is not necessary to demonstrate that they abandoned considerations of self interest. As outlined in Chapter Two morality is regarded as the working of the twin principles of individual creativity and interpersonal unity. The moral person does not abandon one of these principles in favour of the other, but tries to work out a solution whereby both can be expressed within existing constraints.

Finally, it is worth noting the importance of my belief in the morality of pupils. Without this belief it would have been difficult to engage in the discussions with Steve, Brian and Mike; difficult to accept their challenges, and their determination to have equal control over the situation; and difficult to accept the bargain. Equally, without a belief in their intelligence it would have been difficult to listen seriously to their views, and difficult to accept that I should take them into account, or provide convincing reasons why they were wrong. Finally it would have been difficult to accept that the card playing compromise need only be temporary, and that together we might find something of interest with more educational value and that, even if this did not happen, making and sticking to a bargain was an appropriate way for moral and intelligent persons to proceed when their interests were diametrically opposed.

Notes

1   Woods, P. (1979) p. 266.
2   Hargreaves, D. *et al.* (1975) p. 67.
3   Hargreaves, D. *et al.* (1975) p. 87.
4   For a discussion of 'switch signals' see Hargreaves, D. *et al.* (1975). Briefly he describes them as '. . . an action taken by the teacher, typically in the form of a verbal statement, which puts an end to one task (or phase) and initiates a subsequent task' (p. 65).
5   In Cosin, B.R. *et al.* (Eds) (1971) p. 42.
6   See plan of classroom location and layout at the end of Chapter 4.
7   Regular breaks are, for example, recommended by Buzan, A. (1974) p. 122.
8   See discussion in Chapter 2, Section 5 of this book.

7   The Relationship Between Classroom Behaviour and the Curriculum

In Chapter Two it was demonstrated that if persons are intrinsically moral then long-term conflict must, logically, be a consequence of misunderstanding. One form which this misunderstanding could take was that those involved failed to recognize each other as persons towards whom a moral stance was appropriate. The evidence presented in Chapters Five and Six suggested that, in my first four lessons with 3Y the pupils did see me as some sort of amoral or immoral object, who existed alongside them in the classroom, but whose rights could, therefore, be ignored. As a result of my discussions with Steve, Brian and Mike, however, the perception of these key disruptive pupils seemed to change. They, arguably, began to see me as a person with whose problems they could empathize and towards whom an altruistic stance should be taken. Thus, a bargain was struck and disruptive behaviour was eliminated in lessons five to ten.

However, it was also argued in Chapter Two that a second form of misunderstanding could arise out of the ignorance of one, or both, parties about the mitigating circumstances within which an offending act was committed. This type of misunderstanding, it was suggested, could lead to a confirmation of the opinion that the other was immoral, or even to a re-definition of someone whom one had previously trusted. Indeed, it was also emphasized in Chapter Two that, even when the constraints on the situation were fully understood by all involved, there might still be no easy solution to the moral dilemma of how to achieve an equitable balance between the rights of the self and those of others. It was just such a dilemma which Steve, Brian, Mike and I had tried to solve. On the face of it, therefore, the evidence presented in Chapters Five and Six substantiates the theory that we were all intrinsically moral persons searching, in the light of our combined knowledge of the constraints upon us, for an answer to our problems.

Nevertheless, as was noted at the end of Chapter Six, it is possible to explain our behaviour in a different way. Thus, those who were still unconvinced of the intrinsic morality of our motivation might argue, for example, that Steve was 'caused' rather than 'chose' to conform to my wishes because of some psychological, but irrational, need for approval; or that Brian was 'caused' to work for one lesson and play cards for the next because of some combination of fear of authority, low intelligence, childhood trauma and poor home background, which prevented him from 'acting otherwise'. Indeed, even my own behaviour could be explained as a consequence of psychological 'set' — an inflexibility of mind which made it impossible for me to accept the behaviour of 3Y for what (as any good determinist would tell me) it was, that is the outcome of factors beyond their control. My beliefs could be traced, perhaps, to an over-socialization into Christian thinking at a young and vulnerable age, and my anxieties to the determining effects of environmental factors which made it difficult to act upon those beliefs. The happy outcome of lessons five to ten could, therefore, be dismissed as a 'one-off' consequence of the interaction of a specific set of causal factors which would not necessarily be present in other situations. Thus another teacher, with another class would not, according to this view, be able to rely upon the same result.

As has already been suggested, such alternative explanations can never be finally defeated for both 'determinism', and 'freedom' are metaphysical concepts which, like that of 'intrinsic morality', can only be supported by circumstantial evidence. Fortunately, it is possible to produce additional relevant evidence by looking more closely at the way in which 3Y and I dealt with the constraints upon us. Thus, if we merely 'reacted' to our environment, it might be possible to argue that our behaviour was determined, that there was a clear 'causal' link between factors in our environment and what we did. If, on the other hand, we appeared to act upon a reasoned evaluation of the moral dilemma which was created by significant constraints, so that out behaviour appeared to be an attempt to remove, or circumvent, such constraints in order to maximize the well-being of all concerned, then it could be argued that we were acting freely and altruistically. As was pointed out in Chapter Two, constraints are open to such manipulation. Causes are not. This chapter will therefore present evidence about the way in which 3Y and I reacted to the constraints which were present in the situation in order to further substantiate the case that our behaviour was motivated by intrinsic morality. In particular it will focus upon the ways in which we reacted to one of the most important constraints on the behaviour of persons in classrooms — the official curriculum.

Clearly, the official curriculum is not the only important constraint operating within classrooms. The availability of resources including time, teacher skills and space, as well as equipment, also limit what it is intelligent and feasible to attempt. Nevertheless, the official curriculum is a particularly significant factor, which both teachers and pupils need to take into account. It is ostensibly the reason for them meeting together through the school day; and, being a crystallized expression of the wishes of powerful others, the way in which both teachers and pupils respond to it can either promote, or damage, their future career. A consideration of the way in which 3Y and I responded to the curriculum is, however, useful for another reason. Thus, if it could be shown that 3Y's changed behaviour towards me in lessons five to ten was a result of the fact that they enjoyed doing the work which I had set, then it would be less easy to argue that their change of heart was motivated by altruism.

This chapter is, therefore, divided into four sections. The first considers the way in which pupils responded to the history curriculum which I presented to them. The data is drawn from lessons one to ten and also from three further out-of-class discussions which occurred. The first of these discussions was with Brian and Steve. It took place after lesson six when both boys had demonstrated that they were prepared to stand by our bargain, but when it was clear that Brian, in particular, had little interest in the work he had agreed to do. I was, therefore, anxious to discover ways in which I could engage his interest, not only so that his time in the first of each double lesson could be spent more profitably, but also to try to wean him away from playing cards. Once again, Mr Charles was happy to release the two boys from his lesson. The two final discussions took place in the last week of term. The normal timetable had been abandoned and the week filled with extra-curricular activities and administrative re-organization. I had gone into the school to talk to 3Y as and when I could about the lessons we had shared. This proved to be quite difficult, because 3Y had taken advantage of the unusual circumstances to disappear into remote corners of the school where they could engage in their own activities undisturbed. Nevertheless, I managed to find Brian, Janet and Liz and we went to talk together in a small room. The news clearly got around, for three quarters of an hour later the room began to fill up with other members of the class. In spite of the fact that they were very excited about the imminent end of the school year, and in spite of the cramped conditions and the fact that there were no chairs, but only a table on which Val reclined seductively and a blanket in which two pupils wrapped themselves, something resembling a class discussion about the history curriculum took place.

Section two of this chapter will consider my own responses to the official curriculum. Once again the data will be drawn from lessons one to ten, and from the discussions I had with pupils. In sections one and two, therefore, a case will be made that both I and the pupils of 3Y responded to the curriculum as an important constraint which needed to be taken into account in any resolution of the moral dilemmas which faced us. However, it will be shown that, in spite of the power of this constraint in limiting our behaviour, it never 'caused' us to act in ways which were morally unacceptable. Indeed, where there was a danger that this might happen we all resisted its constraining force, even at the expense of our own interests. Section three of this chapter illustrate this response even more graphically by recounting the events of lessons eleven and twelve. This will be the first time that data from these lessons have been used. They are treated separately not simply because, as the final lessons which I shared with 3Y, they might be considered to have a special significance, but also because they were a dramatic example of the way in which experiments, if they reflect real life, cannot be neatly rounded off and brought to a tidy end. In addition, these lessons, which took place in the penultimate week of term, provide a vivid illustration of how different understandings of the constraints and opportunities present within a situation can lead to conflict, unless there is a firm belief in the morality of the other people involved. They, also, further illustrate how our behaviour in relation to the official curriculum was not a predetermined 'reaction' to an environmental factor, but an intelligent and moral response to our assessment of a total situation. Section four of this chapter will identify the conclusions which can be drawn from all this evidence.

The Pupils' Reactions to the History Curriculum

Typical deterministic explanations of the curriculum behaviour of a class such as 3Y refer to psychological and sociological 'causal' factors. For example, a determinist might argue that disengagement from the official curriculum was the result of, for example, low IQ, personality disorder, or inadequate socialization into the value of education. This latter explanation would be typically linked with social class. Such explanations insist that pupils won't do the work because they can't, or because they haven't been 'programmed' to be interested in it. To anyone who believed in the intrinsic morality of pupil-persons, however, such explanations would be inadequate. Thus, while the concept of intrinsic morality is compatible with the view that persons will have different interests (which may well be grounded in differing cultural experiences) and different skills (which might depend upon the different opportunities for learning afforded by differences in socio-economic position or in physiological make-up and health) it is incompatible with the view that these differences will cause them to reject new knowledge if it offered them new creative opportunities. Knowledge would only be rejected if it failed in this last respect — if it was experienced as 'boring'. (See Chapter Two, Section One (vii)). Intrinsically moral pupils might, therefore, be expected to reject the official curriculum, not because it was 'difficult' or culturally 'alien', but because it neither gave an immediate outlet for their creativity, nor, as far as they could see, opened up new opportunities for them in the future. It would, therefore, be morally repugnant.

However, the response of intrinsically moral pupils to a 'boring' curriculum would also be influenced by their altruism. Thus, any decision about whether, or not, they should actively reject or oppose the curriculum would depend on how such a course of action would affect the rights of other people who were involved. Thus, if 3Y really had come to see me as a person whose interests must be taken into account, it should be possible to demonstrate that their response to the curriculum which I was advocating was tempered with a concern for my interests. Indeed, faced with a set of curriculum tasks, an intrinsically moral pupil might be expected to consider the following questions before deciding on a proper course of action:

(i)   Has the curriculum any interest or value for me? If not:
(ii) What will be the consequence for me of rejecting it? For example, will I be punished so severely that my opportunities for creative expression will be reduced to such an extent that it would, on balance, be better to conform?
(iii) If I conform will this be a cowardly betrayal of my rights in the face of immoral oppression?
(iv) If I fail to conform will the cost to other moral persons be greater than the cost to me of conforming?

Clearly, if the answer to the first question is in the affirmative the pupil faces no moral dilemma in respect to the curriculum and the last three questions would be superfluous. As it turned out 3Y's response to the curriculum tasks I had set ranged from a qualified acceptance to downright disapproval. Thus, the miniatures presented below illustrate how the curriculum responses of different pupils can be represented as their attempt to consider all the questions and thus to find a moral way forward. What is significant about the evidence is the variety of response which is revealed, a variety which is not easily accommodated by cultural or psychological explanations of pupil behaviour. For all these pupils were working class; most came from homes which were disadvantaged; all demonstrated anti-school subcultural attitudes; and all were low achievers.

Steve

Steve's response to the history curriculum which I introduced is interesting, because it changed so dramatically after lesson four. Before our first discussion he was clearly not prepared to engage in the history project in spite of the fact that he was already in serious trouble in school. Indeed, according to him the fact that his mother had been brought in had made him angry rather than penitent. In the first double lesson he created an opportunity for following his own interests and perhaps challenging the official curriculum by asking to do 'sex' as his topic. In the second double lesson, having dismissed my books on sex as uninteresting, he expressed his creativity and his opposition by disruptive behaviour. This behaviour could, of course, be explained by suggesting that he was at the mercy of a cultural background which did not value the study of history, his emerging sexuality, and the psychological stress of his mother's visit to the school. What is less easy to explain through such deterministic arguments is his changed behaviour after our discussions, for such factors would still be present. Moreover, in our earlier interviews Steve had declared that he knew that education was important and, in particular, he had boasted with some pride that, in history, he always got good marks. He was clearly, therefore, not the victim of total socialization into anti-school attitudes.

Steve's response to the tasks I set was, therefore, very complex and apparently full of contradictions. However, once it is represented as the outcome of his attempt to answer the four questions outlined above it begins to make some sense. Thus, Steve's answer to the question: 'Have these tasks any interest or value for me?' was a qualified 'Yes'. For example, he clearly liked getting good marks and the tasks gave an opportunity for him to do this. He, also, knew that if he worked well this would provide a way of getting out of trouble. Moreover, he believed that in the long run his performance at school would affect his job opportunities. He, thus, clearly saw the extrinsic value of the history curriculum. On the other hand he clearly got little intrinsic enjoyment from the work. Like the rest of the class he found writing boring. Unlike most other pupils, however, he had said, in the interviews earlier in the year, that he regarded it as a necessary evil and asked only that it should be kept within limits and be sweetened by other more interesting activities. This complex response to question one meant that, for Steve, the further three questions were still relevant. Thus the question 'What will be the consequence for me of rejecting the curriculum?' would be important in order to decide how far he could go in any given lesson in punctuating work activities with fun. With a strict teacher he might be prepared to abandon all disruptive activities whereas with a weak teacher who he felt would not cause him trouble, he might abandon all pretence of work. Certainly at the end of lesson four he had seemed surprised, as well as angry, when I had put a cross on his report sheet. No doubt having categorized me as a weak teacher who would not affect his long term prospects, he seemed to have put considerable faith in his ability to bribe or bully me into leniency.

However, it was clear from his comments when interviewed, from his behaviour in lessons three and four, and from our discussions, that Steve was, also, concerned about the immorality of teacher oppression (Question (iii)). While in most lessons he seemed prepared, in the light of his complex evaluation of the school curriculum, to tread the delicate path of doing just enough to be able to claim he had done some work, while leaving the maximum opportunity to pursue other interests, he was also prepared to confront teachers if he felt they had unwarrantably ignored his rights. Indeed, throughout, Steve was clearly concerned with human rights, and it was arguably this concern which led him to go far beyond the letter of the agreement we had made after lesson four. Thus, instead of joining Brian for card playing, he worked through each double lesson on the title sheet for the display. This behaviour seemed to be the result of an act of will which stemmed from his belief that the activity represented the optimum solution to his moral dilemma. Thus while, at one level, it was clear that playing cards was a more attractive proposition than the work he undertook, this latter was better than 'writing'. For example, in the discussion which took place after lesson six, when I tried to explore with Steve and Brian ways in which I could make the curriculum more interesting, he had said that he would be interested in doing Rugby for his topic. In lesson seven I took in some books on the subject for him to work from. Although he seemed pleased that I had taken the trouble, he merely glanced through them and then went back to the title sheet. As he had said with some firmness during the discussion: 'I'm doing that "HISTORY: 1870 to 1910", you know'. In continuing to work on the title sheet, therefore, Steve appeared to have made a deliberate choice of an activity which would allow him to keep out of trouble by conforming to the bargain we had made, while at the same time avoiding the stultifying boredom of the other tasks I had suggested. Nevertheless, in spite of these quite legitimate motivations I was left in no doubt that Steve also conformed because he had come to regard me as a person who no longer need be opposed on principle. His attitude towards me after lesson four was constantly cheerful and often protective. The impression he gave, therefore, was of a pupil who had deliberately chosen a course of action which would result in the optimum balance between my rights and his.

Barbara, Janet and Liz

From lesson one these three girls appeared to accept my right to ask them to engage in the curriculum. They quickly chose a topic and began to produce charts. This was consistent with Janet and Barbara's views expressed in the earlier interviews when they had given some support to school work, complaining mainly that some pupils were allowed 'to get away with it', and that teachers did not help them sufficiently. Liz, however, had complained at that time that school work 'wastes all the day'.

In spite of the fact that these three girls completed a substantial amount of work, it was clear that Liz's view was shared by Janet and Barbara as far as my lessons were concerned. For example, Barbara, who exuded vigour and mischief, argued in the discussion in the last week of term that even staying in bed would be better than doing history. Janet was equally unenthusiastic. She argued that they had too many history lessons and indicated that she would have been more interested in another subject. Thus, in the last week of term she said:

Janet: Miss. Did you have any books on trampolining?

KC: There are some in the library.

Janet: Did you have some though? If I would have asked you, would you have got me some of those books?

KC: Yes. I mean — that was one of the problems wasn't it, that we were doing the dates 1870 to 1910.

This lack of interest in the curriculum was further demonstrated by the fact that although they claimed to have learned something, they could see no real point in it. In the discussion in the last week of term I asked them to criticize the lessons so we could see how they could have been improved. At one point I asked:

KC: Do you think you learned anything?

Janet: Yea.

Liz: Yea.

KC: What sort of thing do you think you learned?

Liz: About the olden days.

Janet: About how people used to live and what clothes they used to wear.

Later I asked:

KC: Do you see any point in looking back and seeing how earlier people lived? I mean, do you think it helps at all to understand what's going on now? [Long silence] I mean, people say — let me tell you what people say — people say you ought to do history to know what's happened in the country before ...

Janet: Mmm.

KC: ... and they say that between 1870 amd 1910 there were a lot of poor people who had a terrible time trying to make a living. And so you can look back and see why it happened, and how they tried to cope with it. And then if some people today are poor we can learn some lessons about why, and what we ought to do. But — I mean — is that not a good reason for everyone to learn history? [Silence]

KC: It doesn't seem interesting that? Does it to you Liz?

Liz: No.

But in spite of this lack of commitment to the curriculum *per se*, as Janet pointed out she completed four charts, and Liz was prepared to make a suggestion about how I might have avoided wasted time.

Liz: It would have been better if we'd had books.

Janet: We did have books!

Liz: No. I mean exercise books to do it in.

KC: Would it?

> *Liz:*   Yea. Like an exercise book. One each. Then you wouldn't have to keep running out of glue.

In the light of the girls' lack of interest in the curriculum their conforming behaviour needs some explanation. It did not seem to be the result of a fear of unfortunate consequences nor because there were no alternative activities available. For example, both Barbara and Liz said to me on different occasions that they knew that if they misbehaved I 'wouldn't tell'. Moreover, they were clearly aware that every second lesson Brian played cards. At the end of term I asked them about this:

> *KC:*   I let them play cards, but what did you feel about it? Did you think I ought to have made Brian work?
> *Janet:*   We don't mind. It's alright. You let him do what he wanted.

This change from their earlier complaint that teachers allowed pupils to get out of work, together with the fact that although they knew that they could have done the same they continued working, seemed to be explained by an empathetic perception of my position and problems, and by a belief that I had done the best I could. In the earlier interviews Barbara had acknowledged that many of the teachers' difficulties were not of their making and, in negotiating some time out of the classroom in lesson ten, they had demonstrated an understanding of my fears. This empathy was further illustrated by their comments in the discussions in the last week of term. I asked what I could have done to improve the lessons.

> *Liz:*   Nothing.
> *Janet:*   Nothing. It was good.
> *KC:*   There must have been something wrong though.
> *Janet:*   [Indignantly] There wasn't!
> *KC:*   I mean — what about the work? Could the work have been better?
> *Janet:*   No. It was alright.

By which she seemed to mean, as she later more accurately commented,

> *Janet:*   You can't do more than what you have already done, Miss, can you?

Thus, although these girls found little of interest or value in the history curriculum, their conformity cannot be explained through fear of punishment. Rather they appeared to feel that I had done the best I could within the constraints imposed by the official curriculum; and that in providing tasks which allowed them some choice and liberty of movement I deserved to be treated morally in return.

Howard, Dave, Jim and Robert

The response of these boys to the curriculum was different from that of both Steve and the three girls. This seemed to derive from a more positive response to the first question: 'Has the work any interest?' All four boys sought and found something which they wanted to do. In Howard's case he chose to enlarge a complicated picture of a street scene in the late nineteenth century. He was the only pupil who chose to do his work in a way which I had not directly suggested. His commitment was demonstrated by the fact that he worked at this task for ten lessons, taking time off at intervals for a rest, but then returning to work of his own accord. He also often asked for help, so that sometimes we worked side by side on a difficult figure. At other times he brought his work up for approval.

Dave, Robert and Jim also found subject matter to interest them. Perhaps because of this, they did not do much drawing and writing. Whereas the girls had, as they chatted, mechanically completed several charts, these three boys only produced two charts between them. This was due, however, to the fact that they spent a lot of time reading the books, and discussing what they found with each other and me. They undoubtedly learned more than the girls. Dave's interest was demonstrated by his suggestion in the final discussion about how the lessons could have been improved.

> *Dave*: We should have had more time. Like you on a Monday and Wednesday, or on Wednesday and Thursday, or something like that. Two double periods, so in the end four lessons a week.
> *KC*: Would that have been better?
> *Dave*: We'd have got more work out of it.

Robert and Jim, who worked together, had discussed their attitude to topic work in the earlier interviews. At that time they had distinguished between work which was useful (though often boring) like 'punctuation and things like that' and work which was interesting. Project work fitted into this latter category. Robert argued that in ordinary lessons, where they had to do what the teacher said:

> *Robert*: You're not getting rid of any of your tension, so it's good to have a lesson where you can do what you want.
> *KC*: Would you like to do a project all the time?
> *Robert*: No. But it takes off all the hard work.
> *KC*: You seem to be saying that a project isn't hard work.
> *Robert*: No. Cos you like it, and you're interested in the subject you're doing. You're doing what you want really. One week you can read, and the other week you can write. With Mr Charles we write all the time.

Given then that Howard, Dave, Robert and Jim seemed quite interested in the work, the question of my rights in the matter, or a consideration of the consequences of not doing the work, did not arise.

Frank

Frank's response to the curriculum was again unlike that of any other member of 3Y. Unlike the girls, he was not prepared to do work unless it was interesting in itself, apparently getting little pleasure from the production of charts. Nevertheless, he was prepared to spend a lot of time looking for something of interest. However, the problem which he identified in lesson two, when he said 'I want to do something, but I can't find nothing *to* do' was never resolved. I spent a considerable amount of time discussing possible alternatives with him, but after sampling a topic he would return to me asking for something else because it was boring. In lesson seven he asked if he could do the Romans. He had found some pictures of Roman legionaries in a book on weapons. I pointed out to him that if he did that, we wouldn't be able to include his work in a display depicting life between 1870 and 1910, but he said he would do it anyway. By the end of lesson nine his interest in this topic had waned too, and he finally joined the card players.

His behaviour was interesting. Clearly the question of finding something which he would enjoy doing was important to him and one upon which he was not prepared to compromise easily. On the other hand he seemed to have enough faith in my moral integrity to think that there must be something in the books to interest him, if only he could find it. This persistent search did not appear to be the consequence of a fear that retribution would follow if he did not do the work. He, like other members of the class, saw Brian playing cards every second lesson with my consent, and he could have joined him earlier. That it took nine lessons for him to decide to do this is arguably evidence that he saw me as a person whose wishes should be respected as far as possible.

Brian, Mike and Val

These three pupils gave a clear indication that they had no interest whatever in the history curriculum. Their opposition to it was total and was demonstrated by a resistance to even talking about the problem. It was as if they did not wish to consider that I might be able to improve it. Val had been away in lessons one and two. When she returned in lesson three I attempted to discuss with her what she might do, but her eyes never met mine, and she merely said that she would join the other girls. In the melée of lessons three and four I lost sight of her, but she gave in no work. In lesson five I tried to engage her in a further discussion but again she quickly said that she would join the girls. This time she did some writing which she brought to show me at the start of lesson six with a request that she could join Brian in playing cards. She had copied out the acknowledgements at the beginning of the book she was using and, clearly, what she had written was of no relevance on a chart. I asked her if she could tell me what she had written about. She either could not, or would not. I explained the meaning of her writing and why it was irrelevant. She said she had done it because 'It was in the book'.

In spite of her sullenness I began to suspect that part of her problem was illiteracy, rather than simple opposition. This was too sensitive a subject to be approached directly so I said she could join Brian and that we must talk again. The following lesson she was away. In lesson nine she sat behind Brian and Mike, ostensibly looking at a book. In lesson ten she joined them again to play cards.

Perhaps because I never managed to engage Val in conversation, my impression was that her superficial engagement in curriculum work in the first of each double lesson was a result of a belief that if she did not conform the consequences would be unpleasant. In the life of the experiment I certainly failed to discover where she was as a person, and I felt equally sure that she did not perceive me as a person either.

With Mike and Brian the position was rather different. Although they, too, totally rejected the curriculum, their conformity for half of the double lesson appeared to be a consequence of a belief that I was a person with rights, and, moreover, one with whom they had struck a bargain which should be honoured. In addition, however, they were undoubtedly of the opinion that if they did not conform to the bargain I would punish them. There had certainly been enough talk of punishment in the discussions following lesson four to suggest that, in spite of my protests, I would use it.

A peace based upon a legalistic and exact division of time between their preferred curriculum and mine was clearly uneasy no matter what the reasons were for its continued existence. I was, therefore, concerned to pursue discussions which might lead to the discovery of work in which Brian and Mike would be interested. As a result I arranged to meet Brian, Steve and Mike on the Monday morning following lesson six. In the event, Mike was away and Steve had decided that his best course of action would be to work at the title sheet. Most of the discussion, therefore, took place between myself and Brian. It provided an important illustration not only of the complexity of Brian's response but also of how the failure of a teacher to perceive this complexity could cause conflict. It began:

KC: Last lesson when I came in.... I thought you and Steve and Mike were very good and everything seemed to go very well.

Brian:	Yea.
KC:	But the one thing that worried me about it, and I thought 'Right. This is probably something that I can do' was that you weren't very interested in the work.
Brian:	No.
KC:	Am I right in thinking that? Because, you know, you did do some didn't you? You did that list of cricket successes. But what I wondered was whether there was anything that you would be interested in, in History, that you could do and I could organize for you, you know, so that you would be interested. Because it seems such a waste of time if you're not interested doesn't it? Really what sort of thing would you like doing best?
Brain:	Football.
KC:	How would you do it then?
Brian:	The history of football or something like that.
KC:	Would that be interesting? How would you like to do it? Would you like to do drawing and writing ... or making models?
Brian:	Mike would do football an' all.
KC:	Would he? Cos he's not here today is he?
Brian:	No.
KC:	But I mean, the thing is, how would you like to do it ... cos I'll need to find the stuff for you won't I? So how would you like to do it, remembering that at the end of term what I'm hoping to do is have a big display of all the work. So it needs to be something that can go on display, to show people who look at it something about football.
Brian:	I don't mind, Miss.
KC:	Well would you rather do a poster, or would you rather do a model?
Brian:	Just do drawing and writing and that.
KC:	You'd like to do drawing and writing ... Now, if we're doing the years 1870 to 1910, now what sort of things do you think people ought to know about football at that time if they were to understand what football was like?
Brian:	There wasn't no teams and that. Well — there was just one big team, about a hundred people in each team, and they use to play on the streets.
KC:	Did they?
Brian:	Yea — just kicking it about and that.
KC:	So. About the sort of teams. You probably know quite a bit about it already don't you?
Brian:	Yea.
KC:	Oh. That's good. So that will give us a start then won't it?

	Now what other sorts of things? I mean, did the teams change? When did the FA cup start? When did the Football Association start?

Now what other sorts of things? I mean, did the teams change? When did the FA cup start? When did the Football Association start?

Brian: Eighteen — um — eighteen seventy-two was when the cup started.

KC: Oh that's good, cos that's right in our dates isn't it?

Brian: Yea. 1872 when the FA cup started, and the first one was the Wanderers versus the Engineers.

KC: Was it?

Brian: Yea. The Wanderers versus the Royal Engineers.

KC: Right, so then we'll need something about the start of the FA cup. Right. So that means that the teams had been sorted out by that time doesn't it?

Brian: Yea.

KC: Do you know how that happened?

Brian: There weren't that many. There was about twelve teams....

KC: ... So we need to find out when the teams started and which teams there were at that time. What other sorts of things ought people to know about ...? What about the strips they wore?

Brian: Oh yea — the colours.

KC: That would be interesting wouldn't it?

Brian: You could do a drawing like, and then name them underneath. You could do like a top and colour it in, and do like the name then underneath — like Crystal Palace or something like that.

KC: So. The colours.

Brain: ... Miss, you know in our library, in our library they've got a good book, haven't they? [Addressed to Steve] on football.

KC: Can you take books out? Of the library?

Brian: Yea. When you're a member or something.

KC: Can you join, or not?

Brian: No. Not now.

KC: ... I'll ask somebody ...

Brian: ... In 1981, Miss, there was the first, the first non-league team to win it (the FA Cup)

KC: Was there?

Brian: Yea. Tottenham. They were the first non-league team to win the cup.

KC: (At the end of further discussion) Now, the question is, 'Are you going to be interested in this?'

Brian: Yea.

KC: Good. But anyway you can tell me when it comes whether you are or not.

> *Brian*: And Mike would be, wouldn't he? [Addressed to Steve.]
> *Steve*: Yea.

Although I experienced this discussion as difficult at first, by the end I began to feel that we had found a subject which Brian would enjoy and, perhaps, even one which would wean him away from playing cards. This belief was based on the change in his contributions from monosyllables to lengthier statements. My comment that Brian could tell me, when the time came, whether he was interested or not was, to some extent, formal. I believed that as long as I found attractive books the problem would be solved.

It was not. The next lesson I produced a set of books which ranged from clear, simply written children's books on the history of football, to expensive glossy encyclopaedias on the subject. They were tied up with string and had Brian's name on them so no other pupil could take them first, and they were accompanied by a typed sheet giving the page numbers on which different types of information could be found. The result was that Brian looked through the books in a desultory manner in his work lessons, produced one minimal piece of writing from them, and was still clearly more interested in the advent of the card-playing session.

The apparent incongruence between what Brian said and what he did is open to different interpretations. For example, it could be argued that because his behaviour was 'determined' he could not plan his future behaviour, or, alternatively, that he never intended to do the topic on football, that he was just playing me along. However, other evidence indicated that that would be an over-simplification of his position. For example, a major part of the problem was his dislike of history. In the discussion in the final week of term he argued that he would have been interested if it had been 'Like 1970 to 1981. Like that. Then you can go through all the records and all that. You done the wrong year.' He also said to Janet 'We do too much history, don't we?'

Even this, however, did not explain why he did not appear to find the books interesting, whereas he had been enthusiastic about '. . . the good book in the library'. The book I had taken in contained contemporary, as well as historical, information which he could have looked at. Perhaps he felt partially bound by our agreement, knowing that I would not consider a study of recent football as appropriate 'work'. Moreover, unlike Barbara, Janet and Liz who equally disliked History, Brian appeared to find no pleasure in the production of charts for its own sake. In the initial interviews, like the other pupils, he had complained about the boredom of writing. Perhaps more importantly, he was like Robert and Jim, whose main source of pleasure in the curriculum came from a discussion of ideas. Twice in considering football as a possible topic Brian had stated that Mike would do it too. In the event, Mike was away for the following lesson and when he came back, chose to continue with his original topic. Brian was, therefore, isolated, having no-one with whom he could discuss the books. In the final week of term he even said that the lessons would have been better if I had taught them from the front — a process which would have allowed an interchange of ideas. To some extent I led him into making this statement. Discussing the lessons,

Janet: It was alright as it was.
KC: What about you, Brian? Cos you didn't really enjoy it did you?
Brian: No. It was boring.
KC: That's right. Well can you tell me why you thought it was boring, cos it's important.
Brian: I don't know. I don't know what was the matter with it, but it was just boring.
KC: Well — I wonder. Let's try and help you think why it was boring. I mean, would you have preferred it if I'd taught a lesson from the front? You know — like what normally happens.
Brian: What — read a story or something like that?
KC: Either read a story, or told you about something.
Brian: Yes. It would have been better like that, Miss.

Although I had led Brian into this position he did not seem to be agreeing blindly. He checked what I meant first, and even though Janet said she disagreed with him, was prepared to repeat the suggestion when we were discussing the lessons with the whole class saying 'You should have taught us, Miss'.

That the key to interesting Brian in the history curriculum would have been through the use of more oral work was also strongly suggested by his behaviour at the end of the discussion on football. There had been still ten minutes of that lesson left, and he and Steve began their usual practice of punching each other when they had time to spare. Wanting to avoid the tiresome experience of watching them and wondering what they would do next, I said I would tell them a story. I told them *The Beast with Five Fingers*. It was the only time that I felt I had Brian's complete attention. Both he and Steve listened in total silence. The bell went before I had finished. Steve said curtly, 'Keep going'. I hurriedly did so, until Brian said:

Brian: Oh yea. And then it nailed him to the thing.
KC: That's right. It killed him.
Brian: Yea.

He then quickly went on to tell me a story of his own.

Brian's response to the curriculum can, therefore, be represented in the following way:

(a)   He felt that the timetable was over-burdened with history in which he saw little value.

(b)   Although he was interested in football, he was mainly interested in the contemporary scene.

(c)   Although he was not opposed to using books, he wanted to discuss ideas. Without discussion he found information to be inert and boring.

(d)   He, therefore, found nothing of interest, value or pleasure in the curriculum I offered.

(e)   In spite of this he was prepared to sit grimly through a lesson of total boredom, quietly going through the motions of conformity, in exchange for a lesson where he could play cards. This seemed to be a direct result of the agreement we had made. His reason for keeping to this agreement was, however, as much to do with a belief that I would punish disruptive behaviour as with empathy with my problem. Discussing the improvement in 3Y's behaviour, he commented, 'I expect it was because you threatened us, Miss'. This perception was especially interesting when laid alongside the comments of Janet and Liz that they knew I 'wouldn't tell'. Undoubtedly I had reacted towards Brian in a way which had prevented him from perceiving my intentions.

Overview of these Curriculum Responses

From the examples of pupil responses to the curriculum outlined above, a number of limited conclusions can be drawn. In the first place it is apparent that the general improvement in classroom behaviour noted in Chapter Six was not a consequence of an increased enthusiasm for History. Key disruptives such as Steve found it only marginally rewarding, and others such as Barbara, Mike and Brian continued to be bored. There seemed, therefore, to be no direct causal link between classroom behaviour and interest in the curriculum. Some more important factor seemed to be at work.

Secondly it was apparent that this factor was not culture. Given the pupils' common working-class background and anti-school attitudes, it would be difficult to find a cultural explanation which could account for both conformity and non-conformity to the set tasks. Nor did the factor appear to be academic achievement. Not only were all the pupils low achievers, but even within the limited range which they represented, the most academically successful — Brian, Barbara and Janet — responded differently, as did the least successful — Liz and Val.[1] Equally the responses could not be categorized by sex. It would, of course, be possible to argue that it was a sophisticated, but mechanical, interaction between such factors, which, being in a different combination for each pupil produced different results. However, such an explanation would seem to be unnecessarily complex, and would, moreover, leave teachers with nothing to do but sophisticated factor analyses to discover the differential importance of variables (such as age, sex, home background and IQ.) but over which, as teachers, they had no control. The simpler view, that 3Y were responding morally to a total situation, avoids this problem. By demonstrating that their behaviour can be validly explained by reference to moral criteria, the search for an explanation of differences becomes a search for reasons (not causes) and thus, for constraints which might possibly be removed.

The Effects of the Curriculum on My Behaviour

Although it will be demonstrated that my behaviour was also open to interpretation through other perspectives, my relationship with the curriculum will be portrayed, like that of the pupils, as a moral one, in which I was responding to such questions as: 'Have I the right to ask 3Y to do this?'; 'What will happen if I fail to insist that they do it?'; and 'Am I being fair?' Answers to such questions always took priority over purely curriculum questions such as: 'Will this action help the pupil to learn some history?' As with the pupils, therefore, my behaviour was arguably a moral response to a total situation, of which the curriculum was only one aspect, and at no time did I consider it proper to pursue curriculum objectives at all costs. As a result, an analysis of my behaviour which used a purely curriculum logic would inevitably reveal contradictions which, because they seemed irrational, might be put down to the effects of causal factors, but which disappear once a moral logic is employed.

My initial task had been to produce a curriculum which would be flexible enough to accommodate the varying interests and current skills of 3Y. The degree to which this was possible was of course constrained by the availablity of resources (including time), by the syllabus laid down by the school and by the limitations of my own skills and imagination. Nevertheless, within these constraints, I attempted to provide opportunities for the pupils to do something which they and I would feel was worthwhile. In lessons three and four my objective of encouraging 3Y to learn some history was clearly superceded by my desire to persuade them to take a moral stance towards me. I felt personally affronted by their disruptive behaviour but tried to maintain a moral stance towards them by inviting them to discuss with me the reasons for their actions. Had curriculum objectives been paramount I would perhaps have taken a firmer line.

With the decrease in disruptive behaviour after lesson four, I spent much of my time helping pupils with difficulties, advising on alternative topics, and discussing ways in which their work could be made more interesting. From lesson five onwards my behaviour would have appeared to an observer to be directly linked with my curriculum objectives, and on the basis of such an assumption they could have argued convincingly that I was engaged in strategic survival rather than education and that my commitment[2] to the curriculum led me to apply deviant labels to pupils who rejected it, rather than treating them as persons whose non-conformity was based on moral principles. For example:

(i) Even when it had become apparent that several pupils could find nothing of interest within the limits set by the curriculum, I did not relax those limits in spite of the fact that this would have been possible. Thus, although the school had laid down a nineteenth century syllabus for 3Y, it is unlikely that I would have met any strong opposition if I had let them study a different period. Schools often allow considerable flexibility of curriculum for difficult, non-examination classes, and Mr Charles would no doubt have been satisfied if I had got these pupils to do anything. Instead of which, I insisted that Brian's football topic should lie within the dates 1870 to 1910, and told Frank that if he did the Romans, he would not be doing what I wanted. I was, thus, clearly committed to my original curriculum in a way which prevented a maximization of learning for some pupils. At face value such behaviour seems neither rational nor moral.

(ii) Secondly, my negative perception of Brian seemed to be associated with a commitment to the curriculum. I undoubtedly did regard Brian more negatively than any other pupil, and this was certainly linked with the amount of time and effort which I had given to finding a topic which he would enjoy. Although I had invited Brian to change his mind about the football topic if it did not prove interesting, I was irritated when he did so, and my feelings would have inevitably communicated themselves to him. It would, therefore, be possible to argue that my commitment to the curriculum had promoted a classic example of the effects of labelling and that far from attempting to understand and empathize with his point of view in our discussions, I was merely trying to 'manipulate' him, so that he would act in a way which fitted in with my preconceived ideas.

(iii) Thirdly, an observation of my behaviour could have led to the conclusion that I was unreasonably committed to a display of work at the end of term, even after it became apparent that this encouraged mechanical production. My behaviour appeared to be based on the educationally indefensible view that the girls' prodigious, but mindless output was of more value than, for example, Dave's slow, but thoughtful engagement with the subject matter. As the lessons progressed, I increasingly emphasized 'getting the charts finished'. This commitment could plausibly be linked with Woods' description of 'routine mongering' and 'therapy' as survival strategies.[3]

(iv) Finally, in spite of the fact that I did not allow pupils to redefine the limits of the official curriculum, tenaciously emphasizing the dates 1870 to 1910, I did allow them to 'opt out'. Once again this behaviour can be interpreted as the result of an over-commitment to the curriculum, coupled with a need to survive. Thus, rather than legitimating work other than that I had proposed, I preferred pupils to learn nothing. As an educational rather than a survival strategy such behaviour appears to be totally irrational.

While such interpretations are plausible and at one level contain some truth, they are inadequate explanations of my behaviour because they rest upon a number of inaccurate assumptions. They assume, for example, that I was unaware of the limitations of the tasks I had set as a vehicle for learning, whereas, as the lessons progressed I was increasingly conscious of this. They also assume that my desire to survive over-rode my concern for the interests of the pupils, whereas my concern was to survive within a framework of classroom justice which took pupil interests into account. Finally, they assume that I was at liberty to change the curriculum within the limited opportunities that the constraints on me allowed.

In one sense, of course, I could have changed it and a purely educational logic would have required me to do so on the basis that any learning is better than none. However, this did not appear to be an option which was open to me. The curriculum, once stated, did not remain a neutral object. It quickly became enmeshed in the more fundamental reality of classroom justice and in so doing became public property. Pupils began to judge their own and each other's behaviour in relation to it. Thus Barbara admonished Tony for still being on the same piece of work after two lessons; Janet used it as a justification for leaving the room; and Steve used it as a means to salvation. Clearly the curriculum was no longer mine to change at will, and it did not need much imagination to envisage the righteous indignation which would follow a change of mind about the set tasks. Public justice, therefore, required that the definition and status of the official curriculum remained intact in recognition of the commitment of some of the pupils. On the other hand, the rights of those pupils who found the work intolerably boring had to be met. They, therefore, were allowed time out which brought personal but no public rewards. The superficial contradiction in my behaviour can, therefore, be explained as a principled attempt to balance the rights of both conforming and non-conforming pupils with my personal need to survive.

My determination to mount a display at the end of term can be explained in a similar manner. In spite of the lack of interest of some pupils, and in spite of some pessimism about whether anyone would want to look at their work, other pupils clearly found the idea rewarding. Exchanges like that in lesson nine reinforced my perception that this was the case.

KC:	(To the class) Now — so far we've got about seven or eight charts completely finished, so we need to work very hard.
Robert:	Where will we put it?
KC:	[Pointing to the classroom walls.] We'll put it all round here.
Robert:	Not worth it.
KC:	It will be. You wait and see.
Robert:	I bet they won't even come to see it.
KC:	Well, we'll put it up and get someone to come and look at it.
Andy:	Put it in the exhibition hall.
Chris:	Put it in the 'Special' room.
Steve:	No.
Barbara:	Yes. Put it in the 'Special' room.
Steve:	Well, none of us will see it then.
KC:	Well, we'll see where we're going to put it. I'll ask Mr Charles, and see which is the best idea.

The combination of cynicism and enthusiasm expressed here, convinced me that, whatever the cost in educational terms, the display should be mounted. I had made a promise and pupils had acted upon it. Morally speaking, I had no choice.

Equally my negative attitude towards Brian can be represented as a moral judgment of him as a person, rather than the result of my over-commitment to the curriculum. Indeed, it was not his rejection of history, or the football topic, which offended me. Rather it was his apparent refusal to view me as a person. His rejection of the football books in lesson seven was not accompanied by an explanation. His attitude seemed surly and, in contrast to Steve, he seemed careless of the personal effort I had made. As already noted, I later believed that I had misunderstood his position but this was not apparent at the time. I believe I communicated my displeasure to Brian in subtle ways, and a process of mutual reinforcement of our dislike of each other began, which I failed to bring out into the open. This finally erupted into open confrontation in lesson twelve.

More will be said about this incident in the next section. What is important here is that the labels I applied to Brian derived from my view of him as an unsatisfactory person rather than as someone who disliked the curriculum. This emphasizes, again, the way in which misconceptions are created in action. With theory to support me, I ought to have been more aware of what was happening. In the event, it took a further angry scene before Brian and I began to express our feelings openly, each charging the other with immorality.

The effect of the curriculum on my behaviour, therefore, closely paralleled its effect on the pupils. Because it quickly became an external object, no longer mine to alter at will, it became one factor amongst others which I needed to take into account in my relationship with the pupils. It was clearly a very significant factor because it defined the goals towards which our behaviour was officially directed. But the power which it derived from its official status was not absolute. Indeed, its dictates were only heeded if they were acceptable within a moral evaluation of the whole situation. Ironically, this sometimes led to an acceptance of the official curriculum when it was defeating its own ends, which was to encourage the learning of history. But my acceptance of the curriculum on such occasions, like that of the pupils, was arguably neither 'determined', nor contradictory, but a coherent moral response to a heavily constrained reality of which we were all aware. This is certainly how it seemed to me at the time, and the behaviour of, for example, Steve, Barbara, Liz, Janet and Frank, suggests that this is how it seemed to many of the pupils, too.

The Events of Lessons Eleven and Twelve

These were the last two history lessons which I took with 3Y and so far no evidence has been drawn from them. They were important because they were different from any other lesson which 3Y and I had shared. As the theory upon which this research has been based proposed, nothing stands still and the pleasant routine which 3Y and I were developing together was at this time interrupted by a change of circumstances, calling for new assessments of the way in which it was proper for us to behave. Moreover, the change which occurred was not only unplanned, but unforeseen, and, therefore, provided an important test of the strength of the person-to-person relationship which I had been attempting to build.

Additionally it provided further support for a number of claims which have been made in this chapter, *viz*:

1 that both 3Y and I responded to a total situation, rather than in a direct way to the curriculum;
2 that our responses to this total situation, which included the curriculum, were moral responses; and therefore,
3 that the engagement in the curriculum of a significant number of pupils was a consequence of their empathy with my position.

If these claims were valid, one would expect that in a situation where the curriculum remained the same but other significant factors changed: firstly, that our curriculum responses would change significantly; secondly, that these changes would be compatible with a moral assessment of the new total situation; and, thirdly, that although we might come to different decisions about the best moral solution to the new situation, we would seek to make compromises.

These expectations were not only largely fulfilled in lessons eleven and twelve, but were fulfilled in a situation which was impregnated with all the ingredients necessary for misunderstanding and which, therefore, invited conflict rather than empathy. For although both 3Y and I knew that the situation had changed, we believed it to be changed in different ways. They did not know what I knew, and vice versa. Thus, we began the lessons with different perceptions of the situation in which we were placed, and had come to different views of the sort of behaviour which would be appropriate. A successful outcome required an interpersonal stance. For example, it was necessary to believe that the behaviour of the other, although in our view inappropriate, was morally conceived. We also needed to be prepared to revise our initial assessments of the situation and acknowledge that they were based on inadequate information. To do this we needed to communicate on a person-to-person basis in the midst of a potentially explosive situation.

I came to the lesson with two pieces of information of which 3Y seemed to be unaware. Firstly, I had just discovered that the official timetable for the last week of term had been cancelled to make way for end-of-term activities. Because of my commitment to an end-of-term display, I was not prepared merely to survive this final double lesson. I wanted 3Y to work hard to get their charts finished. Secondly, on entering the classroom Mr Charles had told me that the pupils were not allowed to sit out on the grass. This had been communicated to me as an institutional regulation and, therefore, as a constraint against which I had no means of fighting. Not to comply would have invited institutional disciplinary action. 3Y seemed unaware of this constraint on their behaviour.

Equally the pupils came to the lessons with information of which I was unaware. They knew that work in school had virtually ceased. The staff-pupil cricket match had been played the day before, and on the following day they were going on school trips — some of them to France. That very afternoon they had a half-day holiday in order that the new intake from the junior schools could be shown round the premises. Because of this morning school was to finish early. In addition, it was Brian's birthday the next day and because he was going on a different trip to Barbara and Mike my lesson was their last chance to 'give him the bumps'. I had known none of this.[4]

3Y's understanding of the situation which was the context in which lessons eleven and twelve took place was therefore radically different from my own. My information — that these were our last lessons and that the school was restricting non-work activities such as sitting out on the grass, led me to believe that we should work hard. 3Y's information that to all intents and purposes school work had been abandoned, and that in any case we still had two lessons the following week in which to complete our display, led them to the conclusion that we should relax and enjoy ourselves. The evidence from lessons eleven and twelve, therefore, demonstrates how we:

(a) began the lesson with different objectives;
(b) communicated to each other our different assessments of the situation;
(c) accommodated in some instances to each other's views; and
(d) failed to accommodate in other instances, with an inevitable result.

3Y arrived at the lesson hot, but cheerful. They said:

Janet:	All I want to do is sit down.
Howard:	(Flopping into a chair) Phew! I'm hot, Miss.
Mike:	Will you read us a story, Miss?
Barbara:	Miss. Can we play cards, Miss? Cos I did that big one (chart) last week, didn't I?
Steve:	I don't want to do no work today, Miss.
Liz:	Miss. Can we go and sit on the grass?

This last request reminded me of Mr Charles' warning. I felt constrained to reply 'No, love'.

Mike:	Miss — we're allowed.
KC:	I don't think so.
Brain:	It's too hot in here.
Frank:	Can we go outside, Miss?
KC:	No, love. Not today.
Frank:	Oh — go on, Miss.

A little later Janet came back with the same request.

Janet:	Can I sit on the grass?
KC:	No, love. I can't let anybody....
Janet:	Oh, please.
KC:	... cos Mr Charles says you aren't allowed.
Liz:	[Voice rising in anger.] Oh God! Mr Charles never lets us go out. Other classes do.
KC:	Well, I can't help that, can I?

From my point of view this was a bad start. I tried to put across my problem.

KC:	Now, listen all of you a moment. We've only got this one lesson now to finish all the work. Now, at the moment, we've got eight charts finished and ten charts nearly finished. So we need to get the rest of them done as quickly as possible.

This was clearly new information for the pupils.

Howard:	How come this is the last one (lesson) cos we've got next week?
KC:	No. Not next week. So we've got to make sure we've got everything together.
Frank:	Why ain't we got it next week?
KC:	I think you've got something else.

Later Brian asked for confirmation of the news.

Brian:	[Calling across the room] Is this the last lesson with you? Miss — is this the last lesson with you? Howard — is this the last lesson with her?
Howard:	Yea.
Barbara:	No it ain't. We've got next week.
Howard:	No we ain't.
KC:	I'll be in next week, but we shan't be able to have a lesson.

In this way 3Y and I communicated to each other early in the lesson eleven our different view of the situation. Moreover our behaviour reflected our different views. I began to harry pupils into completing the charts, and 3Y began to entertain themselves. The tape recorder once again became a centre of attraction with even the girls using it for the first time. Barbara and Janet sang into it in chorus, for Brian, 'Happy Birthday to you....' etc., and:

Barbara:	Hi-di-hi. Hello campers. It's a lovely Butlins morning, and breakfast will be served in half an hour. Ding, dong, ding.

My impression was that the classroom had, indeed, become a holiday camp, with pupils avidly discussing leisure activities.

Chris:	[to Dave] Going down to the nudist beach tonight?
Dave:	Yea.
Chris:	Thought so. Robert — you're going to the nudist beach, ain't yer?
Robert:	No.
Dave:	No? Oh, come on! We'll have some fun. All tits and fannies.

In addition, the girls began to play a game of happy families and Brian roamed around the classroom annoying other pupils.

Within this ferment of activity communication became a problem. At one level the pupils were communicating with me directly through their behaviour, and I was doing the same. They were saying — this is a joyous occasion not to be wasted in drudgery; and I was saying — this is our last chance to complete something worthwhile and should not be wasted in pure fun. Both messages were valid but, because they contradicted each other, they needed discussing. For example, I did not feel at liberty to accept their behaviour as an argument against mounting a display fearing that, in retrospect, they would see this as another example of a teacher who failed to deliver promised goods.

Unfortunately, proper discussion was difficult for several reasons. Firstly, we were short of time. To have stopped and attempted a class discussion would have meant that there would have been no time left to complete the display. Secondly, 3Y were in no mood to engage in a discussion. Without the force of sanctions it is doubtful whether it could have been operationalized. Thirdly, by the time the problem had become apparent I, too, would have found an open discussion difficult. I was feeling hot and irritable. I had been irritated by 3Y's declaration that they did not want to work, especially as, at first, I did not understand the reasons for this change in behaviour. By the time I understood I was feeling threatened by the old spectre of disruptive noise. 3Y seemed unable to enjoy themselve quietly. Loud outbursts of bantering and laughter punctuated the lessons and, as all the doors and windows were open because of the hot weather, I was once again aware of the audience of teachers in other classrooms.

Without the possibility of coming to an agreed solution to the problem, all 3Y and I could do was to try to understand each other's positon and respond to it on an individual basis. The degree of compromise which we reached would be a measure of our interpersonal stance. In the event this seemed to be considerable. For example:

(a) Although there were regular outbursts of noise, they immediately stopped once I reminded the pupils involved. The noise did not appear to be directed against me, but rather to be a spontaneous outburst of excitement. When the bell rang between lessons eleven the twelve someone said 'Only got thirty minutes left. How's that then! Only thirty minutes left'. With the freedom of one and a half days of holiday so imminent, it was perhaps more surprising that they heeded, however temporarily, my requests for quiet than that they made a noise in the first place.

(b) In spite of my scarcely veiled irritability, pupils seemed prepared to tolerate me. For example at one point I said to Howard:

KC: Why's everyone in such a funny mood today?
Howard: Eh?
KC: Why is everyone in such a funny mood today?
Howard: Heat.
KC: Is that what it is?
Howard: It's the first time we've had heat.

> KC: It is really. It's the first time this summer. Were you the same yesterday, cos it was hot yesterday?
> Howard: Yea. We were the same yesterday.

Howard's civil response to my negative definition of the pupils' behaviour was remarkable. He might equally have asked me 'Why are you in such a funny mood today?' Even more significant was his response to my over anxious attempts to prevent noise and get him to do some work. On one occasion he was standing watching the girls play cards. Knowing that he liked to poke them and provoke squeals I said:

> KC: Howard. Come and sit down away from the girls, please.
> Howard: Why? I ain't done nothing — yet.

He laughed as he said this, but came across to me good-humouredly enough. I suggested that he did a small picture to fill up a chart.

> Howard: I don't want to do nothing.
> KC Well just sit down quietly.
> Howard: I am quiet. I've done what I want to do. That's it isn't it? (Pointing to his large picture) Whatever I do now, it's going to take more than one lesson to do isn't it? Look how long it took me to do that picture.

Everything which Howard said was true. To him my remark must have seemed provocative and senseless and totally inappropriate on a hot summer's day. In spite of this he sat and drew a picture.

(c) Howard's willingness to help with completing the display was matched by the behaviour of other pupils. Thus, although the girls spent time playing cards and talking into the tape recorder, they only engaged in these activities once they had ensured that their charts were finished. Dave, Frank and Steve helped arrange the charts in order, and check them, and Robert and Jim completed their one chart. Steve was still concerned with ensuring he did not get into trouble. When he finally felt he could do no more in the circumstances, he appoached me and said 'I can't do any more, Miss'. He gave as his excuse that he had a bad thumb. I laughed and said 'I don't think that's the problem really is it?' But I was able to accept that he had sufficiently respected my interests and, therefore, to agree that he could do something else, without this resulting in a 'cross' on his Report Sheet. This willingness of the pupils to accept my definition of the situation alongside their own was ultimately demonstrated by the fact that at the end of the lesson all the charts were completed, and the display was mounted.

(d) Finally, in spite of my frustration and anxiety, I, too, made concessions. All the pupils, despite their feelings of injustice about Mr Charles' ban on them sitting on the grass outside the classroom, had accepted the situation. When, with the commencement of lesson twelve, it became clear that pupils from other classes were being accorded this privilege, it was my suggestion that pupils who had finished their work could do the same. I did this because I felt I had been given no good reason by Mr Charles for discriminating against 3Y, and justice seemed to demand that they were allowed to go out. However, I did this feeling a degree of anxiety. In their present mood I had no confidence that they would 'behave' once they got outside. In fact, like the pupils from other classes, they sat in twos and threes and talked quietly.

The evidence from these two lessons, therefore, seems to support the central claims being made in this chapter. It is clear that both 3Y and I were responding to a total situation, and that our curriculum behaviour was a consequence of our evaluation of the whole. It is equally clear that both the pupils and myself were using moral criteria in our evaluation, weighing our own interests against the interests of the other, so that conflict was largely avoided.

There was one significant exception to this, however. Brian had been challenging me all lesson. Unlike the other pupils who had told me cheerfully when they intended to stop work, often giving their reasons and continuing to talk to me through the lesson about other things, Brian's stance towards me had seemed surly and offensive. Confrontation, however, did not occur until two minutes before the final bell. Barbara and Mike seemed to have realized that this was the last chance they would get to give Brian the bumps. They cornered him close to the windows. Barbara kicked out to bring Brian down. Brian kicked back but lost his balance giving Mike the opportunity to grab hold of him. I moved quickly across took hold of Brian and Mike by the arm and dragged them apart. Brian began to shout angrily at me. I raised my voice, told him I would not have fighting in the room. and ordered him out. He went. I learned later that he went to Mr Charles to complain that I had hurt him. It was significant in the light of such a serious charge that I was not asked by the school to explain my behaviour. This would no doubt have been seen by pupils as further proof that the school was on the side of the teachers. As a pupil had said in the earlier interviews 'No-one listens at this school, do they?'

Once again this incident can only partially be laid at the door of an inadequate curriculum. Thus, although a solution to Brian's boredom with the history lessons might have prevented the build-up of our negative feelings towards each other, so that I could have dealt with the incident firmly but more calmly, it is unlikely that this in itself would have prevented Mike and Barbara trying to give Brian the bumps. Moreover, I could not have ignored this. I believed that giving the bumps was danger-ous and, as Brian had had 'glarss in his arse' already once that term, I could not have countenanced a scuffle, however friendly, next to the windows.

The factor which turned a piece of preventative action into conflict was the anger involved. In a discussion with Brian, Janet and Liz in the last week of term it was possible for Brian and me to communicate about the source of our anger. The discussion nicely illustrates the way in which we had assessed each other at that time. It also contains Janet's comments on our assessment. I began by explaining how the lesson had seemed to me.

KC:	I hated that lesson, because everyone came in, and they were all hot, and no-one wanted to work. I'd come in and I'd thought 'Great. This is the last lesson we've got, so we must work hard and finish all those things'. And then nobody wanted to work, so I was disappointed. Right? And yet I could see that you were all hot, so in a way couldn't help it either. And then people wanted to go out and Mr Charles had said nobody was supposed to go out. And then people were noisy and things.
Janet:	Yea — but other classes do though. (ie. go out)
KC:	That's right. Yes. But you can see how I felt. Becuase, you see, I'm not a proper teacher in the school, so I'd only been able to hear, you know, what he said. And it made me feel weird. And I didn't know what to do.
Janet:	Yes.
KC:	I mean that's how the lesson seemed to me. So I felt 'Good-ness' you know. 'Ought I to let them go out, or ought I to insist they stay in?' And then you started getting on at Brian because it was his birthday the next day. I mean, how did that lesson seem to you?
Janet:	Alright.
Liz:	Boring.
Brian:	Crap.
Janet:	Oh — that's nice!
Brian:	Rubbish! I'd rather have played cards.
	[He had forgotten to bring his cards that day]
KC:	Did you know you were annoying me that lesson, Brian?
Brian:	No. You were annoying me.
KC:	How did I annoy you?
Brian:	Because you hurt my arm.
KC:	No. Before that. Did you know that you were annoying me throughout the lesson?
Brian:	What, cos I did no work?
KC:	Well — that. But it was also the *way* you didn't do any work. We'd agreed that you could have free time. I was

disappointed that people didn't want to work, but you were
being — I mean to me it looked as if you were being cheeky
and rude.

Janet: A right pest!

KC: You'd got that expression on your face, and I thought you
were being horrible. Did you know that you were doing
that?

Brian: Yea.

Janet: Well, why did you do it then? Why did you do it if you knew
you were being annoying?

Brian: I dunno.

Janet: You must know!

Brian: Cos it was boring. All the lessons were boring that day.
There wasn't nothing to do, so I thought I might as well
annoy you, see?

Janet: Oh. That's nice!

Taken at face value Brian's comments seem to indicate that it was the
failure of the curriculum which caused his attitude toward me. While
acknowledging that he had deliberately annoyed me, he justified this in
terms of boredom and resisted my appeal to the personal level, even
though Janet clearly thought that his attitude was wrong. However, as the
discussion progressed it became clear that Brian justified his behaviour
not merely as a response to the curriculum, but as a response to what he
perceived as my immorality. In his view I had broken our agreement. For
example he claimed that I had not made my dissatisfaction clear 'You
didn't tell us off'. Moreover, he said that if he was doing wrong 'You
should have sent me to Mr Hardy'. He accused me of violence 'You're
not supposed to get hold of anyone's arm, or things like that'.

Brian's objection to my behaviour was not, however, based on a
simple dislike of violence. For example, he described with pleasure playing cards which was:

Brian: ... good. Cos when you playing cards and someone loses,
you cut the pack. And if you get diamonds you can scratch
their hand. If you get spades you can dig their hand. When
you get clubs you can pinch them. And when you get hearts
you can punch them.

My violence in getting hold of his arm was different because it was unjust.
It was unjust because the incident was Barbara's fault not his 'She kicked
me, so I kicked her back' and because the power relationship was one-
sided. I said:

KC: Brian you're a fraud ... If you enjoy scratching and pinching and punching people, why did you object to me getting
hold of your arm?

Brian: I wouldn't mind if I could hit you back.

Thus even in the case of Brian, where the curriculum was clearly a major factor in the problems we experienced, it was not the only cause of conflict. Had I stuck exactly to our agreement as Brian perceived it, that is, had I given clear warnings that I would send him to Mr Hardy, the legalistic peace between us would still have been uneasy but it might have been preserved. Clearly had the lessons been continuing Brian and I would have needed to do a lot more talking in the way outlined above before we could sort out our difficulties. The fact that we had talked, and talked quite openly, demonstrated that this would be possible. Importantly, although my theoretical beliefs had not helped me to avoid this incident they did help me to make a constructive response. Typically, an angry outburst at a teacher, such as that which Brian directed at me, is either punished, or forgiven and ignored. The first would be to devalue the pupil's anger, and the second to devalue the teacher's point of view; both of which lead to confusion and resentment and fail to encourage those involved to find new ways of behaving. In the present instance although no solution had been found, and perhaps never could be, Brian and I were 'still talking'.

Conclusions

The purpose of this chapter was to illustrate the way in which the curriculum affected my relationship with 3Y. Although it is difficult to draw secure conclusions from the type of evidence presented here, it does seem possible to argue that our behaviour was never a pure response to the set tasks, but that it was a response to a constellation of factors which constituted an existential moment. Moreover, while there were clear links with other analytical perspectives, it did seem possible to characterize that response as a moral one, in which all involved attempted to find solutions to their conflicting rights. That the pupils' stance towards me was a personal one was substantiated by evidence that although they found the curriculum only minimally rewarding, many of them were not only prepared to engage in it, but were also prepared to significantly moderate their general behaviour. Moreover, given that many of them did not fear punishment, and given that the card-playing sessions were proof that I would allow them to opt out, their conformity seems inexplicable unless they were empathizing with my rights as a teacher-person. Thus, although the curriculum was clearly an important factor in the interaction between 3Y and myself, a more important factor appeared to be the interpersonal framework within which the lessons took place. Where this failed, as in Brian's case, both the pupil and I experienced most problems.

If this analysis of our curriculum behaviour is correct it leads to some further important conclusions. For example, in spite of the fact that the curriculum *per se* was not the over-riding cause of a reduction in disruptive behaviour, it can be argued from the evidence that my decision to offer topic work was important. The argument here is not that the tasks I set promoted an understanding of History. Indeed the conclusion must be that most of 3Y learned very little. However, because the development of an interpersonal ethos required that the pupils and I should talk and listen to each other, and because 3Y were not prepared to engage in the sort of class discussion which I could tolerate, topic work did provide me with the space I needed to communicate with individuals and small groups. As a result, not only did our relationship improve, but the pupils' willingness to take discussion seriously increased too. In the initial interviews I had discussed with some pupils the possibility of holding class discussions. None of them thought that it would work. For example:

Janet: It would be awful.
Val: I don't think half the class would listen.
KC: They wouldn't listen to each other?
Val: Not really. They'd take no notice of yer.

This view was corroborated by Robert's comment:

Robert: If you had a discussion they'd go eccentric and have an excuse to shout. Once or twice we've had a discussion, but it doesn't really work out, cos some pupils can't be sensible.

The events of lessons three and four supported these views. Nevertheless, by the end of the experiment, and arguably as the result of the in-depth discussions which topic work had allowed me to hold with individual pupils (as well as the out of class discussions with Steve, Brian and Mike) the situation had changed. Thus, in the unplanned class discussion which took place in the last week of term, it was clear that 3Y were more prepared to abide by the minimum rules which a group discussion requires. For example when, early in the meeting, scuffling and banter threatened to disrupt any serious exchange of ideas about the curriculum, I switched off the tape recorder and said 'OK. If you don't want to talk about it, I'll go'. As a result they settled down with Steve and Dave keeping order through such comments as 'Shut up! We're talking. OK. What do you want, Miss?' Progress might be slow with a class like 3Y, but a curriculum based on a discussion of ideas such as is advocated, for example, by Willis[5] seemed to be a possible way forward once a person-to-person relationship had been forged.

Thus, by creating space for me to talk with pupils, the use of topic work helped me to develop relationships with the class which in turn made it possible to engage in curriculum activities which had previously failed. As a result it is possible to argue that a teacher who wishes to introduce a class to a curriculum which she thinks is important, but which the pupils do not, need not despair. Steve, Barbara, Janet and Liz did not cooperate because they found the work attractive, but because they believed I had done my best; whereas Brian's uncooperative behaviour seemed as much to do with his doubts about the morality of my intentions and, therefore, about the propriety of cooperation, as it was to do with boredom. This suggests that, in the last resort, the acceptance of a curriculum has less to do with some superficial idea of the 'relevance' of the subject matter, than with the perceived morality of the teacher. If this is indeed the case, a teacher who was convinced of the importance of what she had to say need not give up, but rather work at developing her relationship with the pupils so that, at a later time, she can return to introducing pupils to the important ideas and skills of her own subject.

Finally, the suggested analysis of 3Y's responses to the curriculum provides a way forward for teachers which does not have to wait for sophisticated resources or inservice training. It provides a human, low-technology solution. However, it does not do this at the cost of over-simplifying the situation. For if teachers help their pupils to explore the four questions: 'Has the curriculum any interest or value for me?'; 'What would be the consequences of rejecting it?'; 'If I conform will this be a betrayal of my rights?'; and 'What will be the cost to others of my rejecting it?' then an infinitely complex reality will be revealed, as pupils and teachers bring into consciousness and share their, perhaps unconscious, evaluations of the situation and each other. This uncovering of a complex reality would, indeed, be a valuable curriculum in itself, and certainly any teacher, who chose to listen and learn, would be in no danger of subscribing to simplistic cures for curriculum ills.

Notes

1   I am basing this evaluation of pupil achievements on statements given to me by their form tutor.
2   The type of 'commitment' to which I am referring here is that described by WOODS P. in Chapter 7 of *The Divided School* (1979). There he argues that teachers become committed to the official curriculum and other aspects of the school's organization, because this is the only way that they can both prosper and look themselves in the face. Their commitment is, therefore, essential for the preservation of their self-concept and, rather than responding intelligently to evidence which would undermine their belief, they resist such knowledge.
3   WOODS, P. (1979) PP. 161–4.
4   My ignorance of these circumstances may seem both extraordinary and unforgivable. My excuse can only be that I had been heavily involved with duties outside the school; and also, perhaps, I had become complacent about my relationship with 3Y. In the event it was a fortunate lapse in my efficiency for it created a fruitful experimental situation.
5   WILLIS, P. (1977) pp. 188 and 191.

8   Conclusions

Buber wrote,

> What counts is not the products of analysis and reflection but the
> genuine original unity (of) the lived relationship.[1]

This idea has been at the heart of this research. Yet in the act of writing,
in the need to make selections from evidence, and, now, with the need to
draw general conclusions, the principle embedded in Buber's words is
endangered. Indeed, this book will only be persuasive if the total vibrancy
of my relationship with 3Y has been communicated, a vibrancy which
does not permit the identification of a linear progression from disorderly
to orderly behaviour from the beginning to the end of our time together,
for this was not how it was. Each moment was full and we experienced it
in different ways; and each moment was lived for itself. The past and the
future were an important context, but it was the felt 'now' which was
paramount until it, too, splintered into a kaleidoscope of new moments
each demanding our fullest attention.

In presenting the evidence from my lessons with 3Y, it has, therefore, been necessary to resist the temptation to organize what happened
into neat categories. That would have been to distort the reality and to
destroy the message of the theory which underpins this research, which
claims that by sharing, rather than controlling life, a creative order, not
chaos, will ensue. Nevertheless, looking back over the term that I spent as
3Y's History teacher in which I attempted to work without models of who
they were and predictions about how they would behave, some conclusions can be drawn in spite of the untidiness of the evidence.

For example, there is no doubt that a change took place in the quality
of the relationship between 3Y and myself as the lessons progressed. This
change, moreover, was not a consequence of increased control. Indeed, at
least from lesson three onwards 3Y were, by any criteria, out of my
control. Yet, after lesson four, this did not lead to disorderly and disruptive
behaviour; and with all the other constraints on the situation remain-

ing intact, this reduction in disruptiveness seemed to stem directly from the discussions I had with Steve, Brian and Mike which produced a bargain we were all prepared to honour. Moreover, the bargain was not merely a reaffirmation of an obvious solution to an easy problem. The rights of the pupils and my rights did encroach upon each other, and the moral dilemma was very real. In addition, it had to be solved by persons who initially disagreed about the best way out, requiring each of us to shift our original positions. That we achieved this and put our achievement into practice seemed to be due, at least partly, to an increased acceptance of the personhood of the other.

Unfortunately, however, the bargain included my right to punish the boys, and although this right was accorded to me against my explicit wishes, it did create problems. Being a factor in the pupils' perception of our relationship, it made it difficult to detect the degree to which their conformity was due to fear rather than empathy, and produced intractable questions for this research such as 'What if Brian had not believed that I would punish him — would he have been more disruptive?' Or 'What if Steve had not been in trouble with the school authorities? Would he then have been so supportive?' Such questions are, of course, unanswerable — and inevitably so in an experiment which took a natural setting as its laboratory. However, as has been argued in the main body of this book Brian's belief that I would punish appeared to make the situation worse not better. It was accompanied by a wary reserve which made communication between us difficult, so that even in face to face discussion, I had to rely on an interpretation of his non-verbal behaviour in order to guess how he felt. This contrasted strongly with the other members of 3Y who, arguably, were less concerned with a fear of punishment, either because they believed, like the girls, that I wouldn't use it, or believed, like Steve, that in some situations its use would be appropriate. These pupils showed no reserve towards me, either treating me with a cheerful but inoffensive familiarity, or telling me forcefully when I had offended them.

Nevertheless, 'What if . . .' questions are awkward. They allow those who are sceptical about the morality of persons to cling to their scepticism, and those who are unsure to remain on the fence. Moreover, they are compounded by other possible objections of the 'If only' or 'But that wasn't really' variety; for example: 'If only you'd managed to talk to all the pupils . . .'; or 'If only you'd been their teacher for a year instead of a term'; or '. . . had taken them for the last two lessons on a Friday afternoon' — then evidence would have been more convincing. Or alternatively 'But 3Y's behaviour did not really change in any significant way' or 'But they weren't really typical members of an anti-school subculture'.

Attempts to counter such objections have, of course, already been made as they arose within the research. Nevertheless, the nature of the available evidence was such that it would always be open to alternative interpretation. This fact cannot, however, be used as an argument that the experiment should have been conducted in a different manner. The aim of this research was to apply a person-centred approach to classroom conflict in a way which any teacher, in any school without any extra resources, could attempt tomorrow. As was argued earlier, to manipulate the natural setting would have been to undermine this aim.

More importantly, it would have been to deny the view of life which is necessary if the concept of free moral persons is to have any meaning. Moral persons cannot exist in a world where 'What if's' and 'If only's' have been analyzed out of existence, for the assumption behind such analyses would be that reality can be described and explained by identifying and controlling causal factors. It would be to subscribe to the doctrine of determinism. Likewise to choose precise definitions of conflict and empathy, in order to demonstrate that what occurred 'really was' what it was claimed to be, would be to view such things as objects which could be modelled, rather than as infinitely variable expressions of the holomovement, which has been regarded throughout this research as the only permanent reality.

Thus, rather than engage in an illogical and spuriously scientific attempt to argue that the evidence was anything more than highly suggestive, this study took what was considered to be a more honest and powerful way forward. Firstly, the evidence has been presented as fully as space would allow, so that on occasions transcripts of an entire piece of interaction were included where this was necessary if criticism was not to be aborted by over-editing. Secondly, however, an attempt was made to present the strongest possible theoretical case for interpreting the evidence in a particular way. For example, a wide variety of circumstantial evidence and opinion was drawn upon to demonstrate that the claims which I wished to make about my relationship with 3Y would not do violence to the insights of other perspectives, including those of the natural sciences. The appeal to the natural sciences, however, was not for the purpose of setting up a hypothesis which would be tested by a controlled experiment such as is typical of their methodology. Indeed, the theory which emerged prohibited the use of such research methods. Equally, however, it was not possible to engage in 'inductive' theorizing, where the evidence is scrutinized, in the hope that a convincing theory will emerge. The evidence which has been presented is too open to alternative interpretations for such an approach to yield convincing results. The view which has been taken, therefore, is that, in the last resort, neither theory nor evidence can stand as an objective yardstick against which the other can be judged. Rather it is believed that the persuasiveness of each is a function of the reciprocity of their relationship.

The strength or weakness of this research, therefore, rests upon the degree to which it has succeeded in demonstrating the coherence of (a) a body of theory which proposes a particular set of logical relations between phenomena; with (b) substantial bodies of circumstantial evidence. It has been argued that the preferred theory is more powerful in this respect than some of its rivals, firstly because, like the concept of education, it speaks of persons whose mind and body are a unitary phenomenon; and, secondly, because it is capable of explaining all observed behaviour and not merely that which falls into statistical categories. Moreover, it is capable of doing this not only with evidence derived from my interaction with 3Y, but also with evidence from published sociological studies into teacher-pupil conflict as well with that from the physical sciences. The circumstantial support for the theory, it is argued, is overwhelming even if, in the last instance, it cannot be proved.

Alongside an attempt to demonstrate the validity of interpreting large bodies of evidence in a particular way, however, has been a concern to investigate the implications of such a theory for professional practice. At one level, as the argument outlined above implies, the implications are spontaneous not analytic. Thus if the proposed theory is a valid summation of reality, persons, including teachers, will act morally, and an alternative interpretation of the evidence will not affect that issue one iota. At another level it has been demonstrated that a belief in the morality of others is at times seriously threatened by their behaviour, coupled with an ignorance of the mitigating circumstances. In ordinary life this ignorance is fostered by socio-spatial divisions which prevent interaction between different social groups so that through ignorance each can write the other off as immoral. In public life it is encouraged by political rhetoric; in academic life by Habermas's scientific subcultures; and in the life of professional teachers by a literature which presents causal models of persons, or fails to make the logic of their freedom clear. In heavily constrained situations, where disagreements about optimum solutions are inevitable, this failure to recognize the morality of others can produce and sustain bitter conflict with each side seeking victory at all cost. This research demonstrates that, in such situations, an intellectual theory of personal morality is a powerful tool. It enabled me to resist 3Y's attacks on my well-being and break through the vicious circle of confrontation. I was able to remind myself of, and so reinforce, my belief in the morality and rationality of 3Y's behaviour, and thus maintain a specific course of action. At the same time it enabled me to make clear statements of my belief to disruptive pupils. It was this process which occurred in and after my fourth lesson with 3Y. An important conclusion of this research, therefore, is the need to bring into consciousness and share the logic of morality, so that this can be used to sustain persons against evidence, which superficially contradicts it, and prestigious theories which deny it.

At yet another level this study has implications for day to day practice. It suggests that teachers need to talk with and listen to their pupils on a regular basis, especially about problems of classroom interaction. It demands that if pupils become angry with teachers, responding emotionally rather than intellectually, the intelligent and moral basis of that anger must be assumed, and pupils should be helped to verbalize the reasons behind their feelings so that they can be discussed. It requires, however, that those discussions are truly open-ended and not merely a means of enforcing the teacher's point of view and, therefore, it requires a belief that pupils will understand the constraints on the situation if these are explained and that they will not deliberately choose to act in a way which would hurt a teacher who was taking a moral stance towards them. In short, it demands that teachers should not merely understand their pupils. They should give those pupils the opportunity to understand them.

All this, of course, has implications for the use of time. Certainly in using three free lessons for discussion with the boys in 3Y, many would argue that I had moved beyond the resources available to a typical teacher. The dramatic reduction in disruptive behaviour which resulted from those discussions and the immediate reduction in stress which I experienced, so that I began to look forward to meeting the class each week, suggests that somehow time should be found, and that if schools do not find it they must hold themselves responsible for the continuation of conflict. A number of suggestions immediately present themselves from the evidence. For example, if 3Y were in any way typical, it is clear that they would have gladly exchanged a cold dinner-hour out on the field for the warmth of a room inside and the chance to express themselves freely. Alternatively, the speed with which I was invited to the local youth club suggests that there, too, might be a time and a space for talking with individuals and small groups of friends. At an institutional level the evidence suggests that the role of senior staff might be changed, so that rather than allotting to them the unenviable task of enforcing discipline, or papering over the cracks of a broken relationship, their expertise and status could be used to facilitate open discussion between the offended parties. At its most minimal, this might take the form of freeing a member of staff for a lesson so that she could talk with one or two pupils.

All these suggestions, however, assume that discussion in class would not be possible. A far more obvious and far-reaching solution would be to prevent such a situation arising. This would require that teachers instigated a person-to-person relationship with pupils as soon as they entered the school; that they encouraged skills of class discussion, which would make time-costly small group and individual discussions less necessary. If pupils knew that they could always criticize a teacher, or the curriculum, without being accused of rudeness; indeed, if they were taught ways of phrasing and presenting criticism which minimized the hurt to the person involved, while still making the point; if they were asked on a regular basis to evaluate lessons and suggest ways in which their teachers could improve their method; if teachers then took these criticisms seriously, and in exchange gave reasons for their own actions; and if all this were done on a routine basis, and solutions to differences of opinion were worked out together; then, if the arguments embodied in this study are correct, entrenched teacher-pupil conflict would never arise. This is not an argument for school councils, nor an argument for individualized learning, though both, or either, might arise out of discussion. Rather it is to suggest that joint pupil-teacher evaluations of the educative process should be woven into the fabric of their relationship so that it was the natural basis of their life together. It could consist of such minimal interchanges as the teacher asking pupils at the end of a lesson whether they had found it of value or interest — as long as the response was listened to and taken seriously. It might, on a more formal basis, consist of pupils being invited at the end of a course to write down their views about its interest or value; or, in each subject, the last lesson of every term might be devoted to a class discussion of how the course had been experienced so far, and how it might be improved. It would certainly require teachers at the beginning of each term to make explicit the value, as they saw it, of what they intended to teach, their aims and objectives, and how pupils would be evaluated. And if pupils were unimpressed, teachers would need to be prepared to pick up this discussion again and again, although they might also have to say 'Sorry, folks. I know you don't agree,· but the constraints on us are such that we have to do this'.[2]

In fact, as the evidence from my lessons with 3Y demonstrates, even habitual disruptives are prepared to go along with teachers if they feel they are not being immorally oppressed. This is perhaps the most worrying feature of this research. For although teachers who engage in the proposed method must expect a period of acute discomfort before calm is restored, there may be a danger that, in that calm, they become complacent. One of the most secure conclusions which can be drawn from the evidence presented in this research is that, whatever else did, or did not happen, 3Y learned very little history. Yet this was a class which already had a complex grasp of key historical concepts, having important insights into the relationship between power, punishment, social control, economic and social constraints, negotiation, justice and human dignity. Moreover, within this one class of low academic achievers there was a wide spectrum of views about social reality from those who believed that the *status quo* was invidious and should be changed (Brian); through those who believed it could not be changed and looked for their salvation within it (Steve, Barbara, Janet and Liz); to those who believed it gave adequate opportunities for human expression (Dave, Robert and Jim). If all these insights and perspectives could have been brought to bear on the years 1870 to 1910 some real history could have been learned. Instead of which most pupils engaged in mechanical tasks.

That such mechanical tasks were in the first instance productive because they provided space in which I could begin to talk to pupils in lessons cannot be denied. However, such tasks would need to be regarded as a means to a further end in which the promise of the teacher's role could be realized. It was argued in Chapter One that education had at its centre the concept of persons and the concept of knowledge, which could be used by persons to maximize their creative potential. If teachers merely choose to relate to pupils as persons, conflict may indeed be avoided. If they then use the space which the reduction in disruptive behaviour provides to introduce and discuss important ideas, their teaching role will be fulfilled. They will be instrumental in increasing their pupils' liberty.

Notes

1 BUBER, M. (1970) p. 70.
2 ROGERS, C. (1983) p. 28 makes a similar point. He writes: 'I should never *say* I was granting some degree of freedom ... that I was not willing to back up with my whole being.... Where freedom ... was limited in certain ways, I had found those limits had better be *explicit*'. 'I want this course to be as free as possible, but the department requires that we cover these two texts, and an examination written and graded by the department will be given on those texts ...' (NB. Rogers is using the term 'freedom' whereas this research would have used the term 'liberty' in this context.)

Appendix: The Concept of Intelligence

The term intelligence has been used throughout this work to identify a state of being or quality of persons, which is indivisible (and, therefore, immeasurable); uncaused by more primitive factors (and therefore not determined by factors within the environment of the person); and so closely allied to the concepts of purposiveness and creativity that it can be regarded as a dimension of these latter qualities and they of it. This usage of the term intelligence so contravenes the way it is used in much educational literature, that it has been felt necessary to provide some justification in order to avoid a charge of eccentricity.

My justification rests upon a brief analysis of the way the term is currently used, which reveals that common usage hides some common confusions. These confusions result from the fact that intelligence is a composite term incorporating two distinct concepts which are governed by quite different logical and scientific laws. For example the term intelligence can be used to refer to something which is known. Thus, Elizabeth Bennet, convinced at last of the worth of Mr Darcy, wished to hear news of him when 'there seemed the least chance of gaining intelligence'.[1] Similarly, the 'Intelligence' Corps is not a label applied to a group of soldiers who are necessarily cleverer than others, but to one whose job it is to collect information. Used in this way 'intelligence' refers to something which can be divided and measured. I could conceivably know twice as much of a poem tomorrow as I know today, and I might already know twice as much of it as you. Equally, used in this way, 'intelligence' owes much to the environment of the person. If no-one brings the poem to my notice, I will never learn it. If an Intelligence Officer never infiltrates enemy circles he will never learn their plans; and if Elizabeth Bennet never communicates with persons who have news of Mr Darcy, or better still with the man himself, she will never receive the intelligence which her heart desires — and so on.

However, the term intelligence also carries another meaning, and this second meaning is perhaps the most pervasive in current educational thinking. This second meaning refers to a person's ability. Butcher, discussing the concept of intelligence warns:

> The grammatical form itself can be misleading. 'Intelligence' is a noun, and nouns often refer to things or objects, Even when we know that intelligence is not a 'thing', but a sophisticated abstraction from behaviour, we may sometimes endow it with a kind a shadowy existence distinct and separate from the intelligent organisms which alone give it meaning, or, more insidiously think it is a 'thing' that these organisms 'have', rather than a description of the way they behave.[2]

Clearly, Jane Austen's use of the term intelligence does refer to something which persons 'have' — or in Elizabeth's case something which she had not. What Butcher is identifying is the way in which intelligence is used to describe what persons 'are', something which is indistinguishable from the organisms which 'give it meaning'.[3] Once the term is used to identify an aspect of what persons 'are', however, the concept of intelligence behaves in entirely different ways from those which apply when it refers to something which persons 'have'. My argument will be that, as a quality attributed to persons, intelligence is indivisible and beyond environmental interference. It will be suggested that common usage allows the use of the term intelligence in this way, also that claims to measure, or identify determining causes of this innate ability are both logically confused and scientifically unsound.

In order to substantiate these arguments, one aspect of what it means to 'be' intelligent rather than to 'have' intelligence will be briefly discussed, namely a person's ability to 'know' something. Although many would argue that 'being intelligent' implies much more than this, for example that it implies the ability to see the meaning of what is known, or the ability to learn, or the ability to use what is known to solve problems, for the sake of brevity these additional implications of what it means to 'be' intelligent will not be discussed. This, however, will not detract from the following analysis, for each of these additional aspects of what it might mean to be intelligent are governed by the same set of logical and scientific laws. Thus, if it can be demonstrated that an ability to know (whether it is 'knowing that' or 'knowing how') is indivisible and beyond environmental interference, then by applying the same arguments to the ability to see meaning, or to learn, or to use information to solve problems, it will become clear that all definitions of 'being intelligent' obey the same logic.

Like the term 'intelligence' the phrase 'to know' implies two concepts. Firstly, it conveys the idea that I am able to know, that I have the power of knowing. Secondly, it conveys the idea that something is known. In real life, these two ideas are inseparable, for it would be nonsense to say 'I know' if I didn't know 'something'. That these two concepts cannot logically exist without each other, however, does not mean that they are the same. For example, the human species cannot breathe without air. This does not mean, however, that the presence of air is the same as the ability to breathe. Breathing requires something more than air, just as knowing requires something more than what is known. The statement 'I know', therefore, in referring to a unitary existential moment which includes divisible and determined knowledge, must also include a distinct ability to be knowing. The question to be explored is whether this ability is equally divisible and determined.

In considering this problem, I set myself the task of discovering myself in a state of 'partial knowingness' — for example of 'half-knowing'. Try as I would, I failed to catch myself in this state, or even to imagine what it would be like. I was, however, able to imagine situations which might be confused with such a state. For example, I could imagine making statements of the order, 'I half know the poem'. Here, however, my confusion would be grammatical, for what I would mean would be that I knew 'half the poem'. It would be the poem, not my knowing, which was divided. The bits I knew — a verse, a line, a word here and there — I would know absolutely; and the bits I didn't know I would have absolutely forgotten. Equally, however, I might be in a state where the next line was 'on the tip of my tongue' though I could not quite, just at that moment, bring it into consciousness. In a minute from now, perhaps, it would come to me. Even this state, however, did not seem open to division. What was divided was not the state of knowing, but me — the person who knew; so that although my unconscious mind might have the answer, my conscious mind did not. Of course my unconscious mind might not have the answer either. It might be searching for it, or be engaged on other more pressing business, so that the delay would be a consequence of a current lack of knowing at my unconscious level too. Alternatively my unconscious mind might be playing capricious, prima donna tricks, refusing to come across with the goods which my conscious mind required. But it seemed to me that if it knew, it knew, and if it did not, it did not. However divided I might be, whatever the difficulties in communication between the different levels of my consciousness, the knowingness itself seemed absolute and indivisible.[4] Finally, I was able to imagine a situation in which I was not sure what to believe, not sure whether the solution to a problem was A or B. Indeed, there might seem to be a fifty per cent possibility either way. Once again, however, this could not satisfactorily be described as 'half-knowing', for I would absolutely know that I was not sure.

This failure to discover myself in a state of partial knowingness (no matter how partial, or false, my knowledge, nor how divided 'I' might be) supported my belief that intelligence, conceived as an 'ability to know', was equally indivisible. For example, it would clearly be impossible for 'half-an-ability-to-be-something' to result in 'being-that-something', and, therefore, as long as I was in an absolute 'state of knowing', my ability to be in that state must be absolute too. Nevertheless, this conclusion did leave some problems, for my experience taught me that some people seemed more able than others to know some forms of knowledge (for example mathematics, or music); and that most adults seemed better at everything than most infants. Indeed, if some people were not more able than others, words such as 'gifted' or 'dull' would have no meaning, My problem could be expressed in two contradictory statements both of which seemed to be true. Thus: (1) Knowing is an indivisible (and, therefore, immeasurable) state of being, and the ability to know must be equally indivisible and immeasurable. (2) Some people are more able than others to know some things, and this ability can be increased by learning. The ability to know is, therefore, measurable and divisible.

There seemed to be at least two ways of reconciling this contradiction which would leave the first statement intact. One solution was a temporal/ arithmetic one in which the absolute state of 'being knowing' could flick on and off through time. Thus, the more intelligent person would be the one whose intelligence was 'switched on' more of the time; a gifted person might be one whose intelligence was switched on all of the time; and a person with a specific talent (in mathematics or music) would be one whose intelligence switched on in some situations but not others. Lucky people would be those whose intelligence was activated at critical moments, for example when they happened to be taking the eleven plus exam. This solution to the contradiction between statements one and two would, therefore, leave 'being intelligent' as an absolute state, but allow measurement by adding together the number and periods of time in which a person was in this state. Moreover, although this seemed to be an outrageous solution, something like it could be found in psychological literature which, for example, identifies plateaux interspersed with steep increases in learning. Nevertheless, the solution was not adequate for this study, which requires pupils to be intelligent and free all of the time, so that their morality is never on the blink. The solution also created tremendous problems about what might cause intelligence to flicker on and off in this way, and whether this would, indeed, be possible.

A second way of resolving the contradiction between the two statements, however, avoided the problem of spaces in which persons were absolutely unintelligent. This solution was reached by exploring the different concepts subsumed under the term 'ability'. Even without entering into sophisticated debates about 'cans',[5] it is clear that when I say 'I can do something' I might mean simply that I have a personal capacity which allows me to do whatever it is I claim to be able to do. On the other hand, I might, also, mean that at the moment in time to which I am referring there is nothing in my environment to prevent my performance. For example, if I am asked whether I can translate a letter into French for a friend I might reply 'Yes I can, but I can't do it now'. The 'can' and the 'can't' do not contradict each other because they refer to different things. For the same reason the reply 'Yes I can, I can do it now' is possible without the second 'can' being redundant. In both cases the first 'can' refers to my capacity to translate French, that is it refers to a claim to know enough French to do the job. The second 'can' however, refers directly to the environmental constraints upon my actions, which would include specific plans and promises I had made about how I intended to spend the next half hour. Of the two 'cans' the first is by far the most interesting. For example use of the second 'can' while referring to a different state of affairs, is entirely dependent upon the first, Thus, the sentence 'I cannot translate the letter, and/but I can do it now', would be nonsense; and in the statement 'I cannot translate the letter and I cannot do it now' the second 'cannot' would be redundant. Thus, in 'canny' talk, common usage demands that personal capacity takes precedence over environmental opportunity, and where intelligence is used to refer to certain abilities, it seems justifiable by reference to common usage to link it with this dominant 'can', and to abandon the one which, because it refers entirely to measurable factors in the environment which constrain persons, is not the sort of intelligent ability to which this research wishes to refer.

However, an espousal of the 'can' of personal capacity does not, by itself, solve the problem of identifying abilities which are indivisible and beyond environmental control, and the second possible resolution of the contradictory statements that: '(1) Intelligence is an absolute and, therefore, immeasurable state', and '(2) Some people are more able than others to do some things, therefore, ability is measurable': requires a further piece of analysis before it can be demonstrated. For personal capacities are themselves 'cannier' and 'iffier' than the simple term implies, with the 'I can' of personal capacity referring again to two different states of affairs. Thus, although my ability to translate my friend's letter, like my ability to recite the poem discussed earlier, is in one sense an absolute ability (either I can translate certain French words, or I can not) whether or not I have this ability depends firstly, upon whether I have an intrinsic capacity to see meaning and, secondly, upon whether I have had the opportunity to learn these specific French words. This latter would clearly be a consequence of measurable environmental factors (for example the amount of time I had been exposed to the French language) and such factors would, therefore, be significant in deciding whether I was more able to translate the letter than someone else. If it could be demonstrated, however, that that part of my personal capacity referred to above as 'intrinsic capacity', was not affected by my environment and was indivisible, then a second solution to the contradictory statements (1) and (2) could be that intelligence is indeed an absolute state and that apparent differences in abilities are always a consequence of differing environmental opportunities and constraints. The need for a 'now-we-have-it now-we-don't' type of intelligence would be avoided.

There are, however, major problems in producing such a demonstration. The problem is not merely the methodological one ecountered in the never-ending debate about the relative effects of genetic inheritance and the environment on intelligence; that is, it is not merely a problem of controlling variables, so that a non-environmentally produced factor can be identified. Much more fundamentally, it is a problem of where to draw the boundary between a person and her environment. It is this question which allows me to disassociate myself from the debate between environmentalists and geneticists, for they take the answer as given. Indeed, it is arguable that if they explored the question, the bitterness associated with their debate would disappear, and they would find themselves (almost) on the same side.

For example, both geneticists and environmentalists agree that my socio-economic-cultural-geographical and historical locations provide environmental constraints on my opportunities and willingness to learn French. These environments clearly determine whether I have a personal capacity to translate my friend's letter. But such environmental explanations say nothing about what I could have done had my environment given me the chance. The geneticists, therefore, point to situations in which I am given the opportunity to learn French, when I am motivated to learn it (that is my culture values the skill, I value the skill, and I have a good teacher who encourages me) yet I still do not learn. In this situation it begins to look as if I have less intrinsic ability than other people to learn the offending language, and it is at this point that references to my genetic inheritance, or to the inadequacy of the formation or functioning of my brain might be made, leading to attempts to measure and determine the cause of my intrinsic disability. The question which those who are engaged in the nature/nurture debate generally avoid, however, is, 'Can my genetic inheritance, or brain structure, be regarded as environment?' The discussion in Section Four of Chapter Two suggests that it can. Genetic inheritance was represented there as inherited 'information' which, like cultural information, could be used by the organism, or discarded if it was inappropriate; and parts of the body, such as brains, were represented as objects produced by organisms using this available genetic information.[6] As objects, brains, like genes, would become part of the internal environment of the person and, as environment, they would constrain not act causally on his ability to be knowing. They would determine the liberty of intelligence not threaten its freedom.

In this view persons who appeared to be gifted, or to have a specific talent might well be ones who started life with more, or different, genetic information than their fellows, and they would, therefore, be likely to perform better in situations where that information was relevant. They could, of course, choose to ignore that information — to waste their talent; and, indeed, apparently less talented persons might be doing just that. Equally, in principle at least, a person whose initial genetic information was found wanting in some respect, might be able to compensate by learning enough to produce a performance which was just as proficient as that of his genetically better endowed peer. On the other side of the coin, a person constrained by a malformed, or malfunctioning brain — perhaps that part which dealt with language — would have difficulty with some performances, for example learning French. In such cases in spite of the fact that the severity of the constraint might lead us to talk as if such persons were unintelligent, as if the severity of their brain damage had affected their absolute, intrinsic capacity to be knowing rather than constraining what they could know, we would need to recognize that such talk would result from a confusion. The confusion would be based on a misperception of what was person and what was environment, and a lack of precision about the differing effects of causes and constraints (as defined in Chapter Two).

This second possible resolution of the contradiction between the necessity for knowingness to be absolute and our experience that some people are more able to know some things than others, therefore, depends upon a relegation of our genetic make-up and our brain structure to the role of internal environment. There are a number of advantages associated with this solution. In the first place, while it clearly suggests that common-talk is often imprecise, it does seem to reflect common belief. Thus, most of us have a healthy respect for the intelligence of our common sense, while freely admitting that we have difficulty with, for example, mathematics. A second advantage is that although the conclusion that genetic inheritance and brain structure are environment, not person, appears to contradict some interpretations of psychological data, it does not deny the validity of the data itself. For example, it does not deny that some people are able to do some things better than some other people, and that this may in part be due to genetic inheritance and physical structure. Moreover, it does not deny that genetic inheritance and the physical state of the brain might affect a person's performance throughout a whole life-span. It merely suggests that these are constraining, not causal, effects on his intelligence. The solution also accommodates evidence from developmental theories, so that Piaget's stages in intellectual development would need to be seen as stages in the development of what is known. They would be reflections of the structure of knowledge gradually acquired, or recreated, by persons in their interaction with their environment. Each stage would, of course, increase a person's opportunities, allowing her to interact more successfully with her environment, and so would make her appear more intelligent. That this increase in successful behaviour was a consequence of the person 'having' more intelligence (defined as knowledge) rather that of 'being' more intelligent, would not affect the validity of the research results at all.

Finally, the relegation of genetic and brain structure to 'environment' is supported by the findings of other disciplines which clearly indicate that they are constraints on, rather than determinants of, an ability to know. For example, like all constraints (as defined in Chapter Two, Section One) they are open to manipulation — through brain surgery, drugs, genetic engineering and even hypnosis; and it is when they are thus manipulated that their constraining, rather than causal, effect on the ability to know becomes apparent. For while such manipulations can sensibly be seen as affecting the information available to the person, either by implanting new information (chemical, or genetic, or even propositional statements communicated directly to the unconscious via hypnosis) or by opening up, or mending, channels of communication for the free flow of information (either between parts of a person's internal environment, or between the person and her external environment) there would be exactly no effect if the person did not already have an absolute ability to use the information which was being made available. No doctor or surgeon or geneticist or hypnotist, for example, can ever sensibly claim to be implanting 'knowingness', but only to be giving their patient the chance to use more, or different, data.

The second solution indeed links the concept of an absolute capacity to know with a third way in which the term intelligence is sometimes used, that is as a synonym for life. We speculate whether there are 'intelligences', or living creatures, on other planets; and Popper suggests that '. . . the origin of "life" and the origin of "problems" coincide';[6] so that to be alive is 'to know' a problem. The surgeon's inability to implant knowingness is, therefore, paralleled by his inability to resurrect the dead and the bio-chemist's inability to create life from materials in which the principle of life is not already present.[7] Thus, although the environment provided the opportunities for me, as a member of the human species, to be born, and although it can also kill me by dropping something on my head, or keep me alive by using drugs, or mouth to mouth resuscitation, it cannot turn me on again once I am turned off. If I am born I am absolutely alive, and using this third definition, I must be regarded as absolutely and continuously intelligent, until I am absolutely dead. My environment can only switch my intelligence off be destroying me.[8] It, therefore, seems entirely proper according to common usage to suggest that intelligence can be used to define an indivisible quality of persons which is not determined by more primitive environmental factors, for although the term is sometimes used in other ways all these alternative usages finally depend upon the existence of an absolute capacity to be intelligent. Thus what is known or learned, and the specific problems which are solved, are all products of absolute intelligence acting within its environment. The diagram provides a summary of these arguments.

If the analysis outlined above is accepted, it is a relatively easy task to demonstrate that the concepts of creativity and purposiveness behave in the same way as that of intelligence. Thus the *products* of a creative capacity can clearly be divided and measured, and owe much to the opportunities and constraints in the environment in which they are produced. Equaly the contents of a specific purpose can often be divided into smaller objectives and will depend upon the person's perception of what it is intelligent to attempt at any given moment. But the intrinsic state of being creative, or being purposive, like the state of knowing cannot be divided and owes nothing to the environment, as long as the environment allows the person to live; and this is true even when the environmental constraints on a person are so severe that their purposiveness and creativity cannot easily be expressed.

Indeed, like the constellation of capacities which are commonly subsumed in the concept of 'being intelligent', creativity and purposiveness appear to be unalienable dimensions of life, so that, for example, we would be uneasy about applying the label 'living' to something which could not pursue the minimal purpose of staying alive and reproducing; or which could not adapt, that is respond creatively to new situations.[9] Importantly for this study, if intelligence, purposiveness and creativity are all conceived as dimensions of life, because life is indivisible they must logically be dimensions of each other, not independent capacities.

That common usage allows this conclusion can be demonstrated without difficulty. For example, creativity implies an ability to produce something which is new, whether an action, or a thought, or an artistic or instrumental artefact. However, we would hesitate to apply the label 'creative' to the author of such products, no matter how original the artefact might be, if we felt that it had been produced by chance or was 'determined' by environmental factors. In such a circumstance we would call its author 'lucky'. What we require of creative persons is an ability to manipulate what they know into different patterns of relationships so that new ways of seeing and acting can arise. The creative person, then, is one who can manipulate information, however unconsciously; and in order to do this he must have the capacity to know and see meaning. He must be intelligent. Equally, however, the concept of creativity implies purposiveness. If, while baking, I produced something which could only be used as a new form of solid fuel, I would hardly be classed as a creative person but rather as a bad cook, for the result would not match my intentions. My intentions might have been quite vague in the first place — perhaps I was experimenting in order to produce a new type of cake — but because the flat, black object I retrieved from the oven could not remotely be regarded as edible, it would not remotely fit even these vague intentions,

Diagram Summarising the Analysis of the Concept of Intelligence and the creativity of my performance would be denied. I could only redeem my reputation by setting aside my original intentions and entering, purposefully, into the solid fuel business.

In a similar way purposiveness is an empty concept without intelligence and creativity. Unless I am capable of knowing I could not, in the first place, identify a purpose to be purposive about. Moreover, unless I was capable of manipulating the information I knew into different patterns of relationships, that is unless I could deal with it creatively, I would have to respond to the data I received from my environment in the form it entered my system. I would be a machine responding to a stream of environmental stimuli, and even if I were conceived as a 'knowing' machine, unless I could manipulate what I knew, my actions would be the effects of environmental causes, not my purpose. While it was recognized in Chapter Two of this work that some theorists suggest that purpose, as distinct from environmental causation, is an empty concept, it was argued there that it was unnecessary to draw such a conclusion. Certainly common usage draws a clear distinction between what persons 'purpose' and what they are 'caused' to do, and this distinction rests on the assumption that they can make intelligent and creative choices.

Indeed, the concept of intelligence itself assumes creativity and purposiveness. For in common usage 'to have information' hardly expresses the full force of the phase 'to know'. Thus a book which 'has' information is not regarded as 'knowing', or intelligent, but computers which can manipulate data into different patterns for the purpose of solving problems, are so described. 'To know', therefore, is to be able to construct knowledge and see its meaning in relation to purpose; and to be 'naturally' rather than 'artificially' intelligent is to have these abilities by virtue of being a living organism, rather than an environmentally produced machine.[10]

Finally, although the purpose of this appendix is merely to demonstrate that the term intelligence can properly be used in the way required by this research, it is worth noting that the arguments expressed above have wider ramifications. For if the logic is accepted that apparent differences in ability are always a consequence of the different effects of differing internal and external environments on absolute capacities (which we all hold in common) then no person can ever be regarded as less intelligent than another. Persons are not their brains, nor their psychological set. They are neither epiphenomena of their genetic make-up, nor the consequence of their cultural mileux. They are not what they know, nor what they do. Nor are they a sophisticated mixture of all these things. They are living intelligent organisms whose intelligence is at times horrendously constrained by socio-economic factors, physical deformity or lack of knowledge. But because constraints, unlike determining causes, can be manipulated by human purpose there is always hope, always a chance that some means will be found to increase personal liberty. This is the challenge which faces geneticists, biochemists, medical practitioners, sociologists, psychologists and, of course, educationists. It is a challenge which can be undermined by a belief that some people are intrinsically less intelligent than others.

Notes

1 AUSTEN, J. (1979) *Pride and Prejudice*, Guild Publishing. p. 225.
2 BUTCHER, H.J. (1968) p. 22.
3 In addition to highlighting the fact that the term intelligence is used in psychological literature to describe what organisms 'are', rather than to describe something which they 'have', Butcher also seemed to be suggesting in the passage quoted, that the term is used to describe a way of seeing, rather than to identify something which really exists. Thus he suggested that it could be regarded as 'a sophisticated abstraction from behaviour' or as 'a description of the way (organisms) behave'. Like Eysenck, who also refers to intelligence as a 'concept' rather than a 'thing', (see EYSENCK, H. (1981) p. 13, and Chapter Two, note (9), above). Butcher fails to clarify the implications of this claim. For example, if intelligence exists only as a concept in the mind of the beholder, then claims to measure it are a nonsense, and investigations into the determining causes of intelligence would presumably have more to do with the ideology of the researcher than with the genes of the person who was being studied. In fact, in spite of his protests, Eysenck does believe that intelligence exists, as do most teachers. A purely 'conceptual' definition of intelligence will, therefore, not be discussed further in this appendix, on the grounds that few of those engaged in educational and psychological enterprises use it this way.
4 This argument of course begs the question about whether persons can be divided. The thrust of the argument in Chapter Two, above, was that if persons were to be regarded as free and, therefore, potentially moral, they must logically be regarded as unitary beings who were beyond division. The solution presented in that chapter was that the person should be located at an unconscious level, which would mean that as far as the present argument is concerned if my unconsciousness 'knew' the poem, then 'I' would know it.
5 I am thinking here of Austin's famous essay on 'If and Cans'. (See URMSON, J.O. and WARNOCK, G.J. (1961) pp. 153 to 180.)
6 For example, it was suggested in Chapter Two, Section 4, that in the light of Quantum and Relativity Theory, persons should be regarded as forcefields, rather than as machines of interacting parts. In considering the properties of a forcefield — say a magnetic field — one would not look at the behaviour of a single iron filing, but rather at the behaviour of the whole. Individual iron filings (like brains or livers) would merely be parts of the internal environment of the whole field. They would be objects over which the magnetic field could exert its power, not magnetism itself. And so with intelligence.
7 POPPER, K. (1978) p. 178.
8 See Chapter Two, note (75) in this book.
9 There are a number of interesting variants on this theme which might at first sight appear to be objections, but which I think do not destroy the argument. For example, those who believe in a personal life after death might object that even death would not destroy 'my' intelligence which is a dimension of my soul. This is, however, merely an argument about who the person is and not about whether intelligence is an unalienable dimension of life. Others with a more materialistic

perspective, might argue that because it is technically possible to keep bits of me alive by transplanting them into other bodies, there are problems in equating intelligence with life. For example, DENNETT (1981) pp. 310 to 323, imagines a situation where his brain is kept alive to operate another body after his first body's death, thus raising the question of whether 'he' and his intelligence would still exist. This is, however, not very different from the problem raised by Classical Dualism, For, if Dennett is really just his brain, (like if he is really just his soul,) he would live on. The death of his heart and lungs and liver would be of little significance, except in so far as there would be the practical problem of replacing them. If, however, as this work suggests, Dennett is an intelligent forcefield then he will be destroyed once that forcefield is destroyed, and his surviving brain linked with another body would merely become part of the internal environment of another forcefield, another person. Dennett would be dead.

10 It is perhaps difficult to regard some primitive life forms as creative, because their behaviour appears to be so rigid. Yet Goodwin argues that evolution should be regarded as a creative cognitive development (see GOODWIN, B. (1976) and Chapter Two, Section Four above). Thus if the first primitive organisms had not, within the limited information available to them, been able to act in a creative orderly way, complex organisms whose creativity is more obvious would never have developed.

11 Searle, of course, argues that the real difference between natural and artificial intelligence is that machines are incapable of seeing meaning and that when they appear to do this, for example, when they solve a problem, they are merely operating with syntactical rules. (See SEARLE, J. 1984.) 'Mind' according to Searle 'has more than a syntax, it has semantics, but a computer has, by definition, a syntax alone'. (p. 16) For Searle, as for me, the ability to see meaning is a phenomenon of the natural, biological world.

Bibliography

Texts to which direct reference is made:

ADEY, G. and FRISBY, D. (1976) *The Positive Dispute in German Sociology*, Heinemann.

ARMSTRONG, D.M. (1981) *The Nature of Mind*, Harvester Press.

AYERS, M.R. (1968) *The Refutation of Determinism*, Methuen.

BALL, S.J. (1981) *Beachside Comprehensive: A Case-Study of Secondary Schooling*, Cambridge University Press.

BARTON, L. and MEIGHAN, R. (Eds) (1979) *Schools, Pupils and Deviance*, Nafferton Books.

BENTHALL, J. (Ed.) (1973) *The Limits of Human Nature*, Allen Lane.

BIERSTEDT, R. (1969) *Emile Durkheim*, Weidenfeld and Nicolson.

BIGGE, M.L. (1982) *Learning Theories for Teachers*, (Fourth Edition) Harper and Row.

BOHM, D. (1981) *Wholeness and the Implicate Order*, R.K.P.

BORST, C.V. (1970) *The Mind/Brain Identity Theory*, Macmillan.

BUBER, M. (1970) *I and Thou*, (Third Edition) T. and T. Clark.

BUTCHER, H.J. (1968) *Human Intelligence: Its Nature and Assessment*, Methuen.

BUZAN, T. (1974) *Use Your Head*, B.B.C. Publications.

CALDER, N. (1979) *Einstein's Universe*, Penguin.

CAPRA, F. (1982) *The Turning Point*, Wildwood House.

CATTELL, R.B. AND CHILD, D. (1975) *Motivation and Dynamic Structure*, Holt, Rinehart and Winston.

CHANT, C. and FAUVEL, J. (Eds) (1980) *Darwin to Einstein. Historical Studies on Science and Belief*, Longman.

CHAPMAN, A.J. and JONES, D.M. (1980) *Models of Man*, British Psychological Society.

CORRIGAN, P. (1979) *Schooling the Smash Street Kids*, Macmillan.

COSIN, B.R. *et al.* (Eds) (1971) *School and Society: A Sociological Reader*, R.K.P.

DAWKINS, R. (1978) *The Selfish Gene*, Granada.

DENNETT, D.C. (1981) *Brainstorms: Philosophical Essays on Mind and Psychology*, Harvester Press.

DESMOND, A. (1979) *The Ape's Reflexion*, Quartet Books.

EYSENCK, H.J. and KAMIN, L. (1981) *Intelligence: The Battle for the Mind*, Pan Books.

GIBBS, B. (1976) *Freedom and Liberation*, Sussex University Press.

GOODWIN, B. (1976) *Analytical Physiology of Cells and Developing Organisms*, Academic Press.

HAMPSHIRE, S. (1982) *Thought and Action*, (New Edition) Chatto and Windus.
HARGREAVES, D. *et al.* (1975) *Deviance in Classrooms*, R.K.P.
HONDERICH, T. (Ed.) (1973) *Essays on Freedom of Action*, R.K.P.
HOYLE, F. (1977) *Ten Faces of the Universe*, Heinemann.
LACEY, C. (1970) *Hightown Grammar*, Manchester University Press.
LICKONA, T. (Ed.) (1976) *Moral Development and Behaviour*, Holt, Rinehart and Winston.
MARGULIS, L. (1981) *Symbiosis in Cell Evolution*, Freeman.
MILLER, J. (Ed.) (1983) *States of Mind: Conversations with Psychological Investigators*, B.B.C. Publications.
NASH, R. (1973) *Classrooms Observed: The Teacher's Perception and the Pupil's Performance*, R.K.P.
NIETZSCHE, F. (1913) *The Will to Power*, T.N. Foulis.
PIAGET, J. (1971) *Structuralism*, R.K.P.
POPPER, K. (1978) *An Intellectual Autobiography: Unended Quest*, Fontana.
POPPER, K. (1979) *Objective Knowledge: An Evolutionary Approach*, (Revised Edition.) Oxford University Press.
ROGERS, C. (1977) *On Personal Power*, Delacorte Press.
ROGERS, C. (1983) *Freedom to Learn for the 80s*, Charles E. Merrill.
ROSE, S. (1976) *The Conscious Brain*, Penguin.
RUSSELL, B. (1921) *The Analysis of Mind*, Allen and Unwin.
RYLE, G. (1949) *The Concept of Mind*, Penguin.
SARTRE, J.P. (1948) *Existentialism and Humanism*, Eyre Methuen.
SCHAEFER, G. (1982) *Universe with Man in Mind: The New Paradigm*, Translational Press.
SEARLE, J. (1984) *1984 Reith Lectures — Mind, Brains and Science No. 2 'Beer cans and meat machines'*. In *The Listener*, 15 November, 1984.
SHARP, R. and GREEN, A. (1975) *Education and Social Control: A Study in Progressive Primary Education*, R.K.P.
SKINNER, B.F. (1973) *Beyond Freedom and Dignity*, Pelican.
SMITH, J.M. (Ed.) (1982) *Evolution Now. A Century after Darwin*, Macmillan.
SPINOZA, B. (n.d.) *Ethics*, Heron Books.
STRACHEY, J. (Ed.) (1978) *Sigmund Freud: The Future of an Illusion*, Hogarth Press.
STRAWSON, P. (1974) *Freedom and Resentment, and Other Essays*, Methuen.
SULLOWAY, F.J. (1980) *Freud: Biologist of the Mind. Beyond the Psychoanalytic Legend*, Fontana.
URMSON, J.O. (Ed.) (1975) *The Concise Encylopedia of Western Philosophy*, (Second Edition) Hutchinson.
URMSON, J.O. and WARNOCK, G.J. (1961) *J.L. Austin: Philosophical Papers*, Oxford University Press.
WARN, J.R.W. (1969) *Concise Chemical Thermodynamics*, Van Nostrand Reinhold.
WATSON, L. (1980) *Lifetide*, Coronet.
WEBSTER, G. and GOODWIN, B. (1982) 'The origin of species: A structuralist approach'. In *J. Social Biol. Struct.* 5.
WILLIS, P. (1977) *Learning to Labour*, Saxon Books.
WOODCOCK, A. and DAVIS, M. (1978) *Catastrophe Theory*, Pelican.
WOODS, P. (1979) *The Divided School*, R.K.P.
WOODS, P. (Ed.) (1980(a)) *Pupil Strategies: Explorations in the Sociology of the School*, Croom Helm.
WOODS, P. (Ed.) (1980(b)) *Teacher Strategies: Exploration in the Sociology of the School*, Croom Helm.
YOUNG, M.F.D. (Ed.) (1971) *Knowledge and Control: New Directions for the Sociology of Education*, Collier-Macmillan.
YOUNG, M. and WHITTY, G. (1977) *Society, State and Schooling*, Falmer Press.

Additional Bibliography

ARCHAMBAULT, R.D. (1965) *Philosophical Analysis and Education*, R.K.P.

BENNETT, J. (1964) *Rationality. An Essay Towards an Analysis*, R.K.P.

BENTON, T. (1977) *Philosophical Foundations of the Three Sociologies*, R.K.P.

BERGER, P. (1980) *The Heretical Imperative. Contemporary Possibilities of Religious Affirmation*, Collins.

BLACKHAM, H.J. (1952) *Six Existentialist Thinkers*, R.K.P.

BODEN, M. (1977) *Artificial Intelligence and Natural Man*, Harvester Press.

BOLTON, N. (Ed.) (1979) *Philosophical Problems in Psychology*, Methuen.

CHARDIN, P.T. DE (1970) *The Phenomenon of Man*, (Revised Edition) Fontana.

CHAPPELL, V.C. (1962) *The Philosophy of Mind*, Prentice Hall.

COLEMAN, J.C. (1979) *The School Years. Current Issues in the Socialization of Young People*, Methuen.

COLEY, N.G. and HALL, V.M.O. (1980) *Darwin to Einstein. Primary Sources on Science and Belief*, Longman.

DALE, R. *et al.* (Eds) (1976) *Schooling and Capitalism*, R.K.P.

DWORKIN, G. (Ed.) (1970) *Determinism, Free Will and Moral Responsibility*, Prentice Hall.

FIELD, G.C. (1966) *Moral Theory*, Methuen.

GARDNER, H. (1981) *The Quest for Mind. Piaget, Levi-Strauss, and the Structuralist Movement*, (Second Edition) University of Chicago Press.

HAMILTON, P. (1974) *Knowledge and Social Structure*, R.K.P.

HAMPSHIRE, S. (1972) *Freedom of Mind and Other Essays*, Clarendon Press.

HAMPSHIRE, S. (1975) *Freedom of the Individual*, Chatto and Windus.

HAMPSHIRE, S. (1977) *Two Theories of Morality*, Oxford University Press.

HARSANYI, Z. and HUTTON, R. (1982) *Genetic Prophecy. Beyond the Double Helix*, Granada.

HERSH, R.H., MILLER, J.P., and FIELDING, G.D. (1980) *Models of Moral Education: An Appraisal*, Longman.

HOFFMAN, B. (1963) *The Strange Story of the Quantum*, (Revised Edition) Pelican.

HOYLE, F. and WICKRAMASINGHE, N.C. (1978) *Lifecloud. The Origin of Life in the Universe*, Dent.

KENNY, A. (1963) *Action, Emotion and Will*, R.K.P.

KÖRNER, S. (1955) *Kant*, Penguin.

MACINTYRE, A.C. (1958) *The Unconscious: A Conceptual Analysis*, R.K.P.

PAI, A.C. and MARCUS-ROBERTS, H. (1981) *Genetics: Its Concepts and Implications*, Prentice Hall.

PATON, H.J. (1972) *The Moral Law*, Hutchinson.

PETERS, R.S. (1966) *Ethics and Education*, Allen and Unwin.

RUDDOCK, R. (Ed.) (1972) *Six Approaches to the Person*, R.K.P.

SPICKER, S.F. (Ed.) (1970) *The Philosophy of the Body. Rejections of Cartesian Dualism*, Quadrangle Books.

TAYLOR, C. (1979) *Hegel and Modern Society*, Cambridge University Press.

WILSON, J. (1970) *Moral Thinking*, Heinemann.

Index

ability, concepts of, 215–9, 222
action, human, 35, 45, 49, 50, 51, 96
altruism, intrinsic, 14, 16, 18, 22, 23, 29
  and conflict, 46–7, 48
  and moral law, 25, 27, 28
  teacher-pupil interaction, 170, 172,
    173, 174, 175–6
amorality, 30, 31, 32, 54n13
animate/inanimate phenomena, 47,
  59–60n78
anti-school sub-culture
  see culture
attention, teacher's, need for, 67, 68
authority, opposition to, 63

bargaining, 49, 170, 171, 172, 180, 183,
  206
behaviour, 15, 18, 33, 43, 50–1, 53n4,
  208, 213
  altruistic, 28, 29, 30
  'caused', 20, 44–5, 49, 62, 66–70, 104,
    172–3
  and determinism, 21–2, 27, 34, 35, 49,
    174, 175, 186, 189
  disruptive, 52, 111, 119, 120, 141, 149,
    154–69, 170
    causes, 26, 32, 34, 62, 66–70, 80,
      94, 99
    effect of discussion, **140–71**
  and morality, 14, 16–7, 54n13, 119–20,
    140, 189–93, 208
  predictable/unpredictable, 23–4, 36
  see also boredom; conflict; constraints;
    curriculum; intelligence
    misunderstanding; pupils; research
    responsibility; teachers

Behaviourism: Modification techniques,
  61n95
body, 39, 45, 51
  see also dualism; language; mind
Bohm, David, 43–5, 47, 52, 109
boredom, 26, 30–1, 80, 114, 141, 162
  and curriculum, 92, 99, 175–6, 200–1
Butcher, H.J., 213, 223n3

catastrophe theory, 41, 58n62
categories, statistical, 37–8
  teacher, 99
cause and effect, laws of, 3, 18–20, 27,
  28, 35, 38, 41, 43–4, 46
  and freedom, 40, 49–50
  effects on intelligence, 218, 219, 222
chance, 20–1, 36, 59n68, 220
children: morality, 4, 14, 22–3, 34, 37
choice, personal, 18, 19, 20, 21, 34, 35,
  36, 48, 53n5, 222
classroom reality, 6, 9
  see also conflict
co-existence agreement, 49
'common-sense' views, 34, 35, 36, 62
communication, teacher/pupil, 17, 32, 33,
  62, 97, 101, 102, 110, 118, 129, 194–7
compromise, 72, 140, 149–50, 197
  see also bargaining
conflict, 6–7, 48, 207
conflict, teacher/ pupil, 9, 52
  case study, **62–106**
  evidence from studies, 103–6, 208
  research into, 30–1, **46–52**
  situations creating, 8, 33, 101, 105,
    183, 200, 208
  solutions to, 1–2, 5, 6
  theory: implications, **46–52**, 63

For Product Safety Concerns and Information please contact our EU
representative GPSR@taylorandfrancis.com
Taylor & Francis Verlag GmbH, Kaufingerstraße 24, 80331 München, Germany

www.ingramcontent.com/pod-product-compliance
Lightning Source LLC
Chambersburg PA
CBHW070405270326
41926CB00014B/2707